PLYMOUTH DISTRICT LIBRARY
3 3387 00433 1940

D1073452

Lisa Kahlen

german
grammar
made
easy

HODDER
EDUCATION
AN HACHETTE UK COMPANY

438.24
K

First published in Great Britain in 2005 by
Hodder Education, an Hachette UK Company,
338 Euston Road, London NW1 3BH

www.hoddereducation.com

© 2005 Lisa Kahlen

All rights reserved. No part of this publication may be reproduced or transmitted in
any form or by any means, electronically or mechanically, including
photocopying, recording or any information storage or retrieval system, without
either prior permission in writing from the publisher or a licence permitting
restricted copying. In the United Kingdom such licences are issued by the
Copyright Licensing Agency: Saffron House, 6–10 Kirby Street, London EC1N 8TS.

The advice and information in this book are believed to be true and accurate at
the date of going to press, but neither the authors nor the publisher can accept
any legal responsibility or liability for any errors or omissions.

British Library Cataloguing in Publication Data
A catalogue record for this book is available from the British Library

ISBN 978 0 340 904 961

All illustrations drawn by Chris Blythe/Daedalus Studio

5 6 7 8 9 10
2010 2011 2012

Typeset in 10.5/12pt New Baskerville by Servis Filmsetting Ltd, Stockport, Cheshire
Printed and bound in Malta

What do you think about this book? Or any other Hodder Education title?
Please send your comments to the feedback section on
www.hoddereducation.com

CONTENTS

2 Nouns and Determiners

3 Pronouns

4 Adjectives

5 Adverbs

6 Prepositions

INTRODUCTION

German Grammar Made Easy is a German grammar workbook aimed at adult non-linguists, that is adults with some rudimentary knowledge of German, who do not necessarily know anything about grammar, but need to learn about it so they can progress beyond phrasebook German.

In the past, grammar has been seen as a barrier to language learning. It has put more people off learning a language than it has helped. Because of the way grammar has been portrayed, students were often made to feel that only those who could master 'conjugations' and 'declensions' could learn a language. In fact, you can drive a car without mastering the principles of the internal combustion engine – but if you do learn where to put the oil and how to check the tyres and fill up the windscreen wash, it does help!

Grammar is about recognising word patterns which give you a framework to a language; if you know the framework, you can 'build' new language of your own instead of having to learn everything by heart.

For those who already know some German grammar, short cuts are marked with the ▶▶ to enable you to go straight to the information you need. If you feel you would like to have more in-depth knowledge about a particular grammar point, please refer to *Hammer's German Grammar and Usage*, M. Durrell, 1971/2002, 4th edn.

An interactive CD-ROM accompanies this book for use with a PC. The CD-ROM contains most of the exercises from the book as well as some additional material. Most exercises are recorded so that you can listen to a native speaker saying the sentences and there is a 'click on' facility to allow you to read the English translation. There is also some additional listening material which provides a useful resource and brings the language to life.

A simple guide to the parts of speech

▶▶ **If you know what verbs, nouns, pronouns, adverbs, etc. are, go on to 1.1.**

The most useful categories of words to recognise are:

1 Verbs – 'doing' words

Verbs tell you what someone or something is doing.

> I *am going* to France. My friend *booked* the flight. I *am going* to a meeting.

You also use them to ask questions . . .

> *Have* you *seen* the film? *Are* you all right?

. . . and to give instructions.

> *Fetch* it! *Slow* down! *Help* me! *Wait!*

Verbs usually present the most problems, so the section dealing with them is the longest one and comes first in the book.

2 Nouns – 'naming' words

Nouns are the words which tell you:

- what something is:
  a *timetable*, a *train*, a *station*, a *town*, a *secret*
- who someone is:
  a *steward*, a *bank clerk*, a *baker*, a *student*

3 Pronouns

Pronouns are words which 'stand in' for a noun.

> M. Bleriot is French. M. Bleriot lives in Paris.

Instead of repeating *M. Bleriot*, you can say *he*.

> M. Bleriot is French. *He* lives in Paris.

In the same way, you can say *she* instead of repeating *Florence* in the following sentence.

> Florence works in Strasbourg. *She* works at the European Parliament.

These are also pronouns: *I, you, it, one, we, they, me, us, them.*

4 Adjectives

Adjectives are 'describing' words. They are used to describe something or someone.

the *new* house, the *red* car, a *tiny* flat, a *wet* day, a *busy* secretary

5 Adverbs

Adverbs are words which usually describe a verb, e.g. they describe how something is done. They often answer the question *How?* and in English they often end in *-ly*.

He runs *fast*. She eats *slowly*. It comes *naturally*!

6 Prepositions

Prepositions are words which usually tell you where something is, e.g. *in, under, on*. Words such as *to, for, with,* and *without* are also prepositions.

1 VERBS

1.1 Talking about what you do

▶▶ **If you know what a verb is, go on to 1.1.1.**

You use a verb to talk about what someone or something does, is doing, has done or intends to do. A verb is often called a doing word.

 Ask yourself if it is possible to 'do' something to find out if a word is a verb.

I Which of these words are things you can do?

a run	**f** eat
b jeans	**g** under
c sleep	**h** blue
d make	**i** think
e easy	**j** after

II Some verbs can be used as nouns or adjectives. Which of the words in bold are being used as verbs? Tick each sentence which includes a verb in bold.

a Jason and Lily **run** a homework club in the church hall.
b They both **work** at the local school.
c They go for a **run** every morning.
d After **work** they go straight to the hall.
e Tonight they are having a **meeting** to discuss funding.
f They are **meeting** in the church hall.
g They need more **chairs** for the children.
h Jason usually **chairs** the meetings.
i Lily **records** the proceedings and types them up.
j The **records** show that they have had three meetings this year.

1.1.1 What is the infinitive?

▶▶ **If you know what the infinitive is, go on to 1.1.2.**

When you look up a verb in a dictionary, you will find the infinitive. This is the 'name' of the verb. In English, the infinitive consists of *to* + verb, e.g. *to read, to buy, to travel*.

In German nearly all infinitives end in **-en,** a few end in **-n.**

Infinitives ending in **-en**

find**en**	to find
lern**en**	to learn
helf**en**	to help
üb**en**	to practise
akzeptier**en**	to accept

Infinitives ending in **-n**

wander**n**	to hike
sammel**n**	to collect
lächel**n**	to smile
änder**n**	to change
kletter**n**	to climb

 Try to look for similarities between German and English. Some are obvious, for example **finden** means *to find,* **senden** *to send,* **spekulieren** *to speculate.* Others are less obvious.

III Here are more German infinitives. See how many you can match up with their English counterparts.

a gehen	1 to make/to do
b trinken	2 to bring/to take
c kommen	3 to sing
d sprechen	4 to feed
e waschen	5 to swim
f machen	6 to speak
g füttern	7 to come
h singen	8 to wash
i schwimmen	9 to go
j bringen	10 to drink

IV What do you think the German for these verbs would be? See if you can work it out.

a to organise	1 konzentrieren
b to repair	2 diskutieren
c to type	3 reparieren
d to send	4 surfen
e to surf	5 mailen
f to e-mail	6 senden
g to demonstrate	7 tippen
h to discuss	8 riskieren
i to concentrate	9 organisieren
j to risk	10 demonstrieren

Look out for verbs like **manipulieren** *to manipulate,* **akzeptieren** *to accept,* **studieren** *to study.* The first part of the verb is the same in English as in German.

1.1.2 What is the stem of a verb?

▶▶ **If you already know what the stem is, go on to 1.1.3.**

The infinitive of a verb in German consists of the stem and the ending **-en** or **-n.**

stem	ending	infinitive
geh	+ -en	= gehen
wander	+ -n	= wandern

The stem, or root of the verb, is that part which is left after you take off the ending **-en** or **-n.**

meaning	infinitive	stem
to go	gehen	geh
to look for	suchen	such

V Now try to find the stem of the following verbs. You will see how easy it is.

Just take off **-en** or **-n.**

infinitive	stem	
a to run	rennen	___
b to make/do	machen	___
c to ask	fragen	___
d to phone	telefonieren	___
e to inform	informieren	___
f to communicate	kommunizieren	___
g to change	verändern	___
h to feed	füttern	___
i to treat	behandeln	___

VI More practice at finding the stem.

infinitive	stem	
a to buy	kaufen	___
b to hear	hören	___
c to cry	weinen	___

d to smile	lächeln	____
e to sing	singen	____
f to call	rufen	____
g to meet	treffen	____
h to laugh	lachen	____
i to say/tell	sagen	____
j to understand	verstehen	____

VII Now find the infinitive of these verbs.

English	**stem**	**infinitive**
a to eat	ess	____
b to accept	akzeptier	____
c to run	lauf	____
d to drive/go	fahr	____
e to hike	wander	____
f to look for	such	____
g to do/make	mach	____
h to smile	lächel	____
i to enjoy	genieß	____
j to do	tu	____

1.1.3 The 'persons' of the verb

 If you know about the 'persons' of the verb, go to 1.1.4.

In many languages the verb ending changes according to who is doing the action and you have to learn the pattern of the verb. This is the pattern of the English verb *to talk*:

	singular	**plural**
first person	I talk	we talk
second person	you talk	you talk
third person	he, she, it talks	they talk

In English, we only change the ending when we are talking about he/she or it: *he/she/it talks*, so we don't have to learn our verbs off by heart.

In German, the endings change for each person, so you have to learn them.

ich	-e	wir	-en
du	-st	ihr	-t
Sie	-en	Sie	-en
er/sie/es	-t	sie	-en

	singular	plural
first person	I go ich geh**e**	we go wir geh**en**
second person	you go du geh**st**/Sie geh**en**	you go ihr geh**t**/Sie geh**en**
third person	he/she/it goes er, sie, es geh**t**	they go sie geh**en**

Ich, **du**, **er**, **sie**, **es**, etc. are called pronouns because they 'stand in' for, or represent, a person or thing. Mr Bloggs → *he*; Mr and Mrs Bloggs → *they*; Jim Bloggs and I → *we*.

These are the personal pronouns:

singular		plural	
I	ich	we (my friend and I)	wir
you (informal)	du	you (informal)	ihr
you (formal)	Sie	you (formal)	Sie
he	er	they	sie
she	sie		
it	es		

 Look at the table of personal pronouns again: as you can see, there are different ways of saying *you*.

Du/*you* is only used when talking to a child or a young person under 16, a relation or a very good friend; students use it among themselves as well. It implies a certain degree of intimacy and should not be used to address an adult unless he or she invites you to use it (see page 54).

Ihr is used when talking to more than one person you know well, a group of good friends or children.

Sie (formal) is used when talking to an adult (singular) or more than one adult (plural) and teenagers over 16. You may offend an adult person if you address him or her using the familiar form **du**.

 Sie (formal) singular and plural is written with a capital S.

VIII Which pronoun would you use?

a You are talking about yourself: I am speaking. du/ich/sie
b You are talking about a girlfriend. ich/Sie/sie
c You are talking about a male friend. er/wir/sie
d You are talking about yourself and a friend. ich/sie/wir
e You are talking *to* a child. es/du/er
f You are talking *to* a stranger. du/Sie/er
g You are talking *to* a group of young people. Sie/du/ihr

h You are talking *to* a group of adults.   sie/Sie/ihr

i You are talking about Herr Braun.   er/Sie/es

j You are talking about Herr und Frau Fiedler.   er/sie/Sie

IX Which pronoun would you use when you are talking about the following:

a your friend Peter
b your friend Susanne
c Herrn Meier
d Herrn and Frau Meier
e yourself
f Claudia, Martina und Klaus
g yourself and your friend

1.1.4 Weak verbs (regular verbs)

 If you know about weak verbs, go on to 1.1.5.

In German, regular verbs are called 'weak verbs' and irregular verbs are called 'strong verbs'.

All regular verbs follow the same pattern.

This is the pattern for verbs in the present tense.

Take the **-en** or **-n** off the infinitive of the verb to find the stem, then add the following endings to the stem.

machen – *to do or make*

singular			
I – ich	-e	ich mache	I do
you – du	-st	du machst	you do
you – Sie (formal)	-en	Sie machen	you do
he/she/it – er/sie/es	-t	er/sie/es macht	he/she/it does
plural			
we – wir	-en	wir machen	we do
you – ihr	-t	ihr macht	you do
you – Sie (formal)	-en	Sie machen	you do
they – sie	-en	sie machen	they do

Note that the formal form **Sie** for *you* is exactly like the **sie** – *they* (except that it is written with a capital letter) so you don't have to learn it.

 The endings for **we** – *wir*, **they** – *sie* and **you** – *Sie* (formal) are all the same as the infinitive ending. All you have to memorise are the verb endings for **ich**, **du**, **er/sie/es** and **ihr**.

If you are not likely to be using the **du** and **ihr** forms, you only have to remember that the **ich** form ends in **-e** and that the **er/sie/es** form ends in **-t**; and you probably know that already!

X Now try it yourself with the verb *to live* – **wohnen**.

a ich ____
b du ____
c Sie ____
d er ____
e Frau Meier ____
f das Kind ____
g wir ____
h ihr ____
i Sie ____
j sie (they) ____

XI More practice with the verb *to sing* – **singen**.

a ich ____
b du ____
c es ____
d wir ____
e ihr ____
f Sie ____
g Hannelore ____
h Herr Schmidt ____
i Hans und Ute ____
j Sie ____

XII Match the persons below with the appropriate verb forms.

a ____ telefonieren
b ____ macht
c ____ komme
d ____ sagst
e ____ lacht
f ____ schlafen
g ____ essen
h ____ trinkst
i ____ geht
j ____ buchstabiere

ich, er, wir, du

1.1.5 Strong verbs (irregular verbs)

Strong verbs are verbs which sometimes change their stem. Their endings are the same as those of weak verbs.

The stem changes occurred originally to make some verb forms easier to pronounce.

There are not many verbs that change their stem in the present tense and they only change in the **du** and **er/sie/es** forms. The other 'persons' are not affected by stem changes.

vowel change from -a to –ä

to drive	fahren	du fährst	er/sie/es fährt	wir fahren, ihr fahrt, sie fahren
to fall	fallen	du fällst	er/sie/es fällt	wir fallen, ihr fallt, sie fallen
to guess	raten	du rätst	er/sie/es rät	wir raten, ihr ratet, sie raten
to sleep	schlafen	du schläfst	er/sie/es schläft	wir schlafen, ihr schlaft, sie schlafen

 Read the above verb list out loud so you can hear the difference in pronunciation.

 Here are quite a number of common strong useful verbs. Use the *you* – **du** and *he/she/it* – **er/sie/es** form.

XIII Write down the **du** and **er/sie/es** forms for the following verbs.

a to bake backen du _bäckst_ er _bäckt_
b to roast braten du _brätst_ sie ___
c to dig graben du ___ sie ___
d to booze saufen du ___ sie ___
e to receive empfangen du ___ sie ___
f to catch fangen du ___ er ___
g to hold halten du ___ es ___
h to carry tragen du ___ sie ___
i to grow wachsen du ___ er ___
j to wash waschen du ___ er ___

vowel changes from -e to -ie or -i

to eat	essen	du isst	er/sie/es isst
to give	geben	du gibst	er/sie/es gibt
to help	helfen	du hilfst	er/sie/es hilft
to read	lesen	du liest	er/sie/es liest
to take	nehmen	du nimmst	er/sie/es nimmt
to see	sehen	du siehst	er/sie/es sieht
to meet	treffen	du triffst	er/sie/es trifft

 Remember that there are only changes in the *you* – **du** and *he/she/it* – **er/sie/es** forms.

XIV Now it's up to you to practise again!

a to give	geben	du ___	er ___
b to take	nehmen	du ___	sie ___
c to measure	messen	du ___	es ___
d to steal	stehlen	du ___	er ___
e to die	sterben	du ___	sie ___
f to speak	sprechen	du ___	er ___
g to give orders	befehlen	du ___	sie ___
h to recommend	empfehlen	du ___	er ___
i to throw	werfen	du ___	er ___
j to break	brechen	du ___	er ___

1.1.6 Auxiliary verbs: *Haben* – to have and *sein* – to be

These two verbs are the most commonly used verbs in any language, so it is very important to learn them. They are irregular in the present tense, just as *to be* and *to have* are irregular in English.

 Take some time now to memorise one verb at a time. Start with the verb *to be* – **sein**. You can either read it out loud several times, or write it down a few times and listen to the recording. When learning verbs aloud it is easier to miss out the **Sie** form as it sounds exactly the same as the **sie** plural form.

Haben – to have

 Although the verb **haben** is a strong verb, the plural is regular; so concentrate on the *you* – **du** and *he/she/it* – **er/sie/es** forms of **haben**. If you are not going to need the **du** form, you only have the **er/sie/es** form to learn – which is easy, as they go together. If you know one, you know the others!

haben – *to have*

singular		plural	
I have	ich habe	we have	wir haben
you have	du hast	you have	ihr habt
he/she/it has	er/sie/es hat	you have (formal)	Sie haben
		they have	sie haben

Questions and answers with **haben**:

Haben Sie noch Fragen? Nein, ich habe keine Fragen.
Hat er Kinder? Ja, er hat zwei Kinder.
Hat sie ein neues Auto? Ja, sie hat ein neues Auto.
Haben wir einen freien Tag? Nein, wir haben keinen freien Tag.
Haben Sie eine interessante Arbeit? Ja, ich habe eine interessante
   Arbeit.

XV Fill in the appropriate verb forms of *to have* – **haben**.

a ___ Sie Geld?
b Nein, ich ___ kein Geld.
c ___ du viele Hausaufgaben auf?
d Ja, ich ___ viele Hausaufgaben auf.
e ___ er einen neuen Computer?
f Ja, er ___ einen neuen Computer.
g Ich ___ eine neue Arbeit.
h Wir ___ Besuch aus Deutschland.
i Ich ___ den Vortrag fertig.
j Das Büro ___ neue Öffnungszeiten.

XVI More practice with **haben**.

a Ich ___ keine Zeit. *habe*
b Wir ___ ein altes Auto. *haben*
c Claudia ___ eine neue Wohnung. *hat*
d ___ ihr Lust mit ins Kino zu kommen? *habt*
e ___ du eine Idee, was wir machen können? *Hast*
f Klaus ___ viele gute Ideen. *hat*
g ___ Sie sich im Urlaub erholt? *Haben*
h Frau Klein ___ kein Auto. *hat*
i Ihr Mann ___ kein Geld. *habt*
j ___ Sie ein Auto? *Haben*

Sein – to be
sein – *to be*

singular		**plural**	
I am	ich bin	we are	wir sind
you are	du bist	you are	ihr seid
you are (formal)	Sie sind	you are (formal)	Sie sind
he/she/it is	er/sie/es ist	they are	sie sind

XVII Match the personal pronouns with the corresponding verb forms. Draw linking lines.

a ich	bist
b ihr	sind
c er	bin
d wir	ist
e du	seid

XVIII What do these sentences mean?

a Bist du Deutsche?
b Ja, ich bin Deutsche.
c Bist du verheiratet?
d Ja, ich bin verheiratet.
e Ist er Student?
f Ja, er ist Student.
g Ist sie Krankenschwester?
h Ja, sie ist Krankenschwester.
i Sind Sie guter Laune?
j Ja, wir sind guter Laune.

XIX Fill in the appropriate form of the verb *to be* – **sein**.

a ___ Sie müde?
b Ja, ich ___ sehr müde.
c ___ er müde?
d Nein, er ___ nicht müde.
e ___ ihr müde?
f Nein, wir ___ nicht müde.
g ___ Sie zufrieden?
h Ja, ich ___ zufrieden.
i ___ er glücklich?
j Ja, er ___ glücklich.

XX Fill in the appropriate form of the verb to *be* – **sein**.

In German you don't translate the *a* when talking about what your or somebody's job is. **Ich bin Ingenieur**. I am an *engineer*. **Sie ist Studentin**. – *She is a student.*

a Ich ___ Angestellte bei einer Bank.
b Frau Brinkman ___ meine Chefin.
c Wir ___ bis 6 Uhr im Büro.
d Herr Fischer ___ ein netter Kunde.
e Meine Frau ___ Lehrerin.
f Herr Fink ___ Ingenieur.
g Seine Frau ___ Zahnärztin.

h Ihre Kinder ___ Studenten.
i Mein Vater ___ Rentner.
j Meine Töchter ___ berufstätig.

1.2 Reflexive, separable and modal verbs

▶▶ **If you know what these are, go to 1.2.1.**

Reflexive verbs

Some verbs in German include a reflexive pronoun for their meaning to be complete. Therefore you will say:

I wash myself – **Ich wasche mich** instead of *I am washing*

I shave myself – **Ich rasiere mich** instead of *I am shaving,* etc.

These verbs are called reflexive verbs.

How do I know if a verb is reflexive? In all dictionaries the infinitive reflexive verbs are indicated by the third person pronoun: e.g. **sich setzen, sich fragen, sich wundern**.

 Learn the infinitive and the first person together as a unit: **sich setzen → ich setze mich**, **sich freuen → ich freue mich**.

Separable verbs

In German some verbs are made up of two parts, e.g. *to depart/to leave –* **abfahren**.

ab (first part) + **fahren** (second part)

I leave – **Ich fahre ab**

The separable part of the verb has to go to the very end of the sentence when you use the verb in forms other than the infinitive: **Ich fahre in zehn Minuten ab**.

 In the infinitive, separable verbs are often shown in your dictionary with a slash (/) between the separable part and the main part of the verb: **ab/fahren an/kommen**.

Modal verbs

Modal verbs are verbs which are usually used in conjunction with another verb.

I can go: *can* is a modal verb.

You must eat: *must* is a modal verb.

In German the second verb is the infinitive.

The second verb has to go to the end of the sentence:

Ich kann nicht gleich kommen. (literally: *I cannot straight away come.*)

Du darfst jetzt ein Stück Kuchen essen. (literally: *You may now a piece of cake eat.*)

1.2.1 Reflexive verbs

There are very few reflexive verbs in English; one of them is the verb **sich vorstellen** – *to introduce oneself* → **Ich stelle mich vor** – *I introduce myself.*

However, *sich setzen* translates as *to sit down* → **Ich setze mich** – *I sit down* (literally: *I sit myself down*).

Reflexive pronouns *mich, dich*

Most reflexive verbs take the accusative reflexive pronoun.

ich	mich	myself
du	dich	yourself
Sie	sich	yourself
er/sie/es	sich	himself/herself/itself
wir	uns	ourselves
ihr	euch	yourselves
Sie	sich	yourselves
sie	sich	themselves

sich setzen – *to sit down*	
ich setze mich	wir setzen uns
du setzt dich	ihr setzt euch
Sie setzen sich	Sie setzen sich
er/sie/es setzt sich	sie setzen sich

sich fragen – *to ask oneself/wonder*	
ich frage mich	wir fragen uns
du fragst dich	ihr fragt euch
Sie fragen sich	Sie fragen sich
er/sie/es fragt sich	sie fragen sich

 Remember most reflexive verbs take the accusative.

I Complete the sentences with the appropriate reflexive pronouns: **sich, dich, mich, euch, uns**.

a ich wasche *mich*
b du wäschst *dich*
c Sie waschen *sich*
d er wäscht *sich*
e sie wäscht *sich*
f es wäscht *sich*
g wir waschen *uns*
h ihr wascht *euch*
i Sie waschen *sich*
j sie waschen *sich*

Familiarise yourself with these useful reflexive verbs.

II Match the German reflexive verbs with their English counterparts.

a sich verlieben *7*
b sich treffen *10*
c sich waschen *5*
d sich kämmen
e sich beeilen
f sich erholen
g sich weigern
h sich vorstellen *4*
i sich bedanken *6*
j sich bewerben

1 to refuse
2 to apply (for a job)
3 to hurry
4 to introduce oneself
5 to wash oneself
6 to say thank you
7 to fall in love
8 to comb (one's hair)
9 to have a rest
10 to meet

III Look at the verbs in brackets before completing the sentences.

a Ich ___ ___. (sich beeilen)
b Er ___ ___ gut. (sich benehmen)
c Susanne ___ ___ für das rote Auto. (sich entscheiden)
d Meine Eltern ___ ___ im Moment im Urlaub. (sich erholen)
e Im Winter ___ man ___ sehr leicht. (sich erkälten)
f Du solltest ___ noch ___. (sich verabschieden)
g Ich ___ ___ das Haus alleine zu putzen. (sich weigern)
h Er ___ ___ seiner neuen Kollegin vor. (sich vorstellen)
i Ich ___ ___ sehr herzlich bei dir. (sich bedanken)
j Die Kinder ___ ___ im Garten. (sich verstecken)

IV More practice. Add the appropriate pronouns.

Talking about how you get on with somebody, using the verbs **sich verstehen** and **sich streiten**.

a ___ du ___ gut mit deiner Familie? (sich verstehen)
b Ich ___ ___ sehr gut mit meiner Familie. (sich verstehen)
c Tobias ___ ___ prima mit seinen Eltern. (sich verstehen)
d Meine Schwester ___ ___ nicht so gut mit mir. (sich verstehen)
e Wir ___ ___ sehr gut mit meinen Eltern. (sich verstehen)
f Meine Schwester ___ ___ sehr oft mit meinem Bruder. (sich streiten)
g Mathias Eltern ___ ___ immer. (sich streiten)
h ___Sie ___ oft mit Ihrem Kollegen? (sich streiten)
i Ich ___ ___ selten mit meinem Kollegen. (sich streiten)
j Meine Nachbarin ___ ___ immer mit uns. (streiten)

Reflexive pronouns *mir, dir*

If you don't think you are going to need these or you have had enough of reflexive pronouns, leave them for the moment and come back to them later.

Some reflexive verbs are followed by **mir** (to me) or **dir** (to you), also known as dative pronouns, instead of **mich** (myself) and **dich** (yourself), known as accusative pronouns. Only the **mich** and **dich** form change; **sich**, **uns** and **euch** stay the same.

nominative	accusative	dative
ich	mich	mir
du	dich	dir
er/sie/es	sich	sich
wir	uns	uns
ihr	euch	euch
Sie	sich	sich
sie	sich	sich

The reflexive pronouns **dir** and **mir** may be used if the action refers back to the subject. They are often used in connection with a part of the body (when doing something *with* parts of the body):

Ich wasche mir die Hände.   I wash my hands.
Ich rasiere mir den Bart.   I shave my beard.

They are also used to indicate that you do something to, or for, yourself:

Ich kaufe mir ein Auto.   I buy myself a car.

But you say:

I am washing.   Ich wasche mich.

Mir/dir indicates whose hair is being washed, whose hands are being washed.

Dative	Accusative
Ich wasche mir die Hände.	Ich wasche mich.
Ich ziehe mir die Jacke an.	Ich ziehe mich an.
Ich kämme mir die Haare.	Ich kämme mich.
Ich bräune mir den Rücken.	Ich bräune mich.
Ich ziehe mir die Jeans aus.	Ich ziehe mich aus.

V   Which reflexive pronoun would you use: **dich/dir, mich/mir**?

a I get washed.   Ich wasche ___.
b I comb my hair.   Ich kämme ___ die Haare.
c Sit down!   Setzt ___!
d I sit beside you.   Ich setze ___ neben Sie.
e Buy yourself something!   Kaufst ___ etwas!
f Are you sure?   Bist du ___ sicher?
g I get the salt.   Ich hole ___ das Salz.
h I promise myself that.   Ich verspreche ___ das.
i I take my jacket off.   Ich ziehe ___ die Jacke aus.
j I get dressed.   Ich ziehe ___ an.

 If you get confused between **mich** and **mir** or **dich** and **dir**, don't worry! Everyone will still understand what you wish to say. Even German people make jokes about the 'accusative and the dative' as not all native German speakers get it right. It is more important that you know that the verb is reflexive and you remember to use a reflexive pronoun.

VI   Complete the sentences using the dative reflexive pronoun.

a Ich wasche ___ schnell die Hände.
b Wäschst du ___ die Hände mit der neuen Seife?
c Ich kämme ___ noch schnell die Haare.
d Hast du ___ den Bart abrasiert?
e Wir ziehen ___ schnell unseren Mantel an.
f Kaufen Sie ___ ein neues Auto?
g Ja, ich kaufe ___ ein neues Auto.
h Ich hole ___ ein Eis.
i Nehmen Sie ___ noch etwas Salat.
j Ich nehme ___ noch ein Stück Kuchen.

 Try to remember that you use **dir** and **mir** with the verbs *to buy* – **kaufen**, *to get* – **holen** or *to take* – **nehmen** when you say for whom you buy/take/get something.

Ich hole mir ein Glas.	I get myself a glass.
Hol dir eine Zeitung!	Get yourself a newspaper!
Nehmen Sie sich noch ein Stück Kuchen.	Take another piece of cake.
Kauf dir etwas Schönes!	Buy yourself something nice.

VII Some other useful expressions taking the dative reflexive pronoun – can you match them?

8	**a** sich widersprechen	1 to contract an illness
10	**b** sich etwas versprechen	2 to harm yourself
5	**c** sich sicher sein	3 to imagine/picture something
9	**d** sich etwas gefallen lassen	4 to resolve to do something
6	**e** sich etwas einbilden	5 to be sure
7	**f** sich etwas verbitten	6 to imagine something (unreal)
4	**g** sich etwas vornehmen	7 to refuse to tolerate
3	**h** sich etwas vorstellen	8 to contradict yourself
2	**i** sich schaden	9 to put up with something
1	**j** sich eine Krankheit zuziehen	10 to promise yourself something

VIII Can you match these sentences?

a Ich verspreche mir das.	1 I am not so sure.
b Er verspricht sich das.	2 We are not putting up with that.
c Ich bin mir nicht so sicher.	3 Have you resolved to do that?
d Ich bin mir sicher.	4 Are you putting up with that?
e Ich lass mir das nicht gefallen.	5 I am not putting up with that.
f Wir lassen uns das nicht gefallen.	6 I am sure.
g Du bildest dir das ein.	7 You are imagining that.
h Ich habe mir das vorgenommen.	8 I promise myself that.
i Hast du dir das vorgenommen?	9 He promises himself that.
j Lässt du dir das gefallen?	10 I have resolved to do that.

Some reflexive verbs can be used either with the dative or accusative, but then they change their meaning. The most frequent verb of this kind is **sich vorstellen**.

With the accusative: **sich vorstellen** – to introduce yourself.

Stellen Sie sich bitte vor.	Please introduce yourself.
Ich stelle mich vor.	I am introducing myself.

With the dative: **sich etwas vorstellen** – to imagine something.

Ich kann mir vorstellen, dass
er sich darüber freut.

I can imagine that he will be
pleased about it.

 For more practice using the dative go to 3.3.1.

1.2.2 Separable and inseparable verbs

Separable verbs

Separable verbs are made up of two parts: a prefix – for example **auf** or **ab** – and the infinitive of a verb. The prefix is attached to the front of the verb:

abfahren – *to depart,* **an**kommen – *to arrive,* **vor**stellen - *to introduce.*

These German verbs are similar to English verbs such as *to get up, to go out, to sit down,* but there are more of these verbs in German.

 Some prefixes can be translated literally: **aus** – *out,* **zurück** – *back,* **auf** – *up,* e.g. **gehen** – to go + **aus** – out →
ausgehen – *to go out.* It is useful to learn them by heart.

These are some of the most frequently used separable prefixes, together with their meanings.

usually indicates		infinitive example	example of use
ab	off	abfliegen take off	Das Flugzeug fliegt ab. The plane takes off.
an	at/on	anstellen to switch on	Ich stelle das Radio an. I switch on the radio.
		ankommen to arrive	Der Zug kommt an. The train is arriving.
auf	up /on	aufstehen to get up	Ich stehe um 6 Uhr auf. I get up at 6 o'clock.
		aufheben to pick up	Bitte heben Sie das auf! Please pick it up!
auf	open	aufmachen to open	Machen Sie das Fenster auf! Open the window!
aus	out/off	ausgehen to go out	Wir gehen oft aus. We often go out.

||||➡

usually indicates		infinitive example	example of use
		ausstellen to turn off	Ich stelle das Radio aus. I turn off the radio.
mit	with/along	mitkommen to come with	Kommen Sie mit! Come with me!
		mitbringen to bring along	Bringen Sie Ihren Freund mit. Bring along your friend.
nach	after/to	nachkommen to come after	Ich komme nach. I'll follow.
	imitating	nachmachen to copy	Ich mache das nach. I copy that.
zu	to, towards	zuhören to listen to	Wir hören Ihnen zu. We are listening to you.
zurück	back	zurückgehen to go back	Ich gehe zurück. I'll go back.
zusammen	together	zusammenziehen to move in together	Sie ziehen zusammen. They are moving in together.
weg	away	weggehen to go away	Gehen Sie weg! Go away!

IX Fill in the meaning of these separable verbs with the prefix **aus** – *out*.

origin	separable verb	meaning
drucken – to print	**aus**drucken	to print out
a geben – to give	**aus**geben	*to give up*
b helfen – to help	**aus**helfen	*to help out*
c laufen – to run	**aus**laufen	*to run out*
d probieren – to try	**aus**probieren	*to try out*

 Look up more verbs with the prefix **aus** in your dictionary!

X Fill in the meaning of these separable verbs with the prefix **zurück** – *back*.

origin	separable verb	meaning
geben – to give	**zurück**geben	to give back
a fahren – to drive	**zurück**fahren	*to drive back*
b gehen – to go	**zurück**gehen	*to go back*
c halten – to hold	**zurück**halten	*to hold back*
d rufen – to call	**zurück**rufen	*to call back*

XI Fill in the meaning of these separable verbs with the prefix **auf** – *up*.

origin	separable verb	meaning
essen – to eat	aufessen	to eat up
a wachsen – to grow	aufwachsen	*to grow up*
b geben – to give	aufgeben	*to give up*
c hängen – to hang	aufhängen	*to hang up*
d heben – to lift	aufheben	*to lift up*

 Some separable verbs starting with **auf** or **aus** cannot be translated literally. You just learn them as new words – yet it is always interesting to see where they come from.

origin of the verb

auftauchen – to appear	tauchen – to dive/to dip
aufschließen – to unlock	schließen – to lock
aufteilen – to divide	teilen – to share
aufzählen – to list	zählen – to count
ausgeben – to spend	geben – to give
ausbilden – to train	bilden – to educate
ausladen – to unload	laden – to load
ausfüllen – to fill in (a form)	füllen – fill
auslachen – to laugh at	lachen – to laugh

 When a verb is separable, you can hear it: the prefix is stressed (i.e. you put more emphasis on the prefix). Try it! Read aloud some of the above separable verbs or listen to the CD.

Word order: the structure of a sentence with separable verbs is different from English. In English the prefix comes after the verb; in German it goes to the end of a sentence.

I get **up** at 7 o'clock.	Ich stehe um 7 Uhr **auf**.
I'll be back **at** 9 o'clock.	Ich komme um 9 Uhr **zurück**.
I always wake **up** at 7 o'clock.	Ich wache immer um 7 Uhr **auf**.
I am washing **up** the dishes.	Ich wasche das Geschirr **ab**.
He is phoning **back** later.	Er ruft später wieder **zurück**.

XII Add the relevant prefixes to the following sentences: **auf**, **ab**, **ein**, **aus**, **herein**, **zurück**, **an**.

a Ich komme am Montag *an* I'll arrive on Monday.
b Ich mache den Brief *auf* I am opening the letter.
c Wir kaufen viel *ein* We are buying a lot.
d Susanne ruft Sie *an* Susanne will phone you.
e Ich gebe zu viel Geld *an* I am spending too much money.
f Ich schicke den Brief *zurück* I am sending the letter back.
g Bitte kommen Sie *herein* Please come in.
h Probieren Sie es *aus* Try it out!
i Ruf mich bitte *zurück* Please phone me back!
j Sie fahren bald *ab* They are leaving soon.

XIII Write down the infinitives of the separable verbs in the following sentences and their meanings in English.

	infinitive	meaning
Ich gehe oft mit meinen Freunden aus.	ausgehen	to go out
a Die Busse fahren um 8 Uhr ab.	*abfahren*	*to drive off*
b Wir machen dir die Tür auf.	*aufmachen*	*to close*
c Wir schicken den Brief heute ab.	*abschicken*	*to send off*
d Wir steigen in den Bus ein.	*einsteigen*	*to get on*
e Wir heben Geld ab.	*abheben*	*to withdraw*
f Die Züge kommen heute zu spät an.	*ankommen*	*to arrive*
g Die Konferenz findet heute statt.	*stattfinden*	*to take place*
h Wir kaufen Lebensmittel ein.	*einkaufen*	*to buy*
i Wir holen die Kinder von der Schule ab.	*abholen*	*to collect*
j Wir rufen Sie zurück.	*zurückrufen*	*to call back*

> When reading a sentence in German ensure that you go to the end of the sentence to see if there is a prefix, as the meaning of the whole sentence changes. The same applies when listening to German speakers. Listen carefully to the end of the sentence.

Examples:

Ich nehme das Buch.	I take the book.
but: Ich nehme das Geld **an**.	I accept the money.
Ich ziehe die Schnur.	I am pulling the string.
but: Ich ziehe mich **an**.	I get dressed.
Ich ziehe **um**.	I am moving.
but: Ich ziehe **weg**.	I am moving away.
Ich gehe in die Stadt.	I go into town.
but: Ich gehe mit meiner Freundin aus.	I go out with my girlfriend.
Ich mache das.	I am doing that.
but: Ich mache das **nach**.	I am imitating that.

XIV How would you say the following.

    a She is coming back.   *Sie kommt zurück*

    b She is arriving soon.   *Sie kommt bald an*

    c Open the door. (talking to an adult) *Machen Sie die Tür auf*

    d Close the door. (talking to an adult) *Machen Sie die Tür zu!*

    e Get on the bus! (talking to an adult) *steigen Sie ein!*

    f Get off the bus! (talking to an adult)

    g He wants to fall asleep.

    h He wants to sleep in.

    i Stop it! (talking to an adult)

    j Listen! (talking to an adult)

Inseparable verbs

Some German verbs with a prefix are not separable.

The following prefixes are inseparable.

be-

behalten	to keep
bekommen	to get
bewerben	to apply for a job

emp-

empfangen	to receive
empfehlen	to recommend
empfinden	to feel

ent-

entscheiden	to decide
enttäuschen	to disappoint
entdecken	to discover

er-

erinnern	to remember
erraten	to guess
erwarten	to expect

ver-

verstehen	to understand
verkaufen	to sell
verreisen	to go away

XV Which verbs are not separable?

a entkommen	**f** aufstehen
b versagen	**g** hinfallen
c bestehen	**h** besuchen
d wegfahren	**i** erzählen
e verstehen	**j** entladen

Look up more verbs with non-separable prefixes in your dictionary so that you get used to them.

Verbs with inseparable prefixes are treated in the same way as normal verbs. The verb comes second.

Ich vermiete meine Wohnung.	I am letting my flat.
Ich verstehe Sie.	I understand you.
Wir verkaufen das Auto.	We are selling the car.
Wir behalten das Buch.	We are keeping the book.
Sie bekommen meinen Schlüssel.	You'll get my key.

1.2.3 Modal verbs

Modal verbs are very common in German: it is therefore worthwhile spending time learning them by heart. It is a good idea to learn one at a time and then practise it in various sentences.

There are six verbs known as modal verbs (**Modalverben**):

dürfen	may/to be allowed (to), must
wollen	to want/wish to
müssen	to have to/must/to be obliged to
können	can/to be able to/may
sollen	to be supposed to/shall
mögen	to like

Modal verbs are normally used with another verb that gives meaning to the sentence.

Ich **kann** Englisch *sprechen*.	I **can** *speak* English.
Er **kann** in Deutsch *singen*.	He **can** *sing* in German.

When used in the present tense, the second verb (infinitive) goes at the end of the sentence.

Here the modal verbs are in **bold** print and the infinitive of the verb in *italic,* so it is easy for you to identify them.

XVI Cover up the English sentences. Can you work out what the German sentences mean?

a Sie **dürfen** hier *parken*.   You are **allowed** to *park* here.

b Wir **müssen** Grammatik *studieren*.   We **must** *study* grammar.

c Wir **wollen** Kuchen *essen*.   We **want** to *eat* cake.

d Wir **können** Deutsch *sprechen*.   We **can** *speak* German.

Asking a question:

Dürfen wir hier *essen?*	Are we **allowed** to *eat* here?
Können Sie mir *helfen?*	**Can** you *help* me?
Wollen Sie Tennis *spielen?*	Do you **want** to *play* tennis?
Sollen wir das *machen?*	**Shall** we *do* that?

Exception. The modal verb **mögen** can be used on its own.

Wir **mögen** Pizza.	We **like** Pizza.
Wir **mögen** sie.	We **like** her.

XVII Underline the modal verbs in English and in German in the following sentences.

a Können Sie mir helfen?	Can you help me?
b Ich kann Ihnen helfen.	I can help you.
c Kannst du mir helfen?	Can you help me? (asking a child, relative or friend)
d Können Sie das machen?	Can you do that?
e Ich kann das machen.	I can do that.
f Was kann ich für Sie tun?	What can I do for you?
g Wann können wir uns treffen?	When can we meet?
h Wer kann mir das sagen?	Who can tell me that?
i Wo können wir hier parken?	Where can we park here?
j Warum kann man hier nicht anhalten?	Why is it not permitted to stop here?

können – *can, be able to*

singular		plural	
I can	ich kann	we can	wir können
you can	du kannst	you can	ihr könnt
you (formal) can	Sie können	you (formal) can	Sie können
he/she/it can	er/sie/es kann	they can	sie können

 Modal verbs are irregular in the **ich** – *I* form (remember: normally the **ich** form of a verb ends in **e** → **ich wohne, ich komme**). The **e** has been dropped in the modal verbs. The **er/sie/es** form normally ends in **t** → **er kommt, sie geht**, but not in modal verbs.

 Modal verbs are regular in the plural and the formal *you* (**Sie**). Wunderbar!

 Man – *one* is often used to say what *one* can or must do. It takes the same form as **er/sie/es**.

XVIII Fill in the appropriate form of the modal verb **können**: **können, kann, kannst**.

a Du ___ mir helfen.   You can help me.
b Ich ___ dir das nicht sagen.   I can't tell you that.
c Wir ___ Deutsch sprechen.   We can speak German.
d Er ___ das nicht machen.   He cannot do that.
e ___ wir gehen?   Can we go?
f Petra ___ bald kommen.   Petra can come soon.
g Man ___ das so sagen.   One can say that.
h Sie ___ mir einen Gefallen tun. You can do me a favour.
i ___ du mir sagen, wie spät es ist? Can you tell me what time it is?
j ___ Sie mir sagen, wie spät es ist? Can you tell me what time it is?

dürfen – *may, to be allowed to, to be permitted, must not* (in a negative sentence)

singular		plural	
I	ich darf	we may	wir dürfen
You may	du darfst	you may	ihr dürft
He/she/it may	er/sie/es darf	they may	sie dürfen
You (formal)	Sie dürfen	you (formal plural)	Sie dürfen

Man – *one* is often used to say what one/you must do. It takes the same form as **er/sie/es**.

XIX Underline the modal verb in the English as well as the German sentence.

a Am I allowed to smoke here?   Darf ich hier rauchen?
b You are not allowed to smoke here.   Sie dürfen hier nicht rauchen.
c May I smoke here?   Darf ich hier rauchen?
d We are allowed to play here.   Wir dürfen hier spielen.
e You must not do that.   Du musst das nicht machen.

XX Cover up the English and see if you can guess the meaning of the following sentences. Note: **Dürfen** in a negative sentence means *must not* in English.

a Ich darf das machen.   I am allowed to do that.
b Dürfen wir früher nach Hause gehen?   May we go home earlier?
c Er darf Schokolade essen.   He is allowed to eat chocolate.

d Petra darf ein Eis essen. — Petra is allowed to eat an ice cream.

e Du darfst das nicht machen. — You must not do that. (informal you)

f Wir dürfen hier nicht rauchen. — We must not smoke here.

g Sie dürfen die Tür nicht öffnen. — You are not allowed to open the door.

h Sie dürfen hier nicht schnell fahren. — You are not allowed to drive fast here.

i Sie dürfen das nicht machen. — You are not allowed to do that.

j Man darf hier schwimmen. — One is allowed to swim here.

wollen – *want to/wish to*

singular		plural	
I want	ich will	we want	wir wollen
you (informal) want	du willst	you (informal) want	ihr wollt
you (formal) want	Sie wollen	you (formal) want	Sie wollen
he/she/it wants	er/sie/es will	they want	sie wollen

Example:

Ich will in meinem Garten arbeiten. **I want to work in my garden.**

XXI Cover up the English and see if you can guess the meaning of the following sentences.

a Wir wollen das nicht. — We don't want that.
b Wollen Sie das machen? — Do you want to do that?
c Willst du einkaufen gehen? — Do you want to go shopping?
d Wohin wollt ihr gehen? — Where do you want to go to?

XXII Fill in the appropriate form of **wollen: wollt, will, will, willst, wollen.**

a ___ wir uns um 9 Uhr treffen?
b Was ___ du mit dem kaputten Auto machen?
c Ich ___ das nicht!
d ___ ihr noch etwas essen?
e Klaus ___ mir bei der Arbeit helfen.
f ___ Frau Meier mitkommen?
g Angelika ___ ihr Abitur machen.
h ___ Sie mitkommen?
i Ich ___ in Urlaub fahren.
j ___ du mit ins Kino kommen?

müssen – *must, have to*

singular		plural	
I must	ich muss	we must	wir müssen
you must	du musst	you must	ihr müsst
you (formal) must	Sie müssen	you (formal) must	Sie müssen
he/she/it must	er/sie/es muss	they must	sie müssen

Example:
Ich muss Grammatik studieren.　　**I have to study grammar.**

XXIII　Cover up the English and see if you can guess the meaning of the following sentences.

a Wir müssen aufhören zu telefonieren. We have to stop phoning.
b Ich muss meine Schuhe putzen. I have to clean my shoes.
c Er muss das Auto waschen. He has to wash the car.
d Ihr müsst mir glauben. You have to believe me.
(informal you in plural)

XXIV　Use the appropriate form of **müssen: muss, musst, müsst, müssen.**

a Ich ___ um 8 Uhr nach Hause gehen.
b ___ du den Brief zu Ende schreiben?
c Wir ___ das heute noch erledigen.
d Lisa ___ nächste Woche nach Frankfurt fahren.
e Ihr ___ mir dabei helfen.
f Tobias ___ seine Kunden beraten.
g Jackie ___ um 9 Uhr bei der Arbeit sein.
h ___ Sie auch samstags arbeiten?
i Ich ___ meine Prüfungen bestehen.
j Man ___ hier links fahren.

sollen – *to be supposed to/shall/should*

singular		plural	
I shall	ich soll	we shall	wir sollen
you shall	du sollst	you shall	ihr sollt
you (formal) shall	Sie sollen	you (formal) shall	Sie sollen
he/she/it shall	er/sie/es soll	they shall	sie sollen

XXV Cover up the English and see if you can guess the meaning of the following sentences.

a Du sollst nicht rauchen.

You are not supposed to smoke. (talking to a friend)

b Wir sollen zu Hause bleiben.

We are supposed to stay at home.

c Wo sollen wir uns treffen?

Where shall we meet?

d Wann sollst du am Bahnhof sein?

When are you supposed to be at the train station? (asking a friend)

e Soll ich Ihnen helfen?

Shall I help you? (asking an adult)

XXVI Use the appropriate form of **sollen**.

a ___ ich das für Sie machen?
b Wir ___ die E-Mail abschicken.
c Du ___ Herrn Schmidt anrufen.
d ___ ich das erledigen?
e Wann ___ er dir das Geld bringen?
f Wann ___ wir das fertig haben?
g Wo ___ die Konferenz stattfinden?
h Warum ___ wir das machen?
i Ich ___ am Sonntag arbeiten, aber ich will nicht.
j Sie ___ die Broschüren zur Firma Schmidt schicken.

mögen – *to like (to)*

singular		**plural**	
I like	ich mag	we like	wir mögen
you like	du magst	you like	ihr mögt
you (formal) like	Sie mögen	you (formal) like	Sie mögen
he/she it likes	er/sie/es mag	they like	sie mögen

 The modal verb **mögen** does not require another verb. It is often used with a noun.

Ich mag Pizza.	I like pizza.
Ich mag keine Schokolade.	I don't like chocolate.
Wir mögen ihn.	We like him.
Sie mag Tennis.	She likes tennis.

XXVII Use the appropriate form of **mögen**.

a Ich ___ Fußball.
b Wir ___ Rotwein.
c ___ Sie Musik aus den 60iger Jahren?
d Ich ___ den neuen Film.

e Du ___ ihn, nicht wahr?
f ___ Sie Schnee?
g ___ Sie es in Berlin?
h Ich ___ klassische Musik.
i ___ ihr den neuen Fussballtrainer?
j Frau Schmidt und Herr Schmidt ___ alte Spielfilme.

XXVIII Cover up the English and see if you can guess the meaning
of the following sentences, then cover up the German.

a Ich mag das nicht.	I don't like that.
b Ich mag keine Schokolade.	I don't like chocolate.
c Magst du Milch?	Do you like milk? (asking a friend)
d Was mögen Sie?	What do you like? (asking an adult)

 Mögen is commonly used in the conditional: **möchte** – *would like to*. If you want to say *I would like* to do something, use *ich möchte* (see examples).

What would you like to do? (asking an adult)	Was möchten Sie machen?
I would like to go to the cinema.	Ich möchte ins Kino gehen.
What would you like to do? (asking a child/relative).	Was möchtest du machen?
I would like to sleep.	Ich möchte schlafen.
What would you like to drink? (asking an adult)	Was möchten Sie trinken?
I would like to drink a cup of coffee.	Ich möchte gerne eine Tasse Kaffee trinken.
What would you like to drink? (asking a child)	Was möchtest du trinken?
I would like an orange juice.	Ich möchte gerne einen Orangensaft.
Where would you like to go?	Wohin möchten Sie fahren?
We would like to go to Berlin.	Wir möchten nach Berlin fahren.

Now cover up the left side and see if you can guess the
meaning of the above sentences.

XXIX Fill in the appropriate form of **möchte**.

a ___ Sie mit mir essen gehen?
b Was ___ Sie mir sagen?
c ___ du morgen zu mir kommen?
d ___ ihr noch ein Stück Erdbeertorte haben?
e Ich ___ gerne nächste Woche in Urlaub fahren.

f ___ du mich was fragen?
g Wohin ___ Sie gehen?
h ___ Sie sich die neue Ausstellung anschauen?
i Wir ___ uns die Innenstadt anschauen.
j ___ du zu Fuss gehen?

XXX Fill in the appropriate modal verbs: **muss, müssen, willst, können, soll, kann, kannst, mögen, müsst, wollt.**

a Ich ___ die Musik nicht leiden.   I can't stand the music.
b Wir ___ Vokabeln lernen.   We have to learn vocabulary.
c Ich ___ mein Handy im Kino ausschalten.   I have to switch off my mobile phone in the cinema.
d ___ du mir bei der Gartenarbeit helfen?   Can you help me with the work in the garden?
e Wann ___ ihr euch treffen?   When do you want to meet?
f Wie ___ ich das wissen?   How am I supposed to know that?
g ___ du mir helfen?   Do you want to help me?
h ___ Sie bitte den Bericht lesen?   Can you please read the report?
i ___ ihr schon fahren?   Do you have to leave already?
j ___ Sie die deutsche Sprache?   Do you like the German language?

XXXI Match the English sentences with their German counterparts.

a Can he help me?   Wir müssen den Brief heute zu Ende schreiben.

b She can help me with grammar.   Wir können das verstehen.

c How am I supposed to know that?   Wir können verstehen, was Sie sagen.

d We can understand what you are saying.   Wie soll ich das wissen?

e We can understand that.   Sollen wir die Tür öffnen?

f How are we supposed to know that?   Soll ich das wissen?

g Are we allowed to open the door?   Wie sollen wir das wissen?

h Are we supposed to open the door?   Sie kann mir bei der Grammatik helfen.

i Am I supposed to know that?   Dürfen wir die Tür öffnen?

j We have to finish the letter today.   Kann er mir helfen?

1.2.4 ▶Fast track: verbs

Verbs are doing words: you use them to say what you (or someone/something else) are doing and to ask someone what he/she is doing.

In English when we look up a verb in the dictionary it is preceded by the word *to*: *to go, to drive, to eat,* etc. This is called the infinitive.

In German the infinitive ends in **-en** or **-n**.

In English we just have two main sorts of verbs: regular and irregular. In German these are called weak and strong verbs.

In English regular and irregular verbs change their endings when talking about he/she/it:

I speak → he speaks; I go → she goes; I fly → it flies.

In German the verb ending changes for all the different persons.

The different persons are:

singular		plural	
I	ich	we	wir
You (informal)	du	you	ihr
You (formal)	Sie	you (formal)	Sie
he	er		
she	sie	they	sie
it	es		

Reflexive verbs

Most reflexive verbs include the reflexive pronoun **mich/dich/sich**, known as accusative reflexive pronouns. Some verbs take the reflexive pronouns **mir** and **dir**, known as dative reflexive pronouns.

nominative	accusative	dative
ich	mich	mir
du	dich	dir
er/sie/es	sich	sich
wir	uns	uns
ihr	euch	euch
sie	sich	sich
Sie	sich	sich

Separable verbs

These are separable prefixes. The prefix goes to the end of a sentence.

usually indicates		infinitive example	example of use
ab	off	abfliegen take off	Das Flugzeug fliegt ab. The plane takes off.
an	at/on	anstellen to switch on	Ich stelle das Radio an. I switch on the radio.
		ankommen to arrive	Der Zug kommt an. The train is arriving.
auf	up /on	aufstehen to get up	Ich stehe um 6 Uhr auf. I get up at 6 o'clock.
		aufheben to pick up	Bitte heben Sie das auf! Please pick it up!
auf	open	aufmachen to open	Machen Sie das Fenster auf! Open the window!
aus	out/off	ausgehen to go out	Wir gehen oft aus. We often go out.
		ausstellen to turn off	Ich stelle das Radio aus. I turn off the radio.
mit	with/along	mitkommen to come with	Kommen Sie mit! Come with me!
		mitbringen to bring along	Bringen Sie Ihren Freund mit. Bring along your friend.
nach	after/to	nachkommen to come after	Ich komme nach. I'll follow.
	imitating	nachmachen to copy	Ich mache das nach. I copy that.
zu	to, towards	zuhören to listen to	Wir hören Ihnen zu. We are listening to you.
zurück	back	zurückgehen to go back	Ich gehe zurück. I'll go back.
zusammen	together	zusammenziehen to move in together	Sie ziehen zusammen.They are moving in together.
weg	away	weggehen to go away	Gehen Sie weg! Go away!

Inseparable verbs

The following prefixes are inseparable. They stay with the verb all the time!

be-

behalten	to keep
bekommen	to get
bewerben	to apply for a job

emp-

empfangen	to receive
empfehlen	to recommend
empfinden	to feel

ent-

entscheiden	to decide
enttäuschen	to disappoint
entdecken	to discover

er-

erinnern	to remember
erraten	to guess
erwarten	to expect

ver-

verstehen	to understand
verkaufen	to sell
verreisen	to go away

Ich verstehe Sie.	I understand you.
Wir verkaufen unser Auto.	We are selling our car.

Modal verbs

dürfen	may, to be allowed (to), must (not)
wollen	to want to
müssen	to have to, must, to be obliged to
können	can, to be able to, may
sollen	to be supposed to, shall
mögen	to like

1.3 The present tense

Remember: the present tense is used when talking about what you are doing now, or just about to do, or what you do habitually.

I am going to town. (I am on my way.)

I am going to town. (I am going in a few minutes.)

I go to town on Wednesdays. (I usually go.)

▶▶ **If you know about the ich form, go to the checklist on page 62.**

Remember that in German the verb ending changes according to who is doing what.

When you are talking about yourself you use the **ich** form.

The **ich** form ends in -**e**.

Most verbs end in -**en** in the infinitive.

 The infinitive is the part of the verb that you find in the dictionary when you look a verb up.

To make the **ich** form, take off the -**en** ending and replace it with -**e**:

Infinitive	stem	ich form
fahren	fahr	ich fahre
gehen	geh	ich gehe
laufen	lauf	ich laufe
telefonieren	telefonier	ich telefoniere
schlafen	schlaf	ich schlafe

There are a few verbs which end in -**n**. Take off the -**n** and add -**e**.

infinitive	stem	ich form
wandern	wander	ich wandere
behandeln	behandel	ich behandele
tun	tu	ich tue

You don't have to worry whether a verb is regular or irregular, the **ich** form always ends in -**e** except for the verb *to be* and the modal verbs.

infinitive	ich form	meaning
sein	ich bin	I am
können	ich kann	I can, I am able to
wollen	ich will	I want to
sollen	ich soll	I shall, I am supposed to
mögen	ich mag	I like
müssen	ich muss	I have to, I must, I may
dürfen	ich darf	I may, I am allowed to

I   Fill in the correct form of the verb.

   a Ich ___ in Deutschland. (wohnen)
   b Ich ___ in einem Krankenhaus. (arbeiten)
   c Ich ___ etwas zu trinken. (brauchen)
   d Ich ___ zu viel Kuchen. (essen)
   e Ich ___ das. (kapieren)
   f Ich ___ mich für Kunst. (interessieren)
   g Ich ___ nach Deutschland. (fahren)
   h Ich ___ Deutsch. (lernen)
   i Ich ___ aus der Schweiz. (kommen)
   j Ich ___ ein wenig Deutsch. (sprechen)

II   And some more: fill in the correct form of the verb.

   a Ich ___ gerne klassische Musik. (hören)
   b Ich ___ gerne im Garten. (arbeiten)
   c Ich ___ gerne Briefe. (schreiben)
   d Ich ___ kein Fleisch. (essen)
   e Ich ___ mich auf die Grammatik. (konzentrieren)
   f Ich ___ meinen Hund. (füttern)
   g Ich ___ am Wochenende zu Hause. (bleiben)
   h Ich ___ ein deutsches Buch. (lesen)
   i Ich ___ Deutsch. (unterrichten)
   j Ich ___ mich doch nicht. (blamieren)

> You always pronounce the **-e** at the end of the verb.

III   How would you say these in German? Remember not to
   translate *am*.

   a I speak English.   Ich ___ Englisch. (sprechen)
   b I eat cheese.   Ich ___ Käse. (essen)
   c I am wearing jeans.   Ich ___ Jeans. (tragen)
   d I work in an office.   Ich ___ in einem Büro. (arbeiten)
   e I am watching the news.   Ich ___ die Nachrichten. (schauen)
   f I play tennis.   Ich ___ Tennis. (spielen)
   g I go to school.   Ich ___ in die Schule.(gehen)
   h I am listening to a CD.   Ich ___ eine CD. (hören)
   i I live in England.   Ich ___ in England. (leben)
   j I understand you perfectly. Ich ___ Sie genau. (verstehen)

Now cover up the right-hand side of the page and see if you
can do the exercise again. Say each sentence aloud!

Choose five of the verbs above that you didn't know before (or
had forgotten) and that you think would be useful for you to
learn. Write down the meaning of the verbs. See how many of
them you can remember.

IV   How would you say these in German?

 a Ich ___ meine Patienten.   I am treating my patients.
                              (behandeln)
 b Ich ___ durch den Park.   I am strolling through the park.
                              (wandeln)
 c Ich ___ Briefmarken.   I collect stamps. (sammeln)
 d Ich ___ den ganzen Tag.   I am lazing about all day. (gammeln)
 e Ich ___ das gerne.   I like doing that. (tun)
 f Ich ___ in den Bergen.   I am hillwalking. (wandern)
 g Ich ___ nichts.   I don't change anything. (ändern)
 h Ich ___ mich um ihn.   I look after him. (kümmern)
 i Ich ___ sie   I admire her. (bewundern)
 j Ich ___ die Katze.   I feed the cat. (füttern)

Ich with *haben* and *sein*

Ich habe   I have
Ich bin   I am

V   How would you say these in German? Fill in the correct
    form of **haben** or **sein**.

 a I have an interesting job.   Ich ___ eine interessante Arbeit.
 b Have I got my key?   ___ ich meinen Schlüssel?
 c Am I right here?   ___ ich hier richtig?
 d I am taller than you.   Ich ___ größer als du.
 e I am a journalist.   Ich ___ Journalistin.
 f I have a good idea.   Ich ___ eine gute Idee.
 g I am very interested.   Ich ___ sehr interessiert.
 h Am I next?   ___ ich die nächste?
 i No, I am next.   Nein, ich ___ die nächste.
 j I have a better idea.   Ich ___ eine bessere Idee.

Now cover up the German and see if you can do the
exercise again.

Ich and modal verbs

> If you need more help with modal verbs, go back to 1.2.3

VI   Which modal verb would you use: **soll, kann, will, darf**?

 a Ich ___ das machen.   I can do that.
 b Ich ___ dir das nicht sagen.   I cannot tell you that.
 c Ich ___ ein Stück Kuchen essen. I want to eat a piece of cake.
 d ___ ich mich setzen?   May I sit down?
 e Was ___ ich Ihnen anbieten?   What may I offer you?
 f Ich ___ nicht so viel Salz essen. I am not allowed to eat so
                                        much salt.

g ___ ich das machen?   Shall I do that?
h Ich ___ es gerne anprobieren.   I want to try it on.
i ___ ich Ihnen helfen?   Shall I help you?
j Ich ___ es gerne ausprobieren.   I want to try it.

Ich and reflexive verbs
The reflexive pronoun is **mich** or **mir**.

> If you need more help with reflexive verbs, go back to 1.2.1.

VII   Reflexive verbs with **mich**. How would you say the following?

a I am looking forward   Ich ___ auf Weihnachten. (sich
   to Christmas.   freuen)
b I am afraid of rats.   Ich ___ vor Ratten. (sich fürchten)
c I am interested in Art.   Ich ___ für Kunst. (sich interessieren)
d I hurry up.   Ich ___. (sich beeilen)
e I apologise.   Ich ___. (sich entschuldigen)
f I say good bye.   Ich ___. (sich verabschieden)
g I am catching a cold.   Ich ___. (sich erkälten)
h I am recovering.   Ich ___. (sich erholen)
i I lie down.   Ich ___ hin. (sich legen)
j I decide to do it.   Ich ___ es zu tun. (sich entschließen)

VIII Reflexive verbs with **mir**. How would you say the following?

a I like myself.   Ich ___. (sich gefallen)
b I harm myself.   Ich ___. (sich schaden)
c I imagine that.   Ich ___ das ein. (sich einbilden)
d I trust myself.   Ich ___. (sich vertrauen)
e I am washing my hands.   Ich ___ die Hände. (sich waschen)
f I comb my hair.   Ich ___ meine Haare. (sich kämmen)
g I am cleaning my shoes.   Ich ___ die Schuhe. (sich putzen)
h I am cleaning my teeth.   Ich ___ die Zähne. (sich putzen)
i I am helping myself.   Ich ___ selbst. (sich helfen)
j I am not sure.   Ich ___ nicht ___. (sich sicher sein)

1.3.2 Talking to someone younger or someone you know well: du

This is the *you* form, or the 'second person' of the verb.

There are two forms of *you* in German: the **du** form and the **Sie** form.

You use the **du** form if you are talking to someone you know really well – a friend, a child, a student or an animal.

You do **not** use it when addressing a stranger, a business acquaintance or an older person. You only use it when talking to someone you know well.

▶▶ **If you are not going to need *du* at the moment, go on to 1.3.3.**

 If someone says: **Wollen wir uns duzen?** or **Sie können du zu mir sagen**, it means that this person is inviting you to call him or her **du**. You can answer **Ja, gerne** if you want to, or **Nein, danke**, if you don't want to.

The **du** form ends in **-st**.

Du and regular verbs

The **du** form is very easy to form:

to do/to make – **machen** → **du machst**

to go for a walk/to hike – **wandern** → **du wanderst**

Take the **-en** or **-n** off the verb in order to obtain the stem, e.g. **mach**, and add **-st** (**machst**).

infinitive	stem	*du* form
lachen	lach	du lach**st**
leben	leb	du leb**st**
lernen	lern	du lern**st**
tun	tu	du tu**st**

IX What is the **du** form of these verbs?

   a sagen   (say)
   b trinken   (drink)
   c leben   (live)
   d schwimmen (swim)
   e fragen   (ask)
   f hören   (listen)
   g singen   (sing)
   h spielen   (play)
   I studieren   (study)
   j weinen   (cry)

X Use the right form of the verbs in brackets to tell someone what he/she does.

   a You buy the cake.   Du ___ den Kuchen. (kaufen)
   b You love chocolate,   Du ___ Schokolade, nicht wahr?
       don't you?   (lieben)

c You go swimming, don't you?

Du ___ schwimmen, nicht wahr? (gehen)

d You hate to argue.

Du ___ es, dich zu streiten, nicht wahr? (hassen)

e You watch soaps, don't you?

Du ___ Seifenopern nicht wahr? (schauen)

f You live in Berlin, don't you?

Du ___ in Berlin, nicht wahr? (leben)

g You learn German fast.

Du ___ schnell Deutsch. (lernen)

h You ask many questions.

Du ___ viele Fragen. (stellen)

i You do sport.

Du ___ Sport. (machen)

j You play tennis.

Du ___ Tennis. (spielen)

> Once you have done the exercise, read the answers aloud to get used to the sound of the **du** form.

XI Which verbs are you going to use to complete these sentences: **wohnst, trinkst, machst, hörst, sprichst, schreibst, kochst, spielst, arbeitest, rauchst**?

a ___ du gerne Briefe?

b ___ du in Deutschland?

c ___ du Golf?

d ___ du Urlaub?

e ___ du Tee?

f ___ du Zigaretten?

g ___ du Deutsch?

h ___ du gerne Pop Musik?

i ___ du in einer Bank?

j ___ du gerne Suppe?

Du and irregular (strong) verbs

There are only a few strong verbs which are irregular in the present tense. These verbs change their vowel in the **du** – *you* and **er/sie/es** – *he/she/it* forms.

In some verbs the vowel changes from -**a** to -**ä**, for example:

to drive – **fahren** → **du fährst**
to fall – **fallen** → **du fällst**
to guess – **raten** → **du rätst**

XII What is the **du** form of these verbs? (Some verbs are separable.)

a to hold   halten   du ___
b to stop   anhalten   du ___ an
c to detain   aufhalten   du ___ auf

d to sleep	schlafen	du ___
e to sleep in	verschlafen	du ___
f to fall asleep	einschlafen	du ___ ein
g to catch	fangen	du ___
h to start	anfangen	du ___ an
i to receive	empfangen	du ___
j to carry	tragen	du ___
k to get on	sich vertragen	du ___ dich
l to fill in (a form)	sich eintragen	du ___ dich ein

In some verbs the vowel changes from **e** to **i** or **ie**, for example:

to eat – **essen** → **du ißt**
to see – **sehen** → **du siehst**
to read – **lesen** → **du liest**
to help – **helfen** → **du hilfst**
to meet – **treffen**→ **du triffst**
to kick – **treten** → **du trittst**

 In the case of **treten** the **du** form takes an additional **t** – **du trittst**.

XIII What would you expect the **du** form of these verbs to be?

a to give	geben	du ___
b to enter	eintreten	du ___ ein
c to appear	auftreten	du ___ auf
d to throw	werfen	du ___
e to throw away	wegwerfen	du ___ weg
f to speak	sprechen	du ___
g to promise	versprechen	du ___
h to read	lesen	du ___
i to read out	vorlesen	du ___ vor
j to read through	durchlesen	du ___ durch
k to help	helfen	du ___
l to help out	aushelfen	du ___ aus

Du with *haben* and *sein*

to have – **haben** → **du hast**

to be – **sein** → **du bist**

XIV How would you say these in German? Fill in the correct form of **haben** or **sein**.

| **a** ___ du Zeit für mich? | Have you got time for me? |
| **b** Was ___ du in deiner Hand? | What have you got in your hand? |

c Du ___ sehr freundlich.	You are very friendly.
d ___ du Deutscher?	Are you German?
e ___ du Kleingeld?	Do you have change?
f Du ___ zu viel zu tun.	You have too much to do.
g ___ du schon lange hier?	Have you been here for long?
h ___ du mir böse?	Are you angry with me?
i ___ du Lust, ins Restaurant zu gehen?	Do you feel like going to a restaurant?
j ___ du ehrlich?	Are you honest?

Du and modal verbs

 For more on modal verbs, go back to 1.2.3.

können → **du kannst** – *you can/you are able to*
wollen → **du willst** – *you want/wish to*
sollen → **du sollst** – *you shall, you are supposed to*
mögen → **du magst** – *you like*
müssen → **du musst** – *you have to, you must/you may*
dürfen → **du darfst** – *you may/you are allowed to/you must not*

XV Chatting up. Imagine you have already got to the **du** stage! Match the phrases, then cover the right-hand side of the page and see if you can remember the German equivalents.

a What do you want to drink?	1	Kannst du mir deine Telefonnummer geben?
b Would you prefer a coffee or a tea?	2	Magst du die Musik?
c Do you like the music?	3	Möchtest du mit mir irgendwann essen gehen?
d Do you want to dance?	4	Willst du meine E-Mail-Adresse haben?
e Do you want to sit down?	5	Willst du dich setzen?
f Do you want to meet me again?	6	Willst du lieber einen Kaffee oder einen Tee?
g Do you have to go now?	7	Willst du tanzen?
h Can you give me your phone number?	8	Was willst du trinken?
i Do you want to have my e-mail address?	9	Willst du mich wieder treffen?
j Do you fancy going for a meal with me sometime?	10	Musst du jetzt gehen?

Du and reflexive verbs

The reflexive pronoun is usually **dich**, but some reflexive verbs use **dir** instead.

Du wäschst *dich*. But: **Du wäschst *dir* die Hände. Dir** indicates whose hands are being washed.

> The reflexive pronoun **dir** (dative) is mainly used in connection with a part of the body: e.g. **Du wäschst dir die Hände. Du rasierst dir das Gesicht.**

Giving instructions to a child, friend or relative using the reflexive verb and **dich** is very easy. Take the stem off the verb and simply add **dich**.

infinitive	stem	instruction
waschen	wasch	wasch dich!
freuen	freu	freu dich!

This is how to tell a child, friend or relative what not to do or be:

Ärgere dich nicht!	Don't be annoyed!
Zieh dich nicht um!	Don't get changed!
Beeil dich nicht!	Don't hurry!

XVI   What are you being told to do? Match the German with the English.

a Wash yourself!   1 Freu dich!
b Have a shower!   2 Kämm dich!
c Hurry up!   3 Erinnere dich!
d Apologise!   4 Setz dich!
e Be pleased!   5 Wasch dich!
f Comb (your hair)!   6 Frag dich!
g Get dressed!   7 Zieh dich an!
h Sit down!   8 Dusch dich!
i Remember!   9 Entschuldige dich!
j Ask yourself!   10 Beeil dich!

The reflexive pronoun **dir** (dative) is used in connection with a part of the body. **Du wäschst *dir* die Hände. Du rasierst *dir* das Gesicht.** It is also used to indicate that you do something for yourself. **Du kaufst *dir* ein Auto.** – *You buy (yourself) a car.*

Wasch dir die Hände!	Wash (yourself) your hands.
Kämm dir das Haar!	Comb (yourself) your hair.
Putz dir die Zähne!	Clean (yourself) your teeth.
Kauf dir ein Auto!	Buy (yourself) a car!
Nimm dir Zucker!	Help yourself to sugar!
Mach dir keine Hoffnung!	Don't put up your hopes!

Some reflexive verbs are usually followed by the dative.

to imagine – **sich vorstellen** → **Stell *dir* das vor!**
to get hurt – **sich wehtun** → **Tu *dir* nicht weh!**
to get something – **sich etwas holen** → **Hol *dir* ein Buch!**
to take something – **sich etwas nehmen** → **Nimm *dir* ein Stück Kuchen!**

XVII   Which pronoun would you use: **dir** or **dich**?

a Kauf ___ ein Fahrrad!
b Wasch ___ die Füße!
c Wasch ___!
d Nimm ___ Schokolade!
e Hol ___ ein Glas!
f Mach ___ keine Sorgen!
g Zieh ___ den Mantel an!
h Setz ___!
i Erinnere ___!
j Entschuldige ___!

 For more on reflexive verbs, go back to 1.2.1.

Du and asking questions without a question word

You can make a question by changing the word order and putting the verb first. There is no *do* in a German question, you just go straight to the main verb.

Do you have? → *Have you?* – **Hast Du?**

Do you speak English? → *Speak you English?* – **Sprichst du Deutsch?**

This is one of those times when German is actually easier than English.

Have a look at these sentences. Aren't they straightforward? **Wunderbar!**

XVIII   Match the German sentences with the English.

a Wohnst du in Berlin?	1 Are you a student?
b Spielst du Tennis?	2 Do you like to listen/ Do you like listening to R&B?
c Gehst du gerne ins Kino?	3 Do you speak German?
d Hörst du Musik?	4 Do you live in Berlin?
e Hörst du gerne R&B Musik?	5 Do you take the bus?/ Are you going by bus?

f Verstehst du mich?

g Isst du gerne Pizza?

h Sprichst du Deutsch?

i Nimmst du den Bus?

j Bist du Studentin?

6 Do you like going to the cinema?

7 Do you listen/Are you listening to music?

8 Do you play/Are you playing tennis?

9 Do you understand me?

10 Do you like eating pizza?

> To get used to asking questions, read them aloud and listen to the CD.

XIX Which verb do you need to ask the question: **isst, wohnst, sprichst, trinkst, machst, fährst, reitest, schreibst, spielst, rauchst**?

a ___ du oft Briefe?
b ___ du in Deutschland?
c ___ du manchmal Golf?
d ___ du dieses Jahr in Urlaub?
e ___ du gerne Tee?
f ___ du Zigaretten?
g ___ du gut Deutsch?
h ___ du Currywurst?
i ___ du gerne Aerobic?
j ___ du gerne auf einem Pferd?

> Practise saying the questions aloud to get used to the sound.

XX Practise asking your friend what he/she is going to do. Just add the **du** form of the verb in brackets. Remember that some verbs have vowel changes.

a Do you speak German?   ___ du Deutsch? (sprechen)
b Are you playing golf tomorrow?   ___ du Morgen Golf? (spielen)
c Do you study German?   ___ du Deutsch? (studieren)
d Do you listen to music?   ___ du Musik? (hören)
e Are you going to Germany?   ___ du nach Deutschland? (fahren)
f Do you read many books?   ___ du viele Bücher? (lesen)
g Do you play the piano?   ___ du Klavier (spielen)
h Do you manipulate people?   ___ du Leute? (manipulieren)
i Do you sing often?   ___ du oft? (singen)
j Do you like cooking?   ___ du gerne? (kochen)

XXI Asking a child questions using the reflexive verb. Match the German to the English.

a Are you having a wash?
b Are you combing your hair?
c Are you bored?
d Are you pleased?
e Do you remember?

f Are you having a rest?
g Are you apologising?
h Are you putting on make-up?
i Are you meeting your friend?
j Are you annoyed?

1 Ärgerst du dich?
2 Entschuldigst du dich?
3 Langweilst du dich?
4 Ruhst du dich aus?
5 Triffst du dich mit deinem Freund?
6 Schminkst du dich?
7 Freust du dich?
8 Wäschst du dich?
9 Erinnerst du dich?
10 Kämmst du dich?

1.3.3 Talking about someone or something else: *er/sie/es*

▶▶ **If you know how to use the *er/sie/es* form, go on to the checklist on page 63.**

This form is called the 'third person'. In English it is the *he/she/it* form of the verb.

The third person singular is very easy. Add a **-t** to the stem of the verb.

Remember to use *one* – **man** in the same way.

The **er/sie/es** form usually ends in **-t**.

Er/sie/es and regular (weak) verbs

meaning	infinitive	stem	er/sie/es/man
to go	gehen	geh	geht
to laugh	lachen	lach	lacht
to ask	fragen	frag	fragt
to understand	verstehen	versteh	versteht

Er geht zur Universität.
Sie wohnt in der Schweiz.
Man raucht nicht beim Essen.
Er schreibt eine E-Mail.
Sie besucht eine Konferenz.

XXII Complete the following sentences by filling in the appropriate form of the verbs.

a Anton ___ in einem kleinen Dorf in Österreich. (leben)
b Er ___ regelmäßig auf die Berge. (klettern)
c Bärbel ___ ein interessantes Abendessen. (kochen)

d Sie ___ gerne neue Gerichte aus. (probieren)
e Man ___ den österreichischen Dialekt nicht immer. (verstehen)
f Man ___ ein paar interessante neue Ausdrücke. (lernen)
g Der Schnee ___ dieses Jahr sehr lange liegen. (bleiben)
h Der Schnee ___ nur sehr langsam. (tauen)
i Wann ___ der Bauer mit der Milch? (kommen)
j Er ___ die Milch und die Eier. (bringen)

Er/sie/es and irrregular (strong) verbs

In irregular verbs the vowel changes from **a** to **ä**:

to drive – **fahren** → **er/sie/es fährt**
to fall – **fallen** → **er/sie/es fällt**
to guess – **raten** → **er/sie/es rät**

> The vowel change is the same as for the **du** form.

XXIII   Complete the table.

		er/sie/es	
a to bake	backen	___
b to sleep	schlafen	___
c to dig	graben	___
d to wash	waschen	___
e to carry	tragen	___
f to booze	saufen	___
g to stop	halten	___
h to catch	fangen	___
i to receive	empfangen	___
j to drive	fahren	___

A few other verbs change their vowel from **e** to **ie** or **i**.

Here are the most common ones:

to meet – **treffen** → **er/sie/es trifft**
to eat – **essen** → **er/sie/es isst**
to see – **sehen** → **er/sie/es sieht**
to read – **lesen** → **er/sie/es liest**
to help – **helfen** → **er/sie/es hilft**
to take – **nehmen** → **er/sie/es nimmt**

XXIV   Complete the table:

		er/sie/es	
a to give	geben	___
b to take	nehmen	___
c to measure	messen	___
d to steal	stehlen	___
e to die	sterben	___

f	to kick	treten	——
g	to throw	werfen	——
h	to speak	sprechen	——
i	to read	lesen	——
j	to help	helfen	——

Er/sie/es with *haben* and *sein*

haben → **er/sie/es/man hat**
sein → **er/sie/es/man ist**

XXV   Which verb would you add to the sentence: **hat, ist**?

a Sie ___ Ferien.
b Er ___ im Urlaub.
c Es ___ kalt.
d Sie ___ ein neues Auto.
e Er ___ Schauspieler.
f Es ___ Winter.
g Sie ___ keine Zeit.
h Er ___ müde.
i Es ___ langweilig.
j Sie ___ Kopfschmerzen.

Er/sie/es and modal verbs

The *he/she/it* – **er/sie/es** form of modal verbs is the same as the *I* – **ich** form. It does not have the usual **er/sie/es** ending of the verb. The **-t** is dropped.

Learn the modal verb form of **er/sie/es** by heart as you might use it often. Remember that *one* – **man** is used in the same way as **er/sie/es**.

He/she it can/is able to	Er/sie/es kann
He/she it has to/must	Er/sie/es muss
He/she it shall/is supposed to	Er/sie/es soll
He/she it wants to	Er/sie/es will
He/she it is allowed to/may	Er/sie/es darf

XXVI   Which modal verbs would you use: **kann, muss, soll, will, darf**?

a ___ er dir helfen? (can)
b Sie ___ jetzt gehen. (has to)
c ___ sie mitkommen? (allowed to)
d Er ___ singen. (want to)
e Sie ___ Vokabeln lernen. (has to)
f Er ___ das nicht. (allowed to)

g Es ___ schneien. (supposed to)
h Man ___ hier nicht rauchen. (allowed to)
i Er ___ früh nach Hause gehen. (can)
j Man ___ hier leise sein. (supposed to)

Reflexive verbs in the third person

The reflexive pronoun for **er/sie/es** is **sich**. There is only one reflexive pronoun for the third person, not two as for **ich** and **du**, so it is easier!

sich vorstellen	to introduce oneself
sich setzen	to sit down
sich treffen	to meet
sich fragen	to ask oneself

 Before you do the next exercise look at the reflexive verbs in brackets first. If you aren't sure of their meaning look them up in the dictionary.

XXVII Fill in the correct form of the verb in brackets. **Was macht Robert?**

a Er ___. (sich duschen)
b Er ___ die Haare. (sich waschen)
c Er ___ die Zähne. (sich putzen)
d Er ___. (sich rasieren)
e Er ___ an. (sich anziehen)
f Er ___ die Haare. (sich kämmen)
g Er ___ an den Frühstückstisch. (sich setzen)
h Er ___. (sich beeilen)
i Er ___ den Hut auf. (sich aufsetzen)
j Er ___ mit seinen Freunden. (sich treffen)

For more reflexive verbs practice, go back to 1.2.1.

1.3.4 Talking about yourself and someone else: *wir*

▶▶ **If you are not going to use this form, skip the rest of this section and go to the checklist on page 64, as you need to be able to recognise it when you hear it, even if you don't use it.**

The **wir** form ends in **-en**.

You use the **wir** form (or the first person plural) where you use *we* in English, i.e. when talking about yourself and someone else: *we, my husband and I, my colleagues and I, my friend and I, Mrs Brown and I*, etc.

It is really easy to talk about *us* – **wir** in German as you just use the infinitive of the verb. No changes! **Wunderbar**! This applies to all verbs – weak, strong, reflexive or modal verbs. The only exception is the verb *to be* – **sein** → **wir sind**.

to speak – **sprechen** → **wir sprechen**
to sleep – **schlafen** → **wir schlafen**
to communicate – **kommunizieren** → **wir kommunizieren**
to risk something – **etwas riskieren** → **wir riskieren etwas**

XXVIII How would you say the following? Fill in the missing verbs.

a We are working today.   Wir ___ heute.
b We are playing golf tonight.   Wir ___ heute Abend Golf.
c We are studying German.   Wir ___ Deutsch.
d We are eating in a restaurant.   Wir ___ in einem Restaurant.
e We are communicating   Wir ___ in Deutsch.
   in German.
f We like dancing.   Wir ___ gerne.
g We live in a beautiful house.   Wir ___ in einem
                                       wunderschönen Haus.
h We are cooking.   Wir ___.
i We speak very quickly.   Wir ___ sehr schnell.
j We are reading the newspaper.   Wir ___ die Zeitung.

Wir with *haben* and *sein*

The **wir** form of **haben** is **wir haben** – *we have.*

The **wir** form of **sein** is **wir sind** – *we are.*

XXIX Fill in the right part of the missing verbs (**haben** or **sein**).

a Wir ___ einen neuen Laptop.
b Wir ___ in einer Besprechung.
c Wir ___ eine Besprechung.
d Wir ___ bald fertig.
e Wir ___ miteinander verwandt.
f Wir ___ zurückhaltend.
g Wir ___ glücklich.
h Wir ___ keine Informationen.
i Wir ___ kein Interesse an Politik.
j Wir ___ daran nicht interessiert.

Wir and modal verbs

The **wir** form for modal verbs is the same as the original form – the infinitive:

wir können
wir wollen
wir sollen
wir dürfen
wir mögen
wir müssen

XXX Match the following English sentences with their German counterparts.

a Wir dürfen hier nicht rauchen.	1 We want to eat.
b Wir können das machen.	2 We can smoke here.
c Wir müssen das tun.	3 We are not allowed to smoke here.
d Wir sollen gehen.	4 We can do that.
e Wir wollen essen.	5 We have to do that.
f Wir können hier rauchen.	6 We are supposed to go.
g Wir sollen das machen.	7 We have to go.
h Wir dürfen das tun.	8 We are allowed to do that.
i Wir müssen gehen.	9 We are supposed to do that.
j Wir dürfen essen.	10 We are allowed to eat.

Wir and reflexive verbs

The reflexive form is made by adding **uns**.

Wir beeilen uns.	We are hurrying up.
Wir stellen uns vor.	We are introducing ourselves.
Wir verlaufen uns.	We are getting lost.
Wir verirren uns.	We get lost.

XXXI How would you say the following?

a We are getting changed.	Wir ___. (sich umziehen)
b We are having a shower.	Wir ___. (sich duschen)
c We are having a rest.	Wir ___ aus. (sich ausruhen)
d We are hurrying.	Wir ___. (sich beeilen)
e We are glad.	Wir ___. (sich freuen)
f We are getting lost.	Wir ___. (sich verlaufen)
g We are filming ourselves.	Wir ___. (sich filmen)
h We are mistaken.	Wir ___. (sich irren)
i We are going to be late.	Wir ___. (sich verspäten)
j We are getting lost.	Wir ___. (sich verirren)

Asking questions with *wir*

XXXII Asking questions at work. Which verb would you use so it makes sense: **rufen, besuchen, haben, müssen, machen, ändern, sind, schicken, unterbrechen, buchstabieren**?

a Wo ___ wir bezahlen?
b Um wie viel Uhr ___ wir heute Schluss?
c Wohin ___ wir das Paket?
d Wann ___ wir den Kunden an?
e Wann ___ wir Mittagspause?
f Wann ___ wir unseren Kunden?
g Wir müssen Sie kurz ___.
h Warum ___ wir die Öffnungszeiten nicht?
i Wann ___ Sie fertig?
j Können Sie Ihren Namen bitte ___?

1.3.5 Talking to someone else: *Sie* (you)

▶▶ **If you know all about the *Sie* form, go to the checklist on page 65.**

The **Sie** form ends in **-en**.

You are going to use **Sie** when talking to other adults. It may also be called the polite form. Just like *you* in English, it can be used when addressing one person or more than one person, but it is always followed by the **Sie** form of the verb.

You probably already know a number of expressions that include the **Sie** form:

Sprechen Sie Deutsch? Do you speak German?
Wo wohnen Sie? Where do you live?

It is mostly used for asking questions.

XXXIII Read the following questions before covering up the German column. See if you can remember how to ask the questions in German.

a Are you going to the meeting? Gehen Sie zu der Besprechung?

b Are you coming? Kommen Sie?
c Do you know the agenda? Kennen Sie die Tagesordnung?
d Do you know how to operate the video recorder? Wissen Sie, wie man den Videoapparat benutzt?
e Can you contact your boss? Können Sie Ihren Boss kontaktieren?

f Do you have to go back to the hotel? Müssen Sie zum Hotel zurückgehen?

g Do you want to use
   the OHP?

Möchten Sie den
Overheadprojektor benutzen?

h Can you see the screen?   Können Sie den Bildschirm sehen?

i Do you need an interpreter? Brauchen Sie einen Dolmetscher?

j Do you understand the
   instructions?

Verstehen Sie die Instruktionen?

Asking questions with *Sie*

To ask questions in English you usually use the verb *to do*.
Questions in German are formed simply by inverting the
verb and pronoun.

Do you live in England?   Wohnen Sie in England?

Do you speak German?   Sprechen Sie Deutsch?

Do you drink wine?   Trinken Sie Wein?

Do you have a dog?   Haben Sie einen Hund?

 If you translate the questions literally it sounds funny and that might
make it easier to remember them: **Wohnen Sie in England**? –
Live you in England? or **Trinken Sie Wein**? – *Drink you wine*?

XXXIV Make questions by putting these words into the right order.

a Sie kommen Deutschland aus?

b Zigaretten rauchen Sie?

c Sie verstehen mich?

d Sie kommen mit?

e Sie heissen Frau Schmidt?

f Kaffee Sie trinken?

g Sie mit dem Bus fahren?

h Flugzeug fliegen Sie mit dem?

i Deutschland fliegen Sie nach?

j Sie Humor haben?

Sie (you) with *haben* and *sein*

to have – **haben** → **Sie haben**
to be – **sein** → **Sie sind**

XXXV Which verb makes sense in the following sentences (**haben**
or **sind**)?

a ___ Sie verheiratet?

b ___ Sie eine große Familie?

c ___ Sie Kinder?

d ___ Sie Deutsche(r)?

e ___ Sie berufstätig?

f ___ Sie einen interessanten Beruf?

g ___ Sie geschieden?
h ___ Sie hier geschäftlich oder im Urlaub?
i ___ Sie mit Ihrem Hotel zufrieden?
j ___ Sie Verwandte hier?

Sie and modal verbs

The **Sie** form for modal verbs is the same as the original form – the infinitive:

Sie können
Sie wollen
Sie sollen
Sie dürfen
Sie mögen
Sie müssen

▶▶ **For more on modal verbs, go back to 1.2.3.**

Sie können mir helfen.	You can help me.
Sie dürfen hier nicht parken.	You are not allowed to park here.
Sie sollen ihn anrufen.	You are supposed to phone him.
Sie mögen ihn, nicht wahr?	You like him, don't you?

When asking questions with a modal verb, the modal verb comes first and the infinitive goes to the end of the sentence.

Können Sie mir helfen?	Can you help me?
Sollen Sie hier warten?	Are you supposed to wait here?
Möchten Sie noch etwas trinken?	Would you like another drink?

XXXVI Match the English questions with the corresponding German.

a Wollen Sie ein Stück Apfelkuchen?
b Wollen Sie eine Tasse Kaffee haben?
c Können Sie mir bitte die Milch geben?
d Mögen Sie den Kuchen?
e Wollen Sie etwas Sahne?
f Wollen Sie lieber Kaffee oder Tee trinken?
g Dürfen Sie hier rauchen?
h Können Sie das bitte wiederholen?

1 Do you prefer to drink coffee or tea?
2 Are you allowed to smoke here?
3 Can you repeat that please?
4 Can you please spell that?
5 Can you tell me what time it is?
6 Do you want a cup of coffee?
7 Do you like the cake?
8 Can you please pass me the milk?

i Können Sie das bitte
   buchstabieren?

j Können Sie mir sagen,
   wie spät es ist?

9 Do you want some
   cream?

10 Do you want a piece
   of apple cake?

XXXVII Put the words into the right order to make questions that
you might hear in a hotel.

a Einzelzimmer wollen Sie ein?
b Sie helfen mir können?
c benutzen Sie wollen die Sauna?
d Sie können Schlüssel mir den geben?
e Sie wollen auf dem Zimmer Frühstück?
f Sie einen Balkon wollen haben?
g Sie wollen parken Ihr auf dem Auto Parkplatz?
h Wollen eine lesen Sie Zeitung deutsche?
i Sie wollen 7 frühstücken um Uhr?
j abreisen müssen Sie jetzt?

Sie and reflexive verbs

The reflexive pronoun is **sich**. Remember: A reflexive
pronoun reflects the meaning back to the subject or refers
to the subject.

 If you are not sure about reflexive verbs, go back to 1.2.1.

You have probably already heard some of the expressions,
for example:

Setzen Sie sich, bitte.   Please sit down.

XXXVIII Read these sentences. Then cover up the German and see
how many you can translate.

a Please introduce yourself!   Stellen Sie sich bitte vor!
b Are you going to meet   Treffen Sie sich mit Ihren
   your friends?   Freunden?
c Are you resting?   Ruhen Sie sich aus?
d Hurry up!   Beeilen Sie sich!
e Thank my colleague for it.   Bedanken Sie sich bei meinem
                                     Kollegen.
f Please sit beside me.   Bitte setzen Sie sich neben mich.
g Do you wish to say   Möchten Sie sich verabschieden?
   good bye?
h Don't catch a cold!   Erkälten Sie sich nicht!
i Don't be annoyed.   Ärgern Sie sich nicht.
j Convince yourself!   Überzeugen Sie sich!

1.3.6 Talking to someone else: *ihr* (you)

This is also known as the plural form of **du**.

▶▶ **If you are not going to need this, go on to 1.3.7.**

The **ihr** form always ends in **-t**.

The **ihr** form is made by adding **-t** to the stem. You don't have to worry about any irregularities apart from the verb *to be* – **sein**, which is **ihr seid**. There aren't any vowel changes in any verbs in the **ihr** form. **Wunderbar!**

meaning	infinitive	stem	ihr form
to go	gehen	geh	geht
to come	kommen	komm	kommt
to sing	singen	sing	singt
to stay	bleiben	bleib	bleibt
to phone	telefonieren	telefonier	telefoniert

XXXIX Match the following English sentences with the corresponding German. Then cover the German column and see how many you can remember.

a Kommt ihr aus Glasgow?   1 Do you live in Scotland?

b Wohnt ihr in einer Jugendherberge?   2 Do you speak German?

c Findet ihr Hamburg interessant?   3 Do you find Hamburg interesting?

d Was macht ihr hier?   4 Are you studying at a university?

e Mögt ihr es hier?   5 Are you staying in a youth hostel?

f Sprecht ihr Deutsch?   6 What are you doing here?

g Lebt ihr in Schottland?   7 Do you like listening to live music?

h Studiert ihr an einer Universität?   8 You speak German very well.

i Hört ihr gerne Live-Musik?   9 Do you like it here?

j Ihr sprecht sehr gut Deutsch.   10 Do you come from Glasgow?

XL How would you give instructions to a group of young people trying to find the youth hostel?

Use the verb in brackets.

a Ihr ___ die Strasse. (überqueren)

b Ihr ___ bis die Ampel grün ist. (warten)

c Ihr ___ dann immer geradeaus. (gehen)

d Ihr ___ die dritte Strasse links. (nehmen)

e Ihr ___ an der Kreuzung auf. ((auf)passen)

f Ihr ___ der Strasse nach Süden. (folgen)

g Ihr ___ an dem Park vorbei. (gehen)

h Ihr ___ zuerst nach links. (schauen)

i Ihr ___ jemanden wieder nach dem Weg. (fragen)

j Ihr ___ die Jugendherberge auf der rechten Seite. (sehen)

Ihr with *haben* and *sein*

 While **haben** – *to have* is still regular: **haben** (infinitive) **hab** (stem) **habt** (**ihr** form), the verb **sein** – *to be* changes its ending from **-t** to **-d**: **sein** (infinitive) **sei** (stem) **seid** (**ihr** form).

you have   ihr habt

you are   ihr seid

XLI Fill in the correct verb (**seid** or **habt**).

a ___ ihr müde?

b ___ ihr Hunger?

c ___ ihr Zeit?

d ___ ihr guter Laune?

e Ihr ___ Glück.

f Ihr ___ verrückt.

g ___ ihr Durst?

h Ihr ___ Deutsche, nicht wahr?

i ___ ihr Touristen?

j ___ ihr Freunde?

Ihr and modal verbs

This is easy – just add **-t** to the stem of the modal verb.

ihr könnt   you can

ihr dürft   you are allowed to

ihr sollt   you shall/should

ihr wollt   you want/wish to

ihr mögt   you like

ihr müsst   you have to

XLII Talking to young people, how would you ask the following questions?

a ___ ihr euch im Kino treffen? (wollen)

b ___ ihr mit dem Bus fahren? (müssen)

c Welchen Film ___ ihr euch angucken? (wollen)

d Ihr ___ euch in der Eingangshalle treffen. (können)

e Ihr ___ aber pünktlich sein. (müssen)

f Ihr ___ mit der U-Bahn fahren. (sollen)

g Ihr ___ nicht zu spät nach Hause kommen. (dürfen)

h Ihr ___ auch ein Taxi nehmen. (können)
i Wann ___ ihr euch treffen? (wollen)
j ___ ihr traurige Filme? (mögen)

Ihr and reflexive verbs
The reflexive pronoun is **euch**.

Sit down!   Setzt euch!

XLIII   Match the English with the German.

a Liebt ihr euch?	1 Don't argue!
b Schämt ihr euch?	2 Do you remember?
c Freut ihr euch?	3 You are mistaken.
d Erinnert ihr euch?	4 You are just imagining it.
e Unterhaltet ihr euch?	5 Are you interested in it?
f Benehmt ihr euch?	6 Are you pleased?
g Interessiert ihr euch dafür?	7 Are you ashamed?
h Ihr irrt euch.	8 Do you love each other?
i Ihr bildet euch das ein.	9 Do you talk to each other?
j Streitet euch nicht.	10 Are you behaving?

Now cover up the German and see how many sentences you can remember.

1.3.7 Talking to more than one person: *Sie* (you)

▶▶ **If you know all about the *Sie* form, go to the checklist on page 65.**

The **Sie** form ends in **-en**.

You are going to use **Sie** when talking to other adults. It is sometimes also called the polite form or formal form. Just like *you* in English, it can be used when addressing one person or more than one person, but it is always followed by the **Sie** form of the verb.

As it is exactly the same as **Sie** – *you* in the singular, go to page 65 for practice.

1.3.8 Talking about other people and things: *sie* (they)

▶▶ **If you know all about the *sie* form, go to the checklist on page 65.**

The **sie** form ends in **-en**.

You use **sie** – *they* when talking about more than one person or a group of people.

This is easy to use as the verb endings are all regular for weak, strong and modal verbs.

The only exception is the verb *to be* – **sein** → **sie sind**.

They are going to school.	Sie gehen zur Schule.
They are playing tennis.	Sie spielen Tennis.
They don't have any money.	Sie haben kein Geld.
They are eating too much!	Sie essen zu viel!

XLIV Can you guess what they are saying about the football fans? Match the English with the German.

a Sie gucken heute das Fußballspiel.

b Sie kaufen Ihre Eintrittskarten.

c Sie fahren zum Fußballstadium.

d Sie haben Fußballfahnen dabei.

e Sie unterstützen ihr Team.

f Sie schreien sehr laut.

g Sie sind enttäuscht, wenn das Team nicht gewinnt.

h Sie beschuldigen den Schiedsrichter, wenn sie verlieren.

i Sie sind glücklich, wenn ihr Team gewinnt.

j Sie gehen nach Hause und feiern.

1 They are shouting very loudly.

2 They are carrying football flags with them.

3 They are supporting their team.

4 They are watching the football match today.

5 They are disappointed when their team does not win.

6 They blame the referee when they lose.

7 They are happy when their team wins.

8 They go home and celebrate.

9 They are buying their entrance tickets.

10 They are going to the football stadium.

XLV A group of people is passing by while you are having your coffee in a little café. You are talking to your friend about them. Fill in the appropriate verbs: **tragen, sind, scheinen, essen, sprechen, haben, kommen, trinken, sehen, gehen.**

a Ich denke, sie ___ Studenten.

b Sie ___ relativ jung aus.

c Sie ___ gute Laune zu haben.

d Sie ___ alle moderne Klamotten.

e Sie ___ vielleicht aus Frankreich.

f Sie ___ französisch.

g Sie ___ gerne deutsches Bier.

h Sie ___ Bratwurst mit Kartoffelsalat.

i Sie ___ Hunger.

j Sie ___ in ein Restaurant.

Sie and reflexive verbs

When talking about clients, **sie** is used with reflexive verbs as follows:

Sie treffen **sich** mit unseren Kollegen.	They are meeting our colleagues.
Sie interessieren **sich** für unsere Produkte.	They are interested in our products.
Sie wundern **sich** über unsere niedrigen Preise.	They are surprised about our low prices.

XLVI Talking about a group of small children. Fill in the missing verbs: **kämmen, streiten, verstecken, helfen, ärgern, freuen, waschen, putzen, legen, ruhen.**

a Sie ___ sich die Hände. (wash)
b Sie ___ sich die Zähne. (clean)
c Sie ___ sich die Haare. (comb)
d Sie ___ sich aus. (rest)
e Sie ___ sich ins Bett. (lie down)
f Sie ___ sich über die Süßigkeiten. (be pleased)
g Sie ___ sich. (get angry)
h Sie ___ sich mit den anderen Kindern. (argue)
i Sie ___ sich hinter dem Schrank. (hide)
j Sie ___ sich gegenseitig beim Schuhe anziehen. (help)

1.3.9 ▶Fast track: present tense

Talking about yourself you use *ich*

The *I* – **ich** form of a verb ends in -e: **ich wohne, ich lese, ich studiere.** To make the **ich** form, take off the **-en or -n** ending and replace it with **-e**:

laufen → lauf → ich laufe
gehen → geh → ich gehe

You don't have to worry about whether a verb is regular or irregular, the **ich** form nearly always ends in **-e**. Exceptions are the verb *to be* – **sein → ich bin** and the modal verbs, which are irregular and which you should learn by heart.

infinitive	*ich* form	meaning
können	ich kann	I can/I am able to
wollen	ich will	I want/wish to
sollen	ich soll	I shall/I am supposed to
mögen	ich mag	I like
müssen	ich muss	I have to/I must/I may
dürfen	ich darf	I may/I am allowed to

The reflexive pronoun used with **ich** is **mich** or **mir**. For example, **ich wasche** *mich*, but **ich wasche** *mir* **die Hände**.

Talking to a friend, relative or child you use *du*

The regular **du** form ends in **-st**. To make the **du** form take off the **-en or -n** ending and replace it with **-st**:

machen → mach → du machst
wandern → wander → du wanderst

Irregular verbs have vowel changes in the **du** form:

fahren → du fährst
lesen → du liest

Reflexive verbs: Take the stem of the verb and add the reflexive pronoun **dich** or **dir**.

to hurry up – **sich beeilen → beeil dich!**
to sit down – **sich setzen → setz dich!**

The **du** form of modal verbs is irregular, so learn them by heart:

du kannst
du willst
du sollst
du magst
du musst
du darfst

The **du** form of **haben** and **sein** is irregular:

du hast
du bist

Talking about he/she/it/one you use *er/sie/es/man*

The **er/sie/es/man** form ends in **-t**. To make the **er/sie/es/man** form take off the **-en** or **-n** ending and replace it with **-t**:

gehen → geh → er geht
hören → hör → er hört

There are vowel changes as in the **du** form.

lesen = er/sie/es liest
fahren = er/sie/es fährt

The reflexive verb has only one reflexive pronoun **sich** (and not two different ones as for the **ich** and **du** form):

| Er verliebt sich. | He falls in love. |
| Sie setzt sich. | She sits down. |

The **er/sie/es/man** form of the modal verbs is the same as the **ich** form. It does not have the usual -**t** at the end.

Er/sie/es/man kann
Er/sie/es/man muss
Er/sie/es/man soll
Er/sie/es/man will
Er/sie/es/man darf

Haben and **sein** are irregular, and you will want to learn them by heart.

Er/sie/es/man hat
Er/sie/es/man ist

Talking about yourself and someone else: *wir*

It is really easy to talk about **wir** as you use the infinitive of the verb. No changes! **Wunderbar!** This applies to all verbs – weak, strong, reflexive or modal verbs. The only exception is the verb *to be* – **sein** → **wir sind**.

The reflexive pronoun is **uns**.

| Wir stellen uns vor. | We introduce ourselves. |
| Wir waschen uns. | We get washed. |

Talking about more than one person or a group of young people, relatives or friends: *ihr*

The **ihr** form is made by adding -**t** to the stem: **ihr wohnt, ihr kocht**. An exception is the verb *to be* – **sein** which is **ihr seid**. There is no vowel change in any verb in the **ihr** form: **ihr fahrt, ihr lest**.

The reflexive pronoun is **euch**.

| Setzt euch! | Sit down! |
| Benehmt euch! | Behave yourselves! |

Add a -**t** to the stem of the modal verbs:

ihr sollt
ihr dürft
ihr müsst
ihr wollt
ihr könnt
ihr mögt

The **ihr** form of **haben** is regular (**ihr habt**), but the **ihr** form of **sein** is irregular (**ihr seid**).

Talking to more than one person using the polite form: *Sie*

In the **Sie** form the verb endings are the same as in the infinitive. This applies to all verbs – regular, weak, strong and modal verbs. **Fahren Sie nach Hause? Mögen Sie Rotwein?** It is used in the same way as the **Sie** form (formal singular). The only exception is the verb *to be* – **sein** → **Sie sind**.

The reflexive pronoun for *you* (formal plural) is **sich**.

Fühlen Sie sich wohl?	Do you feel well?
Schämen Sie sich!	Shame on you!

The **Sie** form for modal verbs is the same as the infinitive:

Sie sollen
Sie dürfen
Sie müssen
Sie wollen
Sie können
Sie mögen

Talking about more than one person or a group of people: *sie*

The verb endings are the same as in the infinitive. This applies to all verbs – regular, weak, strong and modal verbs: **sie gehen, sie fahren, sie essen**. The only exception is the verb *to be* – **sein** → **sie sind**.

The **sie** form for modal verbs is the same as the infinitive:

sie sollen
sie dürfen
sie müssen
sie wollen
sie können
sie mögen

The reflexive pronoun for *they* is **sich**.

Sie streiten sich.	They argue.
Sie vertragen sich.	They get on with each other.

1.4 The past tenses

You use the past tenses to say what you have done or what has happened.

▶▶ **If you know when to use the perfect and imperfect tenses, go on to 1.4.2.**

In German there are two main ways of expressing the past tense:

i the perfect tense: **Ich habe gespielt** – *I played/I have played*

Ich habe gespielt.   I did play.
Ich habe gespielt, als ___   I was playing when ___

ii the imperfect or simple past: **Ich spielte** – *I played*

You can use either the perfect tense or the simple past in German. For example, *I flew to London yesterday* is either

- **Ich bin gestern nach London geflogen** or
- **Ich flog gestern nach London**.

The perfect tense is mainly used in conversation while the simple past, or imperfect, is mostly used in written German such as reports, newspaper articles, novels, etc.

1.4.1 The perfect tense

The perfect tense translates:

I played/I have played/ I was playing/I did play.	Ich habe gespielt.
I ate/I have eaten/ I was eating/I did eat.	Ich habe gegessen.
I arrived/I have arrived/ I was arriving/I did arrive.	Ich bin angekommen.
I swam/I swum/ I was swimming/I did swim.	Ich bin geschwommen.

You only need one tense in German to translate three or four different tenses in English.

1.4.2 Formation of the perfect tense

The structure is similar to that of the English perfect tense, e.g. – *I have eaten.*

The perfect tense is made up of:

- *to have* – **haben** + past participle → **Ich habe gegessen** – *I have eaten*
- or *to be* – **sein** + past participle → **Ich bin gelaufen** – *I have* (literally: *am*) *run*

 To have and *to be* are called auxiliary verbs (or helper verbs) as they are used with another verb.

In English the past participle usually ends in *-ed*: *I have danced; you have played; they have laughed.* There are also lots of irregular past participles in English: *sung, eaten, gone,* etc.

In German most past participles begin with **ge-**. For more on past participles see 1.4.6.

All past participles go to the end of the sentence. For more on word order in the perfect tense go to 1.4.7.

1.4.3 The auxiliary verbs: *haben* and *sein*

 If you know how to form the perfect tense with *haben* and *sein*, go to 1.4.6.

Approximately 70% of verbs go with *haben* – *to have*, the rest go with **sein** – *to be*.

 If you are not sure whether a verb takes **haben** or **sein**, use **haben**, as you have a high chance of getting it right. But if you want to learn it correctly, there are easy rules to follow.
As you are going to use the verbs *to have* and *to be* for the perfect tense frequently, here is a reminder of these two important verbs.

 If you have not learnt them yet, spend some time on it now.

singular		plural	
I have	ich habe	we have	wir haben
you (informal) have	du hast	you (informal) have	ihr habt
you (formal) have	Sie haben	you (formal) have	Sie haben
he/she/it has	er/sie/es hat	they have	sie haben

singular		plural	
I am	ich bin	we are	wir sind
you (informal) are	du bist	you (informal) are	ihr seid
you (formal) are	Sie sind	you (formal) are	Sie sind
he/she/it is	er/sie/es ist	they are	sie sind

1.4.4 Verbs with *haben* and *sein*

Here are a few verbs that take **haben** in the perfect tense:
essen, sprechen, denken, buchen, helfen, spielen, wohnen, tanzen.

 Remember that approximately 70% of all verbs go with **haben**.

I have eaten/ate	ich habe gegessen
you have spoken/spoke	du hast gesprochen
you (formal) have thought/thought	Sie haben gedacht
he/she/it has booked/booked	er/sie/es hat gebucht
we have helped/helped	wir haben geholfen
you have played/played	ihr habt gespielt
you (formal) have lived/lived	Sie haben gewohnt
they have danced/danced	sie haben getanzt

I Practise using **haben** and the past participle **gegessen** – *eaten*. How would you say the following?

a I have eaten.   ___ gegessen.
b You (informal) have eaten.   ___ gegessen.
c We have eaten.   ___ gegessen.
d They have eaten.   ___ gegessen.
e He has eaten.   ___ gegessen.
f You (formal) have eaten.   ___ gegessen.
g She has eaten.   ___ gegessen.
h Maria has eaten.   ___ gegessen.
i The children have eaten.   ___ gegessen.
j My husband has eaten.   ___ gegessen.

II Choose the correct form of **haben** to complete the sentences in the perfect tense.

a Ich ___ Tennis gespielt.   I played tennis.
b Du ___ Tennis gespielt.   You played tennis.
c Wir ___ Tennis gespielt.   We played tennis.
d Er ___ viel gelacht.   He laughed a lot.
e Petra und Klaus ___ viel gelacht.   Petra and Klaus laughed a lot.
f Das Kind ___ viel gelacht.   The child laughed a lot.

g Wir ___ beim Film geweint. We cried during the film.
h Du ___ wenig geweint. You cried a little.
i Petra und Klaus ___ nicht geweint. Petra and Klaus did not cry.
j Ich ___ das neue Buch gelesen. I read the new book.

Three groups of verbs take **sein** in the perfect tense. Instead of saying *I have arrived*, in German you say *I am arrived* – **ich bin angekommen.**

Group 1 includes verbs of motion, e.g. *to go* – **gehen,** *to drive* – **fahren,** *to swim* – **schwimmen,** *to come* – **kommen.**

Ich bin nach Hamburg gefahren. I went to Hamburg.

They are sometimes referred to as the 'coming and going' verbs as many of them imply action.

Group 2 are verbs expressing a state of mind, e.g. *to fall asleep* – **einschlafen,** *to wake up* – **aufwachen.**

Ich bin früh eingeschlafen. I fell asleep early.

Group 3 includes the verb *to be* – **sein** and *to stay/remain* – **bleiben.**

Ich bin in Amsterdam gewesen. I have been/was in Amsterdam.

Here are the most common 'going and coming verbs' which take **sein.**

 Read them aloud to get used to saying them and listen to the CD. This has a rhythm and is therefore a good way of learning. Try it out!

meaning	infinitive	past particple	example
to go	gehen	gegangen	Ich bin gegangen.
to come	kommen	gekommen	Ich bin gekommen.
to drive	fahren	gefahren	Ich bin gefahren.
to jog	joggen	gejoggt	Ich bin gejoggt.
to swim	schwimmen	geschwommen	Ich bin geschwommen.
to fall	fallen	gefallen	Ich bin gefallen.
to fly	fliegen	geflogen	Ich bin geflogen.
to travel	reisen	gereist	Ich bin gereist.
to sail	segeln	gesegelt	Ich bin gesegelt.
to hike	wandern	gewandert	Ich bin gewandert.
to run	rennen	gerannt	Ich bin gerannt.

To get used to the sound of the perfect tense choose a short sentence and practise it until you are really fluent.

Below are a few examples, or you can make up one of your own!

Ich bin ins Theater gegangen.	I went to the theatre.
Ich bin nach Berlin gefahren.	I went to Berlin.
Ich bin schwimmen gegangen.	I went swimming.

These are examples of how to use verbs with **sein** and other 'persons'.

I have flown/I flew	ich bin geflogen
you have gone/you went	du bist gegangen
you (formal) have swum/ you swam	Sie sind geschwommen
he/she/it has arrived/he/ she/it arrived	er/sie/es ist angekommen
we have left/we left	wir sind weggefahren
you have been/you were	ihr seid gewesen
you (formal) have left/you left	Sie sind abgefahren
they have come/they came	sie sind gekommen

III Choose the correct form of **sein** to complete the sentences.

a Ich ___ in die Stadt gegangen.
b Er ___ nach Hannover geflogen.
c Wir ___ ins Theater gegangen.
d Petra ___ in den Bergen gewandert.
e Er ___ tief gefallen.
f Tobias und Jackie ___ lange gelaufen.
g Ich ___ lange geschwommen.
h Du ___ weit gesegelt.
i Ihr ___ gestern angekommen.
j Wir ___ nach Amsterdam gefahren.

IV More practice with **sein**. Choose the correct form of **sein** to complete the sentences.

a Ich ___ einkaufen gegangen.
b Sie ___ schnell geschwommen.
c Er ___ dem Bus hinterhergerannt.
d Ich ___ letzten Sommer auf dem Wannsee gesegelt.
e Meine Mutter und ich ___ gestern in ein schönes Restaurant gegangen.
f Ich ___ gestern 20 Minuten im Park gejoggt.
g Martin ___ letzten Sommer auf den Ben Nevis gestiegen.
h Wir ___ um 7 Uhr abgefahren.

i Meine Schwester ___ in einem Pferdeturnier geritten.

j Ihr ___ pünktlich angekommen.

1.4.5 Sentences with *haben* and *sein*

As some verbs take **haben** and others **sein**, it is possible to have sentences with both **haben** and **sein** used as auxiliaries:

Ich **bin** zur Bar gegangen, und ich **habe** ein Bier bestellt.	I went to the bar and I ordered a beer.
Frau Braun **ist** zum Markt gegangen, und sie **hat** Tomaten gekauft.	Frau Braun went to the market and she bought some tomatoes.
Er **ist** ins Kino gegangen, und er **hat** einen Film gesehen.	He went to the cinema and he watched a film.

V Choose the correct form of **haben** or **sein** to complete the sentences.

a Ich ___ in die Stadt gegangen, und ich ___ neue Kleidung gekauft.	I went into town and I bought new clothes.
b Ich ___ zum Bahnhof gegangen, und ich ___ den 6 Uhr Zug genommen.	I went to the station and I got the 6 o'clock train.
c Die Touristen ___ eine Stadtrundfahrt gemacht, und sie ___ danach ins Theater gegangen.	The tourists went for a sightseeing tour and after that they went to the theatre.
d Wir ___ in einem Hotel gewohnt, und wir ___ dort schwimmen gegangen.	We stayed in a hotel and we went for a swim there.
e Regina ___ ihren Freund Klaus getroffen, und sie ___ mit ihm schwimmen gegangen.	Regina met her friend Klaus and she went swimming with him.
f Ich ___ zum Friseur gegangen, und ich ___ einen Haarschnitt bekommen.	I went to the hairdresser and had a hair cut.
g Unser Boss ___ schlechte Laune gehabt und sie ___ uns auf die Nerven gegangen.	Our boss was in a bad mood and she got on our nerves.
h Der Bus ___ unpünktlich gewesen, und er ___ oft angehalten.	Our bus was running late and it kept stopping.
i Ich ___ zu spät gekommen, und ich ___ keine Zeit für einen Kaffee gehabt.	I arrived late and I did not have any time for a coffee.
j Du ___ früh ins Bett gegangen, und ___ früh eingeschlafen.	You went to bed early and you fell asleep right away.

1.4.6 How to form the past participle

▶▶ **If you know how to form the past participle, go to 1.4.8.**

In English, the past participle of regular verbs is formed by adding -*ed* to the infinitive: *play* → *played, watch* → *watched, dance* → *danced*; but irregular verbs have their own participles: *sing* → *sung, read* → *read, tear* → *torn*, etc.

In German, weak (regular) verbs and strong (irregular) verbs form their past participles in different ways.

Most past participles start with **ge-**.

- Weak verbs end in -**t** : **gesagt, gefragt**
- Strong verbs keep their verb ending -**en**: **gefahren, gegessen**.

Some strong verbs also change the vowel.

singen → gesungen	sing → sung
gehen → gegangen	go → gone
finden → gefunden	find → found
trinken → getrunken	drink → drunk

Weak verbs

To form the past participle of a weak verb you simply add **ge-** at the beginning and -**t** to the stem of the verb.

infinitive	stem	add	past participle
machen	mach	ge___t	gemacht
sagen	sag	ge___t	gesagt
fragen	frag	ge___t	gefragt
lachen	lach	ge___t	gelacht

Ich habe das gemacht.	I did that.
Ich habe sie gefragt.	I asked her.
Ich habe das gesagt.	I said that.
Ich habe gelacht.	I laughed.

Verbs which end in -**ten** and -**den** add -**et** instead of -**t** to make them easier to pronounce: **arbeiten** → **gearbeitet**, **öffnen** → **geöffnet, melden** → **gemeldet**.

VI Here are the most common weak verbs. Using the rules above, what would the past participles of these verbs be?

	infinitive	past participle
a to say	sagen	___
b to practise	üben	

c to ask	fragen	—
d to laugh	lachen	—
e to believe	glauben	—
f to search	suchen	—
g to buy	kaufen	—
h to build	bauen	—
i to need	brauchen	—
j to live	wohnen	—

VII More practice! What is the past participle of the following verbs?

past participle

a rauchen	—
b bauen	—
c hören	—
d kochen	—
e putzen	—
f weinen	—
g hassen	—
h melden	—
i öffnen	—
j teilen	—

VIII And more practice: add the past participle.

past participle

a spielen	—
b tanzen	—
c suchen	—
d fragen	—
e zahlen	—
f wohnen	—
g leben	—
h machen	—
i schimpfen	—
j holen	—

IX **Was hat Wolfgang gestern Abend gemacht**? *What did Wolfgang do last night?* Add the right form of the past participle of the verb in brackets.

a Nach der Arbeit habe ich Squash mit Susanne ___. (spielen) — After work I played squash with Susanne.

b Dann habe ich ___. (kochen) — Then I cooked.

c Nach dem Abendessen haben wir Musik ___. (hören) — After dinner we listened to music.

d Wir haben zu der Musik ___. (tanzen) — We danced to the music.

e Wir haben eine Flasche Wein ___. (öffnen)	We opened a bottle of wine.
f Ich habe meinem Freund eine lustige E-Mail ___. (schicken)	I sent my friend a funny e-mail.
g Wir haben viel ___. (lachen)	We laughed a lot.
h Danach haben wir Fernsehen ___. (gucken)	After that we watched TV.
i Wir haben einen schönen Abend ___. (haben)	We had a nice evening.
j Es hat viel Spaß __. (machen)	It was fun.

When you read or hear a past participle and you don't know what it means, simply undo what you did to form it: i.e. take the **ge-** off the beginning and the **-t** off the end and add **-en** to the end. Example: **gemacht**

- take off **ge-** → **macht**
- take off **-t** → **mach**
- add **-en** → **machen**

Now if you don't know what the English meaning is you can look it up in your dictionary.

X Try that with the following verbs. What would the infinitive be?

past participle	infinitive	English meaning
a gehabt	—	—
b geschaut	—	—
c gereist	—	—
d geraucht	—	—
e gesaugt	—	—
f gemacht	—	—
g gehofft	—	—
h gekocht	—	—
i geplant	—	—
j geliebt	—	—

XI What is the infinitive of the following verbs and their English meaning?

	infinitive	English meaning
a gespielt	—	—
b getanzt	—	—
c gesucht	—	—
d gefragt	—	—
e gezahlt	—	—
f gewohnt	—	—

g gelebt	—	—	
h geputzt	—	—	
i geschimpft	—	—	
j geholt	—	—	

The verbs *to have* and *to be* are often used in the simple past in conversation: *I had a wonderful day –* **Ich hatte einen wunderschönen Tag**, instead of: **Ich habe einen wunderschönen Tag gehabt**.

The weather was awful – **Das Wetter war schrecklich**, instead of: **Das Wetter ist schrecklich gewesen**.

Exceptions: verbs starting with **be-**, **zer-**, **ent-** and **er-**

Most verbs starting with **be-**, **zer-**, **ent-** and **er-** do not have **ge-** at the beginning of the past participle, simply because we would not be able to pronounce them. Say them aloud to yourself and see how clumsy they would be.

Examples of verbs starting with **be-**:

to order – **bestellen** → **bestellt**
to visit – **besuchen** → **besucht**

Examples of verbs starting with **zer-**:

There are only a few, so just memorise any you think you might want to use:

to destroy – **zerstören** → **zerstört**
to scatter – **zerstreuen** → **zerstreut**

Examples of verbs starting with **ent-**:

to ventilate – **entlüften** → **entlüftet**
to discourage – **entmutigen** → **entmutigt**

Examples of verbs starting with **er-**:

to talk – **erzählen** → **erzählt**
to expect – **erwarten** → **erwartet**

Verbs ending in -**ieren** don't have the prefix **ge**- in their past participle but they do end in -**t**. They are easy to remember:

to telephone – **telefonieren** → **telefoniert**
to manipulate – **manipulieren** → **manipuliert**
to function – **funktionieren** → **funktioniert**

XII What are the past participles for the following verbs?

   a besuchen
   b betreuen
   c behaupten
   d bezahlen
   e bekommen
   f verhören
   g verkaufen
   h entleeren
   i entkommen
   j entlüften

 Find the English meaning for the verbs you don't know, then cover them up and see how many you get right.

XIII What is the past participle of the following verbs ending in **-ieren**?

   a akzeptieren
   b reparieren
   c kommunizieren
   d experimentieren
   e radieren
   f tolerieren
   g basieren
   h attackieren
   i polieren
   j hereinspazieren

1.4.7 The past participle of strong verbs

The past participle of strong verbs starts with **ge-** and ends in **-en**.

laufen → gelaufen
fahren → gefahren
lesen → gelesen
fangen → gefangen
essen → gegessen

XIV What is the past participle of the following verbs?

   a schlafen
   b blasen
   c graben
   d halten
   e hauen
   f kommen

g raten
h rufen
i sehen
j tragen

Some strong verbs change their vowel in the past participle
from **ei** to **ie**:

leihen → geliehen
speien → gespien
einreihen → eingeriehen

XV Change the infinitive to the past participle by adding **ge-** at
the beginning and change the vowel from **ei** to **ie**.

a schweigen
b schreien
c weisen
d schreiben
e bleiben
f gedeihen
g treiben
h steigen
i scheiden
j reiben

> Look these words up in the dictionary. Spend some time
> memorising them; practise those that you think you might need in
> the future. Read them aloud or listen to the CD. You will soon get
> used to the 'pattern'.

schweigen → geschwiegen
schreien → geschrien
weisen → gewiesen
schreiben → geschrieben
bleiben → geblieben
gedeihen → gediehen
treiben → getrieben
steigen → gestiegen
scheiden → geschieden
reiben → gerieben

Some strong verbs change their vowel in the past participle
from **i** to **u**:

finden → gefunden

XVI Practise the changes from **i** to **u** by filling in the past participle.

past participle

a ringen   —
b klingen   —
c binden   —
d schwingen   —
e singen   —
f sinken   —
g springen   —
h stinken   —
i trinken   —
j zwingen   —

The past participle of separable verbs

To form the separable past participle of weak verbs put -**ge**- between the prefix and the stem of the verb:

auslesen → **ausgelesen** – *to read to the end/to have read to the end*
hineinfahren → **hineingefahren** – *to drive in/to have driven in*

Look at the separable verbs with the stem **kommen** – *to come*:

ankommen – *to arrive*

Er ist sehr spät angekommen.   He arrived very late.

zurückkommen – *to come back*

Wir sind alle spät zurückgekommen.   We all came back late.

XVII What is the past participle of the following verbs?

infinitive	meaning	past participle
a hereinkommen	to come in	—
b herauskommen	to come out	—
c auskommen	to get on with somebody	—
d wegkommen	to disappear	—
e zurückkommen	to come back	—

 The prefixes **herein**, **heraus** and **herunter** are sometimes shortened to **rein**, **raus** and **runter**, so instead of **herauskommen** you may hear **rauskommen**, instead of **hereinkommen** you may hear **reinkommen**, and instead of **heruntergegangen** you may hear **runtergegangen**.

The past participle of verbs with the stem **gehen** is formed in the same way:

Wir sind die Treppe (he)runtergangen.   We went down the stairs.

XVIII Fill in the past participle of the following verbs with the stem **gehen**.

infinitive	meaning	past participle
a weggehen	to go away/to go out	____
b ausgehen	to go out	____
c heraufgehen	to go up	____
d hineingehen	to go into	____
e hingehen	to go to	____

The past participle of verbs with the stem **fahren** – *to drive/go* is formed in the same way:

Er ist aus der Garage (he)rausgefahren.	He drove out of the garage.
Der Zug ist pünktlich abgefahren.	The train left in time.

XIX Fill in the past participle of the following verbs with the stem **fahren**.

infinitive	meaning	past participle
a hinfahren	to drive to	____
b herausfahren	to drive out	____
c hereinfahren	to drive into	____
d abfahren	to leave	____
e zurückfahren	to drive back	____
f wegfahren	to go/drive away	____

The past participle of verbs with the stem **fallen** – *to fall* is formed in the same way, e.g. *to fall down* – **hinfallen** → **hingefallen**.

Ich bin gestern hingefallen.	I fell down yesterday.

XX Fill in the past participle of the following verbs with the stem **fallen**.

infinitive	meaning	past participle
a ausfallen	to be cancelled/ to break down	____
b hereinfallen	to fall for it	____
c auffallen	to stand out	____
d herunterfallen	to fall down	____
e hineinfallen	to fall into	____

XXI How would you say the following in German? Use the verbs in brackets to form the past participle.

a We arrived late. (ankommen)
b We got on well. (auskommen)
c We left quickly. (wegkommen)
d We came down. (herunterkommen)

e We went out. (ausgehen)
f We left. (abfahren)
g We drove away. (wegfahren)
h We fell for it. (hereinfallen)
i We stood out. (auffallen)
j We got on well with each other. (auskommen)

 Notice the difference between:

We went out last night.   Wir sind ausgegangen.

and

We went out of the house.   Wir sind aus dem Haus
herausgegangen (rausgegangen).

When you want to look up a past participle in the
dictionary you have to transform it back to its infinitive by
taking off **ge-** and replacing the final **-t** with **-en**:

aufgeholt → aufholen
zurückgeholt → zurückholen

 Spend some time practising this as you will come across past
participles that you won't know and you will not find them in your
dictionary. You have to find the infinitive first.

XXII   What is the infinitive of the following verbs?

infinitive

a aufgeholt   ___
b aufgesucht   ___
c angesagt   ___
d aufgesagt   ___
e ausgelebt   ___
f zugemacht   ___
g ausgeschimpft   ___
h abgebaut   ___
i angebaut   ___
j weggegeben   ___

 Now look up the infinitive of the past participle of the verbs you
don't know in your dictionary.

XXIII Fill in the infinitive of the following verbs.

		infinitive
a	angehört	—
b	zugehört	—
c	weggehört	—
d	angemacht	—
e	aufgemacht	—
f	kaputtgemacht	—
g	eingekauft	—
h	herausgeholt	—
i	aufgehört	—
j	hingefallen	—

1.4.8 The past tense and word order

The past participle always goes to the very end of the sentence even in longer sentences.

Ich habe **gesungen**.	I sang.
Ich habe unter der Dusche **gesungen**.	I sang in the shower.
Ich habe gestern für 10 Minuten unter der Dusche **gesungen**.	I sang yesterday for 10 minutes in the shower.
Wir haben **gelacht**.	We laughed.
Wir haben ganz viel **gelacht**.	We laughed a lot.
Wir haben den ganzen Abend ganz viel **gelacht**.	We laughed a lot all evening.
Er ist **gegangen**.	He went.
Er ist sehr früh **gegangen**.	He went very early.
Er ist sehr früh ins Bett **gegangen**.	He went to bed very early.

 As the past participle comes at the very end you will only find out what somebody has said if you listen to the whole sentence. Don't interrupt anybody, otherwise you will never find out what he or she was going to say!

XXIV Put the words in the correct order.

a sind am Freitag angekommen wir

b mein Essen ich gekocht habe

c einkaufen ich bin gegangen

d gefrühstückt ich habe

e Tee ich getrunken habe

f habe ich ferngesehen

g uns einen gemacht wir haben Abend schönen

h zu viel gearbeitet ich habe

i bin ich früh gegangen schlafen
j wir lange geschlafen haben

1.4.9 Asking a question about the past

Asking questions with a verb which takes **haben** is similar to English in questions such as:

Have you eaten both sandwiches?

Haben Sie beide belegten Brote gegessen?

You start the question with the verb **haben**. The only difference is the past participle comes at the very end.

Haben Sie den Kuchen *gegessen*?   Have you eaten the cake?
Haben Sie den Wein *getrunken*?   Have you drunk the wine?
Haben Sie den Brief *geschrieben*?   Have you written the letter?

Try to remember that the form *did* does not exist in a German question. The question: *Did you buy the house?* translates as: **Haben Sie das Haus gekauft?** Always remember that questions in the past start with a form of **haben** or **sein** followed by the person: **haben Sie ___?, hast du___?, hat er___?**

XXV Asking questions about somebody's holiday using the **du** form. Put the words into the right order to form a question.

a schöne hast du gehabt Ferien?
b du Tennis hast gespielt?
c gegessen hast du Pizza?
d Limonade hast du getrunken?
e getanzt hast du?
f du oft schwimmen gegangen bist?
g du dich gesonnt hast?
h du neue Freunde getroffen hast?
i geschickt hast du viele Postkarten?
j du gegangen segeln bist?

XXVI How would you ask somebody the following questions about his or her work? Put the words into the right order to form a question.

a ich habe gesagt das?   Did I say that?
b Sie verstanden haben das ?   Did you understand that?
c wir haben bekommen mehr Kunden?   Did we get more customers?

d Sie gelesen haben die Zeitung?	Did you read the paper?
e haben getroffen Sie meinen Kollegen?	Have you met my colleague?
f rausgeschickt Sie die E-Mail haben?	Did you send the e-mail?
g Sie den Brief haben geschrieben?	Did you write the letter?
h Sie angerufen haben ihn?	Did you phone him?
i Sie haben meine bekommen Nachricht?	Did you get my message?

1.4.10 The simple past tense/imperfect tense

The second way of expressing the past is by using the simple past tense, also known as the imperfect tense.

> If you tend to mix up names for tenses, you could remember that the simple past is called the simple tense because it consists of 'simply' one word:
>
> *went* – **ging**
> She *went* to the train station.   Sie *ging* zum Bahnhof.
>
> *read* – **las**
> She *read* the information.   Sie *las* die Information.
>
> *flew* – **flog**
> He *flew* to London.   Er *flog* nach London.
>
> *gave* – **hielt**
> She *gave* a speech.   Sie *hielt* eine Rede.

The simple past tense (imperfect tense) is mainly used in formal writing such as reports, newspaper articles, telling a story, novels and the news to narrate or report events which took place in the past. It is also used to describe a completed action.

Der Außenminister *besuchte* letzte Woche London.	The Foreign Minister visited London last week.
Es *regnete* den ganzen Nachmittag.	It rained all afternoon.
Das Erdbeben *dauerte* drei Stunden.	The earthquake lasted for three hours.

1.4.11 Formation of the simple past or imperfect tense

The majority of weak verbs are formed by adding the following endings to the stem of the verb:

singular		plural	
ich	**-te**	wir	**-ten**
du	**-test**	ihr	**-tet**
Sie	**-ten**	Sie	**-ten**
er/sie/es	**-te**	sie	**-ten**

leben – *to live* singular	plural
ich leb*te*	wir leb*ten*
du leb*test*	ihr leb*tet*
Sie leb*ten*	Sie leb*ten*
er/sie/es leb*te*	sie leb*ten*

XXVII Practise the simple past endings using the verb **fragen** – *to ask.*

a ich ___
b du __
c Sie __
d er/sie/es __
e wir __
f ihr __
g Sie __
h sie __
i Frau Meier __
j Die Besucher __

Verbs ending in **-den** and **-ten** add an additional **-e**. Verbs ending in **-nen** or **-men** after consonants other than **l** or **r** also add an **-e**. (It would be difficult to pronounce these without an additional **-e**.) For example:

arbeiten → ich arbeitete
baden → er badete
atmen → sie atmete

singular		plural	
ich	**-e**te	wir	**-e**ten
du	**-e**test	ihr	**-e**tet
Sie	**-e**ten	Sie	**-e**ten
er/sie/es	**-e**te	sie	**-e**ten

baden – *to bath*, **arbeiten** – *to work*

ich	badete	arbeitete
du	badetest	arbeitetest
Sie	badeten	arbeiteten
er/sie/es	badete	arbeitete
wir	badeten	arbeiteten
ihr	badetet	arbeitetet
Sie	badeten	arbeiteten
sie	badeten	arbeiteten

XXVIII Fill in the simple past using the verb **atmen** – *to breathe.*

a ich ___   **f** es ___
b du ___   **g** wir ___
c Sie ___   **h** ihr ___
d er ___   **i** Sie ___
e sie ___   **j** sie ___ (plural)

XXIX Fill in the simple past form of the verbs in brackets.

a Ich ___ eine Stunde. (warten)
b Er ___ in Deutschland. (wohnen)
c Wir ___ in Berlin. (leben)
d Susanne ___ bei der Bank. (arbeiten)
e Klaus ___ die ganze Nacht. (husten)
f ___ du mit den Kindern? (spielen)
g Wir ___ die Geschenke an die Armen aus. (teilen)
h Anna und Maria ___ die Konferenz. (eröffnen)
i Das Feuer ___ drei Stunden. (dauern)
j Die Kinder ___ in dem gefährlichen See. (baden)

Strong verbs in the simple past

Some strong verbs change vowels in the past tense and may drop the final consonant in the **ich** and **er/sie/es** persons.

present tense	simple past/ imperfect	present tense	simple past/ imperfect
ich sehe	ich sah	ich falle	ich fiel
du siehst	du sahst	du fällst	du fielst
Sie sehen	Sie sahen	Sie fallen	Sie fielen
er/sie/es sieht	er/sie/es sah	er/sie/es fällt	er/sie/es fiel
wir sehen	wir sahen	wir fallen	wir fielen
ihr seht	ihr saht	ihr fallt	ihr fielt
Sie sehen	Sie sahen	Sie fallen	Sie fielen
sie sehen	sie sahen	sie fallen	sie fielen

Try to learn the simple past form of every new verb that you are learning. The best method is to learn a new verb and all its tenses at the same time, e.g.

gehen, ging, gegangen; fahren, fuhr, gefahren.

It will probably stick better in your mind once you have memorised it that way!

Here are a few patterns for common vowel changes. It might help you to learn them, but be careful because they do not always apply.

A common pattern is a change from **ei** to **ie** or **i**.

	infinitive	simple past/ imperfect	past participle
to write	schreiben	schrieb	geschrieben
to stay	bleiben	blieb	geblieben
to bite	beißen	biss	gebissen
to thrive	gedeihen	gedieh	gediehen
to be called	heißen	hieß	geheißen
to lend	leihen	lieh	geliehen
to rub	reiben	rieb	gerieben
to ride	reiten	ritt	geritten
to shine	scheinen	schien	geschienen

Another common change is from **a** to **ie** or **i**.

	infinitive	simple past/ imperfect	past participle
to blow	blasen	blies	geblasen
to roast	braten	briet	gebraten
to receive	empfangen	empfing	empfangen
to catch	fangen	fing	gefangen
to fall	fallen	fiel	gefallen
to hold	halten	hielt	gehalten
to leave	lassen	ließ	gelassen
to sleep	schlafen	schlief	geschlafen
to run	laufen	lief	gelaufen
to guess	raten	riet	geraten

Exceptions: **backen, backte, gebacken; graben, grub, gegraben; tragen, trug, getragen**

 Spend a little time each week learning a few new verbs following the German verb learning pattern: infinitive, simple past, past participle, e.g. *to do, did, done* – **tun, tat, getan**. Choose from the irregular verb list at the back of the book.

XXX What are the simple past/imperfect tense and the past participle forms for the following strong verbs? Guess or look these up in your dictionary!

	simple past (ich)	past participle
a werfen	—	—
b trinken	—	—
c treffen	—	—
d sterben	—	—
e kennen	—	—
f mögen	—	—
g sehen	—	—
h rufen	—	—
i sitzen	—	—
j frieren	—	—

Haben and **sein** in the simple past

The verbs **haben** – *to have* and **sein** – *to be* are often used in the simple past/imperfect tense *instead of* the perfect tense.

haben	sein
ich hatte	ich war
du hattest	du warst
Sie hatten	Sie waren
er/sie/es hatte	er/sie/es war
wir hatten	wir waren
ihr hattet	ihr wart
Sie hatten	Sie waren
sie hatten	sie waren

Instead of saying:

- **Wir haben eine wunderbare Zeit gehabt**, you can say: **Wir hatten eine wunderbare Zeit.** – *We had a wonderful time.*
- **Das Wetter ist sehr prima gewesen**, you can say: **Das Wetter war prima.** – *The weather was great.*

Isn't it easier?!

XXXI Change the sentences from the perfect tense to the simple past/imperfect tense. For example:

Das Wetter ist furchtbar gewesen. → Das Wetter war furchtbar.

Wir sind glücklich gewesen. → Wir waren glücklich.

a	Wir sind in Berlin gewesen.	Wir ___.
b	Das Essen ist sehr gut gewesen.	Das Essen ___.
c	Wir haben einen Unfall gehabt.	Wir ___.
d	Wir haben Glück gehabt.	Wir ___.
e	Ich habe Kopfschmerzen gehabt.	Ich ___.
f	Ich bin nur kurz im Krankenhaus gewesen.	Ich ___.
g	Das Krankenhaus ist fantastisch gewesen.	Das Krankenhaus ___.
h	Die Zimmer sind sehr sauber und schön gewesen.	Die Zimmer ___.
i	Das Wetter ist nicht schlecht gewesen.	Das Wetter ___.
j	Die Museen sind interessant gewesen.	Die Museen ___.

1.4.12 The use of modal verbs in the past tense

The simple past tense/imperfect of modal verbs is formed by adding **-t** to the stem followed by the correct verb ending for each person. The umlaut is dropped.

	infinitive of modal verb					
	dürfen	**können**	**müssen**	**sollen**	**wollen**	**mögen**
Ich	durfte	konnte	musste	sollte	wollte	mochte
Du	durftest	konntest	musstest	solltest	wolltest	mochtest
Sie	durften	konnten	mussten	sollten	wollten	mochten
Er/sie/es	durfte	konnte	musste	sollte	wollte	mochte
wir	durften	konnten	mussten	sollten	wollten	mochten
ihr	durftet	konntet	musstet	solltet	wolltet	mochtet
Sie	durften	konnten	mussten	sollten	wollten	mochten
sie	durften	konnten	mussten	sollten	wollten	mochten

To use the modal verb when talking about the past is easy. The structure of the sentence is the same as in the present tense: the modal verb is in second place and the verb goes to the the end.

ich musste – *I had to*

Ich musste schnell nach Hause gehen.   I had to go home quickly.

ich konnte – *I could*

Ich konnte nicht lange bleiben.   I could not stay for long.

ich wollte – *I wanted to*

Ich wollte nach Hause gehen.   I wanted to go home.

ich sollte – *I was supposed to*

Ich sollte länger arbeiten.   I was supposed to work longer.

ich durfte – *I was allowed to*

Ich durfte eine Pause machen.   I was allowed to have a break.

ich mochte – *I liked*

Ich mochte das sehr gerne.   I liked that very much.

XXXII Which form of the modal verb in brackets do you need?

a Ich ___ gestern in die Kneipe gehen. (wollen)
b Wir ___ ein Eis essen gehen. (wollen)
c Tobias ___ mit dem Hund spazieren gehen. (wollen)
d Du ___ gestern leider nicht kommen. (können)
e Er ___ den Brief nicht abschicken. (können)
f Sie ___ nicht lange telefonieren. (können)
g Ich ___ zwei Stunden auf den Zug warten. (müssen)
h Susi ___ schnell zum Bus laufen. (müssen)
i Wir ___ ein Taxi nehmen. (müssen)
j Ich ___ eigentlich heute das Haus sauber machen. (sollen)

1.4.13 ▶Fast track: past tense

There are two main past tenses in German: the perfect tense and the imperfect, also known as the simple past.

* The perfect tense is used mostly in conversation.
* The imperfect is used more in writing.

The perfect tense is made up of one auxiliary verb (either **haben** – *to have* or **sein** – *to be*) and the past participle, e.g. **gegessen** – *eaten*, **gegangen** – *gone*, **gesagt** – *said*.

The structure is similar to that of the English perfect tense: *I have eaten* – **ich habe gegessen**. But remember that it also covers the other English past tenses.

The past participle always comes at the very end of the sentence, even in longer sentences.

Approximately 70% of verbs go with **haben** – *to have,* the rest go with **sein** – *to be.*

Three groups of verbs take **sein** – *to be.* Instead of saying *I have arrived,* in German you say *I am arrived* – **Ich bin angekommen.**

Group 1 includes verbs of motion, e.g. **gehen** – *to go,* **fahren** – *to drive,* **schwimmen** – *to swim,* **kommen** – *to come.*

Ich bin nach Hamburg gefahren.   I drove to Hamburg.

Group 2 are verbs expressing a state of mind, e.g. **einschlafen** – *to fall asleep,* **aufwachen** – *to wake up.*

Ich bin früh eingeschlafen.   I went to sleep early.

Group 3 includes the verb **sein** – *to be* and **bleiben** – *to stay/remain.*

Ich bin in Amsterdam gewesen.   I was in Amsterdam.

The past participle is made by adding **ge-** to the beginning of the verb.

Weak verbs replace the infinitive ending **-en** with **-t**: **ge+sag+t.**

Strong verbs keep the **-en**: **ge+waschen.**

Separable verbs put the **-ge-** in between the separable prefix and the verb:

weg+ge+laufen (**weglaufen** – *to run away*).

The simple past tense is made by adding the endings: te/test/te/ten/tet to the stem.

singular	plural
ich wohnte	wir wohnten
du wohntest	ihr wohntet
Sie wohnten	Sie wohnten
er/sie/es wohnte	sie wohnten

Modal verbs are mostly used in the simple past/imperfect tense even in conversation – the sentences would be clumsy if they were in the perfect:

Ich konnte nicht schlafen.   I couldn't sleep.
Er durfte nicht gehen.   He wasn't allowed to go.

1.5 Negatives, interrogatives and imperatives

▶▶ **If you know what these are, go on to 1.5.1.**

- Negatives: the negative is used to say *no* you *don't* do something, you *haven't* got something or to tell someone not to do something. A negative sentence is a sentence with a *no, not* or *don't* in it.
- Interrogatives: the interrogative is used to ask questions.

Imperatives: the imperative is used to give orders, directions or instructions; to tell someone what to do or what not to do!

1.5.1 Negatives: how to say what you do or don't want using *nicht*

▶▶ **If you know how to use *nicht*, go on to 1.5.2.**

To say you don't do something, you use **nicht**:

I don't smoke.	Ich rauche nicht.
I don't swear.	Ich schwöre nicht.

Nicht is used with verbs and makes the sentence negative.

The position of **nicht**: The position of **nicht** in a sentence depends on a number of rules. Here, we shall only concentrate on a few rules.

> Don't worry too much about the position of **nicht** in a German sentence. People will definitely understand what you wish to say – as long as your **nicht** is somewhere in the sentence! Here, however, are some easy rules to follow.

i When you are saying what you don't like doing: **nicht** comes straight after the verb in the present tense.

Ich rauche **nicht**.	I don't smoke.
Ich rauche **nicht** gerne Zigarren.	I don't like smoking cigars.
Ich tanze **nicht**.	I don't dance.
Ich tanze **nicht** gerne Salsa.	I don't like dancing the salsa.
Ich schwöre **nicht**.	I don't swear.
Ich schwöre **nicht** in der Gegenwart von Kindern.	I don't swear in the presence of children.

I Make the following sentences negative. How would you say:

a	I drive.	Ich fahre.	I don't drive.	Ich ___
b	He drives fast.	Er fährt schnell.	He doesn't drive fast.	Er ___
c	I am sulking.	Ich schmolle.	I am not sulking.	Ich ___
d	He sulks often.	Er schmollt oft.	He doesn't often sulk.	Er ___
e	The baby is crying.	Das Baby weint.	The baby is not crying.	Das Baby ___
f	Susi is crying.	Susi weint.	Susi doesn't cry in bed.	Susi ___
g	I sleep in.	Ich verschlafe.	I am not sleeping in.	Ich ___
h	He sleeps in often.	Er verschläft oft.	He does not sleep in often.	Er ___
i	I feel cold.	Ich friere.	I am not feeling cold.	Ich ___
j	She feels cold.	Sie friert.	She does not feel cold in the sun.	Sie ___

> In a sentence with the verb *to be* – **sein**, **nicht** comes straight after the verb.

Die Kühe **sind nicht** auf der Weide.	The cows are not in the meadow.
Die Katze **ist nicht** im Haus.	The cat is not in the house.
Der Hund **ist nicht** unter dem Bett.	The dog is not under the bed.
Die Vögel **sind nicht** in dem Baum.	The birds are not in the tree.

II Make these sentences negative.

a Wir sind bei der Arbeit. Wir ___ bei der Arbeit.
b Er ist in einem Krankenhaus. Er ___ in einem Krankenhaus.
c Ich bin zu Besuch hier. Ich ___ zu Besuch hier.
d Du bist in einer politischen Partei. Du ___ in einer politischen Partei.
e Sie sind auf einer Fähre. Sie ___ auf einer Fähre.
f Ihr seid sehr enttäuscht. Ihr ___
g Ich bin sehr glücklich. Ich ___
h Anne ist in Berlin. Anne ___
i Die Musik ist sehr gut. Die Musik ___
j Meine Arbeit ist interessant. Meine Arbeit ist ___

ii When you are describing how somebody feels, or how something makes you feel, **nicht** is placed before the adjective.

Sie scheint **nicht** müde zu sein.	She does not seem to be tired.
Der Film macht mich **nicht** traurig.	The film does not make me sad.
Die Geschichte hört sich **nicht** lustig an.	The story does not sound funny.
Wir sind **nicht** dumm.	We are not stupid.
Ich bin **nicht** konservativ.	I am not conservative.

III Put these sentences in the right order.

a wir nicht nervös sind
b nicht bin unhöflich ich
c seid nicht ihr verrrückt
d ist nicht aufrichtig sie
e er stur nicht ist
f fröhlich Lied das nicht macht mich
g höflich nicht diese Kinder sind sehr
h deprimiert das nicht macht mich Wetter
i Geld nicht glücklich mich macht.
j sich nicht Wolfgang fühlt gut.

iii In short sentences with a modal verb, **nicht** is placed before the second verb in the infinitive form.

Ich kann das **nicht machen**.	I can't do that.
Karin will **nicht schlafen**.	Karin does not want to sleep.
Ich will mit dir **nicht spazieren gehen**.	I don't want to go for a walk with you.
Er darf den Computer **nicht ausschalten**.	He is not supposed to switch off the computer.

IV Put these words in the right order.

a kann ich essen nicht
b will essen das nicht Baby
c darf nicht fernsehen Tochter meine
d soll die Kinder abholen ich nicht
e nicht gehen er möchte
f dürfen nicht hier wir parken
g Frau Schmidt fahren kann nicht
h Der kann nicht abfahren Zug
i Ich nicht lachen kann
j Sie nicht lachen dürfen

1.5.2 Negatives with *kein* and *keine*, etc.

Another negative form meaning *no, not* a, *not any* is **kein**.

Kein is used with a noun.

| I don't have any time. | Ich habe **keine** Zeit. |
| I don't have a cat. | Ich habe **keine** Katze. |

 To make a sentence negative you use **nicht** with a verb and **kein** with a noun.

verb		noun/direct object	
I am not playing.	Ich spiele nicht.	I am not playing tennis.	Ich spiele **kein** Tennis.
I am not eating.	Ich esse nicht.	I am not eating any pizza.	Ich esse **keine** Pizza.
We are not studying.	Wir studieren nicht.	We are not studying German.	Wir studieren **kein** Deutsch.
He is not singing.	Er singt nicht.	He doesn't sing any folk songs.	Er singt **keine** Volkslieder.
She isn't baking.	Sie backt nicht.	She is not baking any biscuits.	Sie backt **keine** Kekse.

 If you want to learn more about how to use **kein**, go to 2.3.3 (determiners).

To say what somebody is not, use **kein** in front of masculine job titles, **keine** in front of feminine job titles and **keine** for the plural.

kein (m)
keine (f)
kein (n)
keine (pl)

Masculine job titles:

Er ist kein Künstler.	He is not an artist.
Er ist kein Automechaniker.	He is not a car mechanic.
Er ist kein Student.	He is not a student.
Er ist kein Schauspieler.	He is not an actor.

Feminine job titles:

Sie ist keine Künstlerin.	She is not an artist.
Sie ist keine Automechanikerin.	She is not a car mechanic.
Sie ist keine Studentin.	She is not a student.
Sie ist keine Schauspielerin.	She is not an actor.

V Complete the sentences using **kein** or **keine**.

a She is not a gardener.	Sie ist ___ Gärtnerin.
b He is not a lorry driver.	Er ist ___ Lastwagenfahrer.
c She is not a teacher.	Sie ist ___ Lehrerin.
d He is not a police officer.	Er ist ___ Polizist.
e She is not a waitress.	Sie ist ___ Kellnerin.
f We aren't students.	Wir sind ___ Studenten.
g Gabi is not a hairdresser.	Gabi ist ___ Friseuse.
h He is not a teacher.	Er ist ___ Lehrer.
i I am not a housewife.	Ich bin ___ Hausfrau.

Kein/keine/keinen

When you say that you don't like something, you use either **keine**, **keinen** or **kein**.

If the thing you don't like is feminine (f) you use **keine**, if it is masculine (m) you use **keinen**, if it is neutral (n) you use **kein** and if it is something plural (pl) you use **keine**.

Ich mag keine Milch (f).	I don't like milk.
Ich mag keinen Käse (m).	I don't like cheese.
Ich mag kein Brot (n).	I don't like bread.
Ich mag keine Katzen (pl).	I don't like cats.

VI What kind of food do you not like? Use **kein**, **keine** or **keinen**.

a Ich mag ___ Fleisch (n).
b Ich mag ___ Kirschen (pl).
c Ich mag ___ Salat (m).
d Ich mag ___ Leberwurst (f).
e Ich mag ___ Tomaten (pl).
f Ich mag ___ Blutwurst (f).
g Ich mag ___ Speck (m).
h Ich mag ___ Schnaps (m).
i Ich mag ___ Fisch (m).
j Ich mag ___ Schnecken (pl).

1.5.3 Interrogatives: asking questions

Asking questions is quite straightforward in German – much easier than in English! The verb takes the first place. *Do you live in England?* → **Wohnen Sie in England?**

Literally: *Live you in England?* Remember not to translate *do!*

You can make a question by:

- inverting the pronoun and the verb
- using a question word

Inverting pronoun and verb: the question starts with the verb

statement	question
Er hat zwei Kinder.	Hat er zwei Kinder?
Susi ist verheiratet.	Ist Susi verheiratet?

VII Change the statements into questions.

    a Sie wohnt in Aachen. ___ in Aachen?
    b Die Kinder sprechen Deutsch. ___ Deutsch?
    c Sie telefoniert gerne. ___ gerne?
    d Tobias und Jackie fahren in Urlaub. ___ in Urlaub?
    e Ihr Mann ist sehr müde. ___ sehr müde?
    f Sie glauben an Gott. ___ an Gott?
    g Wir schicken eine E-Mail an ihn. ___ eine E-Mail an ihn?
    h Er raucht nicht. ___ nicht?
    i Du isst kein Fleisch. ___ kein Fleisch?
    j Sie ist Buddhistin. ___ Buddhistin?

VIII Change the following sentences into questions about sport and leisure time.

    a Sie treibt viel Sport. ___?
    b Sie geht regelmäßig schwimmen. ___?
    c Er spielt gerne Golf. ___?
    d Peter und Gabi gucken gerne Fußball. ___?
    e Du gehst gerne ins Kino. ___?
    f Er hört gerne Musik. ___?
    g Sie fährt gerne Skateboard. ___?
    h Er spielt gerne Gitarre. ___?
    i Er ist DJ. ___?
    j Die Kinder fahren gerne Rad. ___?

Asking questions using a separable verb

Whether making a statement or asking a question the prefix comes at the end.

Example:

Ich kaufe gerne ein. → Kaufe ich gerne ein?

Ich stehe früh auf. → **Stehe ich früh auf?**
Er wacht um 5 Uhr auf. → **Wacht er um 5 Uhr auf?**
Wir laden Freunde ein. → **Laden wir Freunde ein?**
Wir rufen meine Tante an. → **Rufen wir meine Tante an?**

IX   Make these statements into questions.

    a Ihr kauft gerne ein. ___?
    b Anne und Günther sehen gerne fern. ___?
    c Sie fahren heute weg. ___?
    d Wir kommen morgen wieder. ___?
    e Sie packt den Koffer aus. ___?
    f Er wacht um 5 Uhr auf. ___?
    g Wir laden Freunde ein. ___?
    h Wir rufen meine Tante an. ___?
    i Das Flugzeug fliegt ab. ___?
    j Der Zug kommt an. ___?

Asking questions using modal verbs

The modal verb comes first and the verb in the infinitive form comes at the end of the question.

Kann ich Ihnen helfen?	Can I help you?
Können wir bitte bestellen?	Can we order please?
Wollen Sie etwas zu trinken haben?	Do you want anything to drink?
Wollen Sie eine Nachspeise?	Do you want a dessert?
Dürfen wir noch ein Bier haben?	May we have another beer?

X   How would you translate these questions about going shopping and being in a restaurant.

    a Can you help me?
    b Can I do anything for you?
    c Can I try on the trousers?
    d Can I help you?
    e Do you want anything else?
    f Do you want a cup of coffee?
    g Can we order, please?
    h Do you want a starter?
    i Do you want a dessert?
    j Are we allowed to smoke here?

Asking questions with *haben* and *sein* – talking about work

This is when German is really easy. You start a question with a form of **haben** or **sein**. Remember that you do not translate *do*.

Haben Sie eine interessante Arbeit?	Do you have an interesting job? (literally: Have you an interesting job?)
Haben Sie nette Kollegen?	Do you have nice colleagues?
Sind Sie berufstätig?	Are you working?
Sind Sie eine Stewardess?	Are you a stewardess?

XI How do you ask these questions using **haben** or **sein**?

a ___ Sie viele Kollegen?
b ___ Ihre Kollegen alle Ausländer?
c ___ Sie alleine in Ihrem Büro?
d ___ Sie lange Arbeitszeiten?
e ___ Ihre Chefin eine nette Person?
f ___ Ihr Boss immer gute Laune?
g ___ Sie Vollzeit beschäftigt?
h ___ Sie ein Büro für sich alleine?
i ___ Sie ein gutes Gehalt?
j ___ Sie viel Stress bei Ihrer Arbeit?

Asking questions using a question word

Questions asking for information are introduced with a question word. The question word comes first, followed by the verb, followed by the subject.

| Where do you live? | Wo wohnen Sie? (literally: Where live you?) |
| Which languages do you speak? | Welche Sprachen sprechen Sie? (literally: Which languages speak you?) |

The question words are as follows:

meaning	question word
Who?	Wer?
How? What?	Wie?
Where?	Wo?
What?	Was?
Why? How come?	Wieso?
Why?	Weshalb?
Why?	Warum?
How much?	Wie viel?
Whom? Who?	Wen?
To whom?	Wem?
Where from?	Woher?
Where to?	Wohin?
When?	Wann?
What for?	Wozu?

XII   You will have come across a few of these questions before.
Translate the following sentences.

question word	verb	subject
a Wo	wohnen	Sie?
b Wie	heissen	Sie?
c Wo	arbeiten	Sie?
d Wann	kommt	der Postbote?
e Warum	lacht	ihr?
f Wohin	fahren	Sie?
g Warum	bellt	der Hund?
h Was	machen	Sie?
i Wer	ist	Frau Meier?
j Weshalb	lachen	die Kinder?

Have a look at these false friends:
Who in English is **wer** in German.
Where in English is **wo** in German.
A good way to remember might be for you to learn it in phrases
such as:

Who are you? I am Lisa.   Wer sind Sie? Ich bin Lisa.
                                 (using your own name).

Where is Mrs. Meier?   Wo ist Frau Meier? Frau Meier ist
Mrs Meier is in the office.   im Büro.

XIII   Talking to an adult. Complete these sentences with the
correct question word: **wie viel, wer, weshalb, wie, wen,
wohin, wo, wie lange, warum** or **woher**.

a ___ geht es Ihnen?
b ___ kostet das?
c ___ wohnen Sie?
d ___ sind Sie in Frankfurt? (why)
e ___ bleiben Sie in Frankfurt? (how long)
f ___ kommen Sie?
g ___ besuchen Sie?
h ___ fahren Sie Morgen?
i ___ sind Sie?
j ___ lernen Sie Deutsch?

XIV   Talking to a child. Complete the questions with the correct
question word to match the answer: **wie, was, wie viele,
woher, wann** or **wer**.

a ___ heisst du? Ich heisse Paula.
b ___ gehst du zur Schule? Ich gehe um 8 Uhr zur Schule.
c ___ alt bist du? Ich bin 10 Jahre alt.

d ___ kommen deine Eltern? Meine Eltern kommen aus Bremen.
e ___ machst du in deiner Freizeit? Ich spiele Fußball.
f ___ sind deine Freunde? Meine Freunde sind Angelika und Susanne.
g ___ Freunde hast du? Ich habe drei gute Freunde.
h ___ ist deine beste Freundin? Meine beste Freundin ist Claudia.
i ___ Geschwister hast du? Ich habe sieben Geschwister.
j ___ heisst dein Bruder? Mein Bruder heisst Klaus.

XV Meeting someone for the first time. What would you ask?
Match up each question with a suitable answer.

a Wie ist Ihr Name?	1 Ich besuche meine Familie.
b Woher kommen Sie?	2 Das Wetter gefällt mir sehr gut.
c Wie finden Sie Berlin?	3 Ich gehe heute Abend in ein Restaurant.
d In welchem Hotel wohnen Sie?	4 Ich bleibe für drei Tage.
e Wie lange bleiben Sie hier?	5 Ich gehe Morgen ins Theater.
f Wann fliegen Sie wieder zurück?	6 Ich komme aus England.
g Warum sind Sie hier in Berlin?	7 Ich heisse Paula.
h Was machen Sie heute Abend?	8 Ich fliege am Montag wieder zurück.
i Wann gehen Sie ins Theater?	9 Ich wohne im Hotel am See.
j Wie gefällt Ihnen das Wetter?	10 Ich finde Berlin sehr interessant.

1.5.4 Imperatives: giving orders, directions or instructions

▶▶ **If you know how to give orders and instructions, go on to 1.5.5.**

The imperative is the part of the verb you use when you are telling someone to do something, or giving instructions or an order: *Watch out! Stop! Turn left!* etc.

Giving orders, directions and instructions to someone to whom you say *du* (young person, friend, relative or animal)

▶▶ **If you think that you are not going to need this form, go on to 'Giving instructions, commands and directions using Sie'.**

Take the **-en** off the infinitive of the verb to use the **du** form:

Schlaf!	Sleep!
Trink!	Drink!

There are a few exceptions where you add an **-e** to the stem to make it easier to pronounce:

Warte!   Wait!
Erkälte dich nicht!   Don't catch a cold!

Remember also that some verbs have vowel changes in the **du** form, e.g. **lesen → du liest → lies**!

 Whether with an **-e** or without an **-e**, the sounds are nearly the same, so don't worry about that. If you have to tell someone to wait and you shout **Warte**! and you miss the **-e**, he or she would still get the message. More important is to learn some expressions.

XVI Look at these examples. You will probably have heard some of these before. What do these directions, instructions or commands mean?

a Geh!   **f** Komm!
b Lauf!   **g** Pass auf!
c Geh über die Straße!   **h** Schau!
d Fahr rechts rum!   **i** Stop!
e Hör zu!   **j** Probier mal!

XVII How would you tell a friend, relative or child to do these things? Use the **du** form. Remember that some verbs have vowel changes in the **du** form, e.g. **lesen → du liest → lies**!

a Watch less television.   ___ weniger Fernsehen! (sehen)
b Eat more vegetables.   ___ mehr Gemüse! (essen)
c Drink more water.   ___ mehr Wasser! (trinken)
d Go jogging.   ___ jogging! (gehen)
e Close the door.   ___ die Tür! (schliessen)
f Open the window.   ___ das Fenster! (öffnen)
g Show your passport.   ___ deinen Pass! (zeigen)
h Speak more slowly.   ___ langsamer! (sprechen)
i Come with me.   ___ mit mir! (kommen)
j Help me, please.   ___ mir bitte! (helfen)

When giving directions, instructions or commands using reflexive verbs you simply add **dich** after the verb when using the **du** form.

sich setzen – *to sit down*

Setz dich!   Sit down!

sich erholen – *to have a rest*

Erhol dich!   Have a rest!

XVIII Using the infinitives in brackets, how would you say the following?

a Be pleased!	(sich freuen)
b Don't be angry!	(sich ärgern)
c Hurry up!	(sich beeilen)
d Don't hurry!	(sich beeilen)
e Don't catch a cold!	(sich erkälten)
f Sit down!	(sich setzen)
g Wash yourself!	(sich waschen)
h Apologise!	(sich entschuldigen)
i Get dressed!	(sich anziehen)
j Dare!	(sich trauen)

Giving instructions, commands and directions using *Sie*

This is easy: all you do is use the infinitive of the verb and add **Sie**! When using a reflexive verb, just add **sich**.

Sprechen Sie!	Speak!
Lesen Sie!	Read!
Setzen Sie sich!	Sit down!

XIX Give instructions to an adult. Match the German and the English instructions.

a Go!	1 Hören Sie zu!
b Cross the road!	2 Kommen Sie!
c Turn right!	3 Hören Sie auf!
d Listen!	4 Gehen Sie weiter!
e Wait!	5 Gehen Sie!
f Pay attention!	6 Setzen Sie sich hin!
g Sit down!	7 Passen Sie auf!
h Come!	8 Warten Sie!
i Keep on going!	9 Fahren Sie rechts rum!
j Stop it!	10 Gehen Sie über die Straße!

 Did you notice? In separable verbs, the prefix goes to the end of the sentence as usual.

When using reflexive verbs add **sich** after the verb:

sich setzen

Setzen Sie sich!	Sit down!

sich erholen

Erholen Sie sich!	Have a rest!

sich hinsetzen

Setzen Sie sich schnell hin!	Sit down quickly!

XX Tell an adult what to do.

    a Enjoy yourself!   sich amüsieren ___

    b Remember!   sich erinnern ___

    c Imagine!   sich vorstellen ___

    d Talk to each other.   sich unterhalten ___

    e Apologise!   sich entschuldigen ___

    f Be pleased!   sich freuen ___

    g Don't be angry.   sich ärgern ___

    h Don't hurry!   sich beeilen ___

    i Don't catch a cold!   sich erkälten ___

    j Get dressed!   sich anziehen ___

XXI Telling someone what not to do. First match the English and the German, then cover up the right-hand side of the page and see if you can remember the German.

a Please don't smoke here!	1	Öffnen Sie bitte nicht die Tür!
b Don't walk on the grass!	2	Trinken Sie dieses Wasser nicht!
c Don't turn into the one-way street!	3	Überqueren Sie nicht die Strasse!
d Don't leave your luggage here!	4	Warten Sie hier nicht!
e Don't cross the road!	5	Lehnen Sie sich nicht aus dem Fenster!
f Don't lean out of the window!	6	Stellen Sie Ihre Skischuhe nicht auf die Theke!
g Don't drink this water!	7	Lassen Sie Ihr Gepäck nicht hier!
h Don't wait here!	8	Fahren Sie nicht in die Einbahnstrasse!
i Don't put ski boots on the counter!	9	Rauchen Sie hier bitte nicht!
j Please don't open the door!	10	Gehen Sie nicht über den Rasen!

1.5.5 ▶Fast track: negatives, interrogatives and imperatives

Negatives

The negative is used to say *no* you *don't* do something, you *haven't* got something, or to tell someone *not* to do something.

To say that you don't do something, you use **nicht**:

I don't smoke.	Ich rauche nicht.
I don't swear.	Ich schwöre nicht.

Nicht is used with verbs and makes the sentence negative, but if the verb is followed by a noun you use **kein**.

Ich spiele nicht. but **Ich spiele keine Tennis.**
Ich trinke nicht. but **Ich trinke keinen Schnaps.**

When you are saying what you don't like doing, **nicht** comes straight after the verb in the present tense.

Ich rauche nicht.	I don't smoke.
Ich esse nicht gerne Pizza.	I don't like eating pizza.

When you are describing how somebody feels or how something makes you feel, **nicht** comes in front of the adjective.

Sie scheint nicht müde zu sein.	She doesn't seem to be tired.
Wir sind nicht dumm.	We aren't stupid.

Interrogatives

You can make a question by:

* inverting the pronoun and the verb
* using a question word.

Sie hat einen Hund. → **Hat sie einen Hund?**
Er hat ein Auto. → **Hat er ein Auto?**

Whether making a statement or asking a question, the prefix of a separable verb comes at the end.

Ich kaufe gerne ein. → **Kaufe ich gerne ein?**
Ich stehe früh auf. → **Stehe ich früh auf?**

When asking questions with a modal verb, the modal verb comes first and the verb in the infinitive form comes at the end of the question.

Kann ich Ihnen helfen?	Can I help you?
Kann ich bitte bezahlen?	Can I pay, please?

Questions asking for information are introduced by a question word. The question word comes first, followed by the verb, followed by the subject.

Where do you live?	Wo wohnen Sie? (literally: Where live you?)
Which languages do you speak?	Welche Sprachen sprechen Sie? (literally: Which languages speak you?)

Imperatives

The imperative is the part of the verb you use when you tell someone to do something, or give instructions or an order: *Watch out! Stop! Turn left!* etc.

When giving orders, directions and instructions to someone to whom you say **du** (young person, friend, relative or animal) you take the **-en** off the infinitive of the verb.

Schlaf!	Sleep!
Trink!	Drink!

There are a few exceptions where you add an **-e** to the stem to make it easier to pronounce:

Warte!	Wait!
Erkälte dich nicht!	Don't catch a cold!

When giving directions, instructions or commands using reflexive verbs you simply add **dich** after the verb when using the **du** form.

sich setzen – *to sit down*

Setz dich!	Sit down!

sich erholen – *to have a rest*

Erhol dich!	Have a rest!

When giving instructions, commands and directions using **Sie** you use the infinitive of the verb and add **Sie**. When using a reflexive verb, just add **sich**.

Sprechen Sie!	Speak!
Lesen Sie!	Read!
Setzen Sie sich!	Sit down!

1.6 The future tense and the conditional

You use the future tense to talk about something that is going to happen, something you want to do or are going to do in the future. It indicates an action that is going to take place in the future.

In German there are two ways of saying what is going to happen:

- use the auxiliary verb *to become* – **werden**
- use the present tense and say when you are going to do the action.

The conditional implies a condition:

I would (do something) if (something else happens)	Ich würde ___ falls *or* wenn ___
I would like to ___ if ___	Ich hätte gerne ___ wenn *or* falls ___
I could ___ if ___	Ich könnte ___ wenn *or* falls ___

1.6.1 The future tense with *werden*

This form of the future tense is formed with the auxiliary verb **werden** – *to become* and a verb in the infinitive:

subject + **werden** + ___ + verb

 Remember the second verb always has to go to the end of the sentence.

It is used in a similar way to the English future tense *I shall / I will / I am going to.*

Ich *werde* nach Hamburg *fliegen.*	I am going to fly to Hamburg. / I will be flying to Hamburg.

werden – *to become*

singular		plural	
I	ich werde	we	wir werden
you (informal)	du wirst	you (informal)	ihr werdet
you (formal)	Sie werden	you (formal)	Sie werden
he/she/it	er/sie/es wird	they	sie werden

Ich *werde* ein Auto *mieten.*	I am going to rent a car./ I shall/will rent a car. I will be renting a car.
Wir *werden* unsere Verwandten *besuchen.*	We will visit our relatives./ We are going to visit our relatives./We will be visiting our relatives.

I Complete the following sentences with the correct form of **werden**.

a I will go in two hours' time.	Ich ___ in zwei Stunden fahren.
b We will do that today.	Wir ___ das heute machen.
c He will fly to Berlin.	Er ___ nach Berlin fliegen.
d We will buy a house.	Wir ___ ein Haus kaufen.
e You will be there in time.	Du ___ pünktlich da sein.
f We will get up at 9 o'clock.	Wir ___um 9 Uhr aufstehen.
g I will take the bus.	Ich ___ den Bus nehmen.

h The weather is going to be good.

Das Wetter ___ gut sein.

i She is going to arrive late.

Sie ___ spät ankommen.

j They are going to take the train.

Sie ___ den Zug nehmen.

Now cover up the German and see how many you get right.

Asking questions with *werden*

Will you do it?

Werden Sie es machen?

II Complete the following sentences with the correct form of **werden**.

a Will you take the bus?

___ du den Bus nehmen?

b Will you go home tomorrow?

___ du morgen nach Hause gehen?

c Are you going to help me?

___ du mir helfen?

d Will you help me?

___ Sie mir helfen?

e What will you do?

Was ___ Sie machen?

f Are you going to do that?

___ Sie das machen?

g When is he going to do that?

Wann ___ er das machen?

h How will Renate do that?

Wie___ Renate das machen?

i Will she be looking for a new car?

___ sie nach einem neuen Auto suchen?

Do them again – cover up the German and see how many you get right.

1.6.2 Future tense using the present tense

You can use the present tense to talk about future events if you say when it is going to happen. The present tense is most frequently used in conversation when talking about the 'near' future:

this evening

heute Abend

in the next few days

in ein paar Tagen

this year

dieses Jahr

Examples:

In the summer I am (I shall be) going to Switzerland.

Im Sommer fahre ich in die Schweiz.

I am going to send him an e-mail tomorrow.

Ich sende ihm Morgen eine E-Mail.

If you want to talk about something in the future and want to use the present tense, indicate *once* when it will happen and then you can continue the whole story in the present tense.

Dieses Jahr werden wir im Sommer nach Deutschland fahren.	This summer we are going to Germany.
Wir fliegen mit dem Flugzeug.	We shall be flying./We are going to fly.

III Continue the story putting in the correct form of the verbs in brackets.

a Wir ___ nach Hamburg. (fliegen)
b Ich ___ dort meine Tante. (besuchen)
c Wir ___ eine Woche. (bleiben)
d Danach ___ ich mit dem Zug nach Berlin. (fahren)
e In Berlin ___ ich eine Stadtbesichtigung. (machen)
f Mein Freund und ich ___ das Schloss Charlottenburg. (besuchen)
g Am Abend ___ wir auf den Kurfürstendamm. (gehen)
h Wahrscheinlich ___ mein Freund seine Freunde in einer Kneipe. (treffen)
i Wenn wir Zeit haben, ___ wir auf dem Wannsee. (segeln)
j Wir ___ bestimmt einen interessanten Urlaub. (haben)

IV These are some words you can use to indicate the future. See if you can find the matching word or expression.

a morgen früh	1 this summer
b morgen Abend	2 in a week
c nächste Woche	3 the day after tomorrow
d diesen Sommer	4 this year
e später	5 tomorrow morning
f bald	6 next weekend
g übermorgen	7 later
h dieses Jahr	8 tomorrow evening
i in einer Woche	9 soon
j nächstes Wochenende	10 next week

V Continue writing about the visit to Berlin (using the present tense).

Wir werden nächste Woche nach Berlin fliegen. Wir fliegen nächste Woche nach Berlin.

a Wir werden am Montag um 11 Uhr in Berlin ankommen.   Wir ___

b Wir werden die U-Bahn nehmen.   Wir ___

c Wir werden zum Hotel fahren.   Wir ___

d Wir werden unsere Kleidung auspacken.   Wir ___

e Danach werden wir zum Brandenburger Tor gehen.   Danach ___
f Wir werden eine Stadtrundfahrt machen.   Wir ___
g Wir werden eine deutschsprachige   Wir ___
    Stadtrundfahrt machen.
h Am Abend werden wir zum Kurfürstendamm gehen.   Am ___
i Danach werden wir ins Theater gehen.   Danach ___
j Dann werden wir in einen Club tanzen gehen.   Dann ___

1.6.3 The conditional: I would – *Ich würde/Ich hätte*

▶▶ **If you know all about the conditional, or if you have had enough of verbs for the moment, go on to 1.6.5.**

The conditional always includes a condition, whether expressed or not, for example:

I would so much like to go to Switzerland (if I had enough money and time).	Ich würde so gerne in die Schweiz fahren, (wenn ich genug Geld und Zeit hätte).
I would go if you paid me!	Ich würde gehen, wenn Sie mich bezahlen würden!

 The conditional is used to translate *would* in English.

You have probably heard expressions such as:

Wenn ich Zeit hätte, würde ich gerne nach München fahren.	If I had time, I would like to go to Munich.
Wenn ich Zeit hätte, würde ich ein Buch lesen.	If I had time, I would read a book.
Wenn das Wetter gut wäre, würden wir Morgen in die Stadt gehen.	If the weather were good we would go into town tomorrow.

It is also used as a more polite way of stating, or asking for, something: *I would like to* ___ – **Ich hätte gerne** ___

I would like a glass of wine.	Ich hätte gerne ein Glas Wein.
I would like a cup of tea, please.	Ich hätte gerne einen Tee.

1.6.4 How to form the conditional

This is not a tense to express the future but its form is very similar to that of the future tense, and it is really easy to learn.

In German, the conditional is formed with the auxiliary verb **würden** and a verb in the infinitive. It corresponds to the English pattern '*would* + infinitive'.

I *would like to go* to the pub if I had time.	Ich *würde* in die Kneipe *gehen*, wenn ich Zeit hätte.

würden – *would like to*

singular		plural	
I	ich würde	we	wir würden
you (informal)	du würdest	you (informal)	ihr würdet
you (formal)	Sie würden	you (formal)	Sie würden
he/she/it	er/sie/es würde	they	sie würden

Remember: The second verb always goes to the end of the sentence.

Wenn ich einen freien Tag hätte, würde ich den ganzen Tag im Bett *verbringen*.	If I had a day off, I would spend the whole day in bed.
Wenn ich einen freien Tag hätte, würde ich Musik hören und ein interessantes Buch *lesen*.	If I had a day off, I would listen to music and read an interesting book.

VI How would you say ___?

If I had a day off ___	Wenn ich einen freien Tag hätte, ___.
a I would go into town.	würde ich ___.
b I would go work in the garden.	würde ich ___.
c I would play tennis.	würde ich ___.
d I would go to the cinema.	würde ich ___.
e I would bake a Black Forest gateau.	würde ich ___.
f I would meet up with my friends.	würde ich ___.
g I would buy a cheesecake and eat it.	würde ich ___.
h I would go dancing.	würde ich ___.
i I would phone my friends.	würde ich ___.
j I would go shopping.	würde ich ___.

VII What would these people do if they were rich? Fill in the appropriate form of würden + the verb (some can be used twice). Choose from **arbeiten, aufgeben, gehen, investieren, kaufen, legen, machen, verschwenden**.

Example: Petra würde etwas Geld den Armen geben. (Petra
would give some money to the poor.) **111**

Verbs

a Angelika ___ sich ein neues Auto ___
b Peter und Renate ___ eine Weltreise ___
c Du ___ wahrscheinlich deinen Job ___
d Ich ___ in Rente ___
e Wir ___ das Geld nicht ___
f Tobias ___ das Geld auf ein Bankkonto ___
g ___ ihr euch ein neues Haus ___?
h ___ Sie lange in Urlaub ___?
i Ich ___ mit Sicherheit weniger ___
j Manche Leute ___ es in Aktien ___

1.6.5 Polite requests and useful phrases: *hätte gerne*

You might have heard the expression used by sales
assistants in shops, restaurants, pubs, cafés, etc:

Was hätten Sie gerne?	What would you like?

To order something in a restaurant, café or a pub you use:

Ich hätte gerne ___	I would like to have ___
Ich hätte gerne ein Stück Schwarzwälderkirschtorte.	I would like a piece of black forest gateau.
Ich hätte gerne einen Kaffee.	I would like a coffee.

You might hear the question:

Was hätten Sie gerne?	What would you like?
Hätten Sie gerne eine Tasse Tee?	Would you like a cup of tea?
Hättest du gerne ein Eis?	Would you like an ice cream?

I would like to have	ich hätte gerne
you would like to have (informal)	du hättest gerne
you would like to have (formal)	Sie hätten gerne
he/she/it would like to have	er/sie/es hätte gerne
we would like to have	wir hätten gerne
you would like to have	ihr hättet gerne
you would like to have (formal)	Sie hätten gerne
they would like to have	sie hätten gerne

VIII What would these people like to have? Add the correct
form of **hätten**.

a Was ___ Sie gerne?
b Was ___ du gerne?
c Ich ___ gerne ein Stück Schokoladenkuchen.
d Mein Mann ___ gerne eine Tasse Kaffee.

e Wir ___ gerne drei Gemüsesuppen.
f ___ du gerne etwas zu trinken?
g ___ Sie gerne etwas zu essen?
h Karin und Martina ___ gerne eine Nachspeise.
i Martin ___ gerne einen Salat.
j Wolfgang und Timo ___ gerne ein vegetarisches Gericht.

More polite requests and the use of *could*

You might have heard the expression before:

Could you help me?   Könnten Sie mir helfen?

could – **könnten**

I could	ich könnte
you could (informal)	du könntest
you could (formal)	Sie könnten
he/she/it could	er/sie/es könnte
we could	wir könnten
you could (informal)	ihr könntet
you could (formal)	Sie könnten
they could	sie könnten

You translate *could* with **könnten**.

I *could do* that if I had   Ich *könnte* das *machen*, wenn ich
the money.   das Geld hätte.

IX What could they do? Fill in the correct form of **könnten**.

a Nicola could go home.   Nicola ___ nach Hause gehen.
b We could go to the cinema.   Wir ___ ins Kino gehen.
c Nina could go to the   Nina ___ ins Sportzentrum gehen.
leisure centre.
d I could do judo.   Ich ___ Judo machen.
e You could play volleyball.   Du ___ Volleyball spielen.
f Claudia could go riding.   Claudia ___ reiten gehen.
g The children could go   Die Kinder ___ schwimmen
swimming.   gehen.
h We could meet afterwards.   Wir ___ uns danach treffen.
i They could go for   Sie ___ etwas essen gehen.
something to eat.
j We could go back to my   Wir ___ zu mir nach Hause
house.   gehen.

X You might know some of these expressions already. What
are these people saying or asking? Put these words in the
right order.

a könnte ich tun das
b uns treffen wir könnten

c könnte das machen man einfacher
d aufhören könnten wir zu streiten
e könnte mir mein helfen Mann
f mir du helfen könntest
g um 6 könnten wir Uhr da sein
h mit dem Fahrrad fahren ich könnte
i sein es könnte
j kommen er könnte wenn Zeit er hätte

1.6.6 ▶**Fast track:** the future and conditional

The future tense

There are two ways of saying what is going to happen in the future:

- using the auxiliary verb **werden** – *to become*
- using the present tense if you indicate when you are going to do something.

The future tense with **werden** is formed with a verb in the infinitive. It is used in a similar way to the English future tense *I shall/ I will / I am going to.*

Ich *werde* nach Hamburg *fliegen.*	I will fly to Hamburg./I am going to fly to Hamburg./ I shall fly to Hamburg.

The other and even simpler way is to use the present tense. It is frequently used in conversation. You mention once when something is going to happen and then you continue using the present tense.

The conditional: *would* and *could*

This is not a tense to express the future but its form is very similar to that of the future tense, and it is really easy to learn.

In German, the conditional is formed with the auxiliary verb **würden** and a verb in the infinitive. It corresponds to the English pattern '*would* + infinitive'.

I *would like to go* to the pub if I had time.	Ich *würde* in die Kneipe *gehen,* wenn ich Zeit hätte.

The verb in conditional sentences comes at the end of the sentence.

You translate *could* with **könnten**.

I *could do* that if I had the money.	Ich *könnte* das *machen,* wenn ich das Geld hätte.

You use *would* – **hätte** and *could* – **könnte** to make polite requests. You might have heard the expressions:

Was hätten Sie gerne?	What would you like?
Ich hätte gerne eine Tasse Kaffee.	I would like a cup of coffee.
Könnten Sie mir helfen?	Could you help me?

1.7 Useful expressions using verbs

▶ **If you know all these, go on to 1.7.9 Fast track.**

Haben – *to have* is often used in expressions where we would use the verb *to be* in English, for example:

She *is afraid* of spiders.	Sie hat Angst vor Spinnen.

In some expressions you can use either **sein** or **haben**. **Ich bin** hungrig and **ich habe** Hunger both mean *I am hungry*.

Special uses of *haben*

In some expressions using **haben**, the verb *to have* is not used in English.

There is/are – *es gibt*

In German you say *it gives* – **es gibt** instead of *there is/are*.

To know

There are two verbs for *to know* in German: *to know a person or thing* – **kennen**, *to know a fact* – **wissen**.

To like – *mögen* and *gerne*

You use **mögen** with a noun and **gerne** with a verb.

To remember – *sich erinnern*

To remind yourself of something or someone is a reflexive verb in German.

To take/bring

In some expressions *to take* is translated as **nehmen**, and in others as **bringen**.

1.7.1 Special uses of *haben*

Haben is used in some expressions where *have* is not used in English. Here are some examples.

Expressing fear

Ich habe Höhenangst.	I am afraid of heights.
Sie hat Angst vor Spinnen.	She is afraid of spiders.
Wir haben Angst vor Gewittern.	We are afraid of thunderstorms.
Hast du Angst vor Gespenstern?	Are you afraid of ghosts?
Sie haben Angst vor Rowdys.	They are afraid of hooligans.
Ich habe Sorgen.	I am worried.
Haben Sie Sorgen?	Are you worried?

Expressing hunger and thirst

There are two ways of expressing hunger and thirst in German: with the verb *to have* or *to be*.

Ich habe Hunger.	I am hungry.
Ich bin hungrig.	I am hungry.
Hast du Hunger?	Are you hungry?
Haben Sie Hunger?	Are you hungry?
Sind Sie hungrig?	Are you hungry?
Er hat Durst.	He is thirsty.
Er ist durstig.	He is thirsty.
Bist du durstig?	Are you thirsty?
Haben Sie Durst?	Are you thirsty?
Sie sind durstig.	They are thirsty.

Being right or wrong

Recht haben/Unrecht haben – *be right/be wrong*

Ich habe Recht.	I am right.
Sie haben Recht/Du hast Recht.	You are right!
Er hat Unrecht.	He is wrong.
Wir haben Recht.	We are right.
Sie haben Unrecht/Du hast Unrecht.	You are wrong!
Ich habe Unrecht.	I am wrong.

I   How would you say the following (using *haben*)?

a We are right.
b You are wrong.
c She is afraid of dogs.
d He is thirsty.
e They are hungry.
f Are you worried?
g I am thirsty.
h I am right.
i They are wrong.
j I am afraid of rats.

1.7.2 There is/are: *es gibt*

There is and *there are* are both translated by **es gibt** in German.

To say *there isn't* or *there aren't* is **es gibt kein/e/n**.

There was and *there were* is **es gab**.

There wasn't/ there weren't is **es gab kein/e/n**.

There aren't enough of them.	Es gibt nicht genug davon.
In my street there is/ there are ___	In meiner Straße gibt es ___.
There is a park at the end of my street.	Es gibt einen Park am Ende meiner Straße.
There are many building regulations.	Es gibt viele Bauauflagen.
There's not enough space for children to play.	Es gibt nicht genug Platz für Kinder zum spielen.
There was a bakery but as there weren't enough customers it shut.	Es gab eine Bäckerei, aber da es nicht genug Kunden gab, wurde sie geschlossen.
There aren't enough car parking spaces in my street, but there is a cycle lane.	Es gibt nicht genug Parkplätze in meiner Strasse, aber es gibt einen Fahrradweg.

II Now you try it. How would you say the following?

a There *isn't a* bank but *there is* a cash machine.

Es ___ ___ Bank aber ___ ___ einen Bankautomaten.

b There *are lots of* checkouts at the supermarket but *there aren't enough* cashiers. Luckily today *there wasn't a* queue.

Es ___ ___ Kassen im Supermarkt, aber es _____ nicht ___ Kassierer. Heute ___ es glücklicherweise ___ Schlange.

c There *used to be* a shop but now *there is* a pub.

Es ___ da ein Geschäft, aber jetzt ___ ___ da eine Kneipe.

1.7.3 To know: *wissen, kennen*

There are two verbs in German for the English verb *to know* – **kennen** and **wissen**. To know a person, thing or place you use **kennen** and to know a fact you use **wissen**.

kennen – *to know, be acquainted with a person, thing or place*, etc.

Ich *kenne* Frau Schmidt.	I know Mrs. Schmidt.
Ich *kenne* das Gebäude.	I know that building.
Ich *kenne* den Marktplatz.	I know the market place.

ich kenne	wir kennen
du kennst	ihr kennt
Sie kennnen	Sie kennen
er/sie/es kennt	sie kennen

wissen – *to know how to do something/ know a fact/know how ___ , whether ___*

Ich weiß, dass Berlin die Hauptstadt von Deutschland ist.	I know that Berlin is the capital of Germany.
Ich weiß nicht, wo meine Brille ist.	I don't know where my glasses are.
Ich weiß nicht, ob er kommt oder nicht.	I don't know whether he is coming or not.
Er weiß, wie man Leute manipuliert.	He knows how to manipulate people.

ich weiß	wir wissen
du weißt	ihr wisst
Sie wissen	Sie wissen
er/sie/es weiß	sie wissen

III Which verb are you going to use to reply to these questions, **kennen** or **wissen**? Choose the correct form: **weiß**, **wissen** or **kenne**.

a Weißt du was heute im Fernsehen kommt? Nein, ich ___ das nicht.

b Weißt du wie die Hauptstadt von Deutschland heißt? Klar, ___ ich das.

c Kennst du den neuen Song von Nena? Ja, den ___ ich.

d Weißt du was? Was soll ich denn ___?

e Kennst du dich in Berlin aus? Ja, ich ___ mich ganz gut in Berlin aus.

f Weißt du den Unterschied zwischen kennen und wissen? Na, klar ___ ich den.

g Warum weißt du das? Ich ___ es eben.

h Kennst du meinen Bruder? Ja, ich ___ ihn.

i Woher kennst du ihn? Ich ___ ihn von einer Ausstellung.

j Weißt du wo ich wohne? Ja, ich ___ wo du wohnst.

IV Which part of which verb are you going to use, **kennen** or **wissen**?

a Ich ___ Frau Meier schon sehr lange.

b Ihr Sohn ___ meine Tochter.

c Mein Mann ___ ihren Mann von der Arbeit.

d Wir ___ die ganze Familie.

e Mein Sohn ___ auch ihre Tochter.
f Meine Eltern ___ auch ihre Eltern.
g Wir ___, daß ihr Mann im Moment krank ist.
h Sie ___ aber noch nicht, was er hat.
i Er ___ nur, dass er bald ins Krankenhaus muss.
j Wir ___ nicht, ob wir ihn anrufen sollen, oder nicht.

1.7.4 To like: *mögen* and *gerne*

There are two words for *to like*: **mögen** and **gerne**.

You use **mögen** with a noun: *I like pizza* – **ich mag Pizza**, and you use **gerne** with a verb: *I like to read* – **ich lese gerne**.

Reminder: **mögen**

ich mag	wir mögen
du magst	ihr mögt
Sie mögen	Sie mögen
er/sie/es mag	sie mögen

	mögen	gerne
I like wine.	Ich mag Wein.	Ich trinke gerne Wein.
I like trees.	Ich mag Bäume.	Ich klettere gerne in den Bäumen.
I like flowers.	Ich mag Blumen.	Ich kaufe gerne Blumen.
I like tennis.	Ich mag Tennis.	Ich spiele gerne Tennis.

V Which word would you use: **mögen** or **gerne**?

a ___ du deine neue Kollegin?
b Ja, ich ___ sie.
c Gehst du ___ mit deinen Freunden aus?
d Ja, ich gehe ___ mit meinen Freunden aus.
e ___ ihr den neuen Film?
f Nein, wir ___ den neuen Film nicht.
g ___ er Rave Musik?
h Ja, er tanzt ___ zur Rave Musik.
i ___ Sie Walzer?
j Ja, ich tanze ___ Walzer.

1.7.5 To remember: *sich erinnern*

sich erinnern – *to remember* (literally: *to remind yourself of something/someone*)

In German, you remind yourself *of* something.

Ich *erinnere mich* an deinen Bruder.   I remember your brother.
Er *erinnert sich* nicht an mich.   He doesn't remember me.

Erinnerst *du dich* an den Tag, wo er zum ersten Mal zu uns nach Hause kam?		Do you remember the day when he first came to our house?	
Ich erinnere mich daran.		I remember that.	

Sich erinnern an is a reflexive verb and takes the accusative.

Reminder: accusative reflexive pronoun

singular		plural	
ich	mich	wir	uns
du	dich	ihr	euch
Sie	sich	Sie	sich
Er/sie/es	sich	sie	sich

VI   Which reflexive pronoun would you use?

a Wir erinnern ___.
b Du erinnerst ___.
c Ingo erinnnert ___.
d Martin und Christiane erinnern ___.
e Ich erinnere ___.
f Meine Chefin erinnert ___.
g Ihr erinnert ___.
h Erinnern Sie ___?
i Erinnerst du ___?
j Erinnert ihr ___?

To remember something/or someone – **sich erinnern** is followed by the preposition **an**.

Ich erinnere mich *an* meine Kindheit.	I remember my childhood.
Ich erinnere mich *an* deinen Kollegen, Klaus.	I remember your colleague, Klaus.
Wir erinnern uns *an* unsere letzten Ferien.	I remember my last holidays.
Er erinnert sich *an* sie.	He remembers her.

VII   How would you say the following?

a I remember Johann.
b He remembers me.
c I remember everything.
d I remember his wife.
e I remember her smile.
f My children remember her.
g We remember the Sunday in the Black Forest.
h I remember our boat trip.
i I remember the wonderful lunch.
j I remember the romantic evening.

1.7.6 To take – *nehmen* or *bringen*

You probably know how to ask for something in a shop, restaurant or café, etc.

Ich nehme einen Salat. – *I'll have a salad.*
Ich nehme es. – *I'll take it./I'll have it.*

You also use **nehmen** for:

I take the bus.	Ich *nehme* den Bus.
I'll take you with me.	Ich *nehme* Sie mit.
I'll take these trousers.	Ich *nehme* diese Hose.

But: you use **bringen** when you take somebody or something to somewhere, when you use *take* in English. You use **bringen** also when you use *to get* in English.

Please *get* me some chocolate.	*Bring* mir bitte etwas Schokolade.
I take my son to school.	Ich bringe meinen Sohn zur Schule.
I am taking my dog to the park.	Ich bringe meinen Hund zum Park.

VIII Which word would you use: **bringen** or **nehmen**?

a Ich ___ das Auto in die Garage.   I'll put the car in the garage.
b Ich ___ einen Mantel mit.   I am taking a coat.
c Ich ___ die Kinder ins Bett.   I take the children to bed.
d ___ Sie mir bitte eine Zeitung.   Get me a newspaper please.
e Ich ___ einen Salat.   I'll have a salad.
f Ich ___ Ihnen einen Tee.   I'll get you a cup of tea.
g ___ Sie Milch in Ihrem Tee?   Do you take milk in your tea?
h Ich ___ Sie zum Flughafen.   I'll take you to the airport.
i Kann ich meinen Hund ____?   Can I bring my dog with me?
j Wir ___ den Bus.   We'll take the bus.

1.7.7 More negative expressions

Negative statements include saying what you don't do as well as expressions with *no, nothing, never, nobody*, etc.

How to say you don't do something

You already know how to use **nicht** with a verb.

I don't speak fast.	Ich spreche nicht schnell.
I don't like swimming.	Ich schwimme nicht gerne.
They don't live in New York.	Sie leben nicht in New York.
We don't go away.	Wir fahren nicht weg.
Can't you read!	Können Sie nicht lesen!

Some more negative expressions

nicht mehr – *no/not any more*

Wir gehen nicht mehr in die Stadt.	We don't go to town any more.

nicht länger – *not any longer*

Ich kann das nicht länger machen.	I can't do that any longer.

nur – *only*

Er trinkt nur Mineralwasser.	He only drinks mineral water.

noch nie/nie – *never*

Sie war noch nie in Deutschland.	She has never been to Germany.
Ich mache das nie.	I never do that.

nichts – *nothing/not anything*

Ich habe nichts gemacht.	I didn't do anything.

niemand – *nobody/no one*

Niemand hat geantwortet.	Nobody answered.

IX How would you say the following? If possible, say them aloud so that you can get used to the way they sound. Then cover up the English, read them again and think about the meaning. Finally, cover up the German and try and remember the whole sentence.

a I have never been to Germany.
Ich bin ___ in Deutschland gewesen.

b Nobody phoned.
___ hat angerufen.

c We have never eaten in that restaurant.
Wir haben ___ in dem Restaurant gegessen.

d I don't meet Thomas any more.
Ich treffe Thomas ___.

e I don't have anything.
Ich habe ___.

f They don't live in Berlin any longer.
Sie wohnen ___ in Berlin.

g He has never seen Claudia.
Er hat Claudia ___ gesehen.

h They only have a small house.
Sie haben ___ ein kleines Haus.

i I have only ten Euros left.
Ich habe ___ 10 Euros übrig.

j She doesn't ride a bike any more.
Sie fährt ___ Fahrrad.

1.7.8 Since – *seit*

In these expressions, you use a different tense in German from the one you would expect to use in English.

In English, when we want to say we have been doing something for a certain length of time, we use the past tense. In German, when we wish to say that they have been doing it (for a year, etc.) and still are, we use the present tense.

Ich wohne hier seit sechs Jahren.	I have lived here for six years.
Er lernt Deutsch seit zwei Jahren.	He has been learning German for two years.
Ich habe dieses Auto seit einem Jahr.	I have had this car for a year.
Sie warten seit einer Stunde.	They have been waiting for an hour.
Ich bin hier seit zwei Tagen.	I have been here for two days.

X How would you answer these questions? Remember to use the present tense in your answers.

a Seit wann wohnen Sie hier? Ich ___ hier ___ 5 Jahren.

b Seit wann sprechen Sie Deutsch? Ich ___ Deutsch ___ einem Jahr.

c Wie lange kennen Sie schon Ihren Mann? Ich ___ meinen Mann ___ sieben Jahren.

d Wie lange haben Sie Ihr Auto schon? Ich ___ mein Auto ___ 8 Jahren.

e Wie lange sind Sie schon hier? Ich ___ hier ___ 1990.

f Wie lange wartet er schon hier? Er ___ hier ___ 3 Stunden.

g Wie lange wohnt Ihre Nichte schon in Göttingen? Sie ___ ___ zwei Jahren da.

h Wie lange sind Sie schon in Glasgow? Ich ___ ___ 1998 in Glasgow.

i Seit wann rauchen Sie nicht mehr? Ich ___ nicht mehr ___ 5 Monaten.

1.7.9 ▶**Fast track**: useful expressions using verbs

Haben

In German **haben** is used in some expressions where the verb *to be* is used in English.

Ich *habe* Angst vor Schlangen.	I am scared of snakes.
Ich *habe* Recht.	I am right.

Es gibt

There is and *there are* are both translated by **es gibt** in German:

es gibt – *there is/there are*

es gab – *there was/were*

Es gibt viele Bäume in unserer Straße.	There are many trees in our street.
Es gab nicht genug davon.	There weren't enough of them.

Kennen and wissen

There are two verbs for the verb *to know* in German: **kennen** and **wissen**. To know a person/thing or place you use **kennen** and to know a fact you use **wissen**.

kennen – *to know, be acquainted with a person, thing or place, etc.*

Ich kenne Frau Meier.	I know Mrs. Meier.
Ich kenne die Kneipe.	I know the pub.

wissen – *to know how to do something/ know a fact/know how ..., whether ...*

Ich weiß, dass Berlin die Hauptstadt von Deutschland ist.	I know that Berlin is the capital of Germany.

Mögen and gerne

There are two words for *to like*: **mögen** and **gerne**.

You use **mögen** with a noun: *I like pizza.* – **Ich mag Pizza**, and you use **gerne** with a verb: *I like to read.* – **Ich lese gerne**.

Sich erinnern

In German, you remind yourself *of* something: **sich erinnern an**.

Ich *erinnere mich* an deinen Bruder.	I remember your brother.
Ich *erinnere mich* an meinen letzten Urlaub.	I remember my last holiday.

Nehmen and bringen

You use **bringen** when you take somebody or something to somewhere, when you use *take* in English. You use **bringen** also when you use *to get* in English.

I *take* the books to the library.	Ich *bringe* die Bücher in die Bibliothek.

Please *get* me some chocolates. *Bring* mir bitte etwas Schokolade.

Some more negative expressions

nicht mehr – *no/not any more*
nur – *only*
nicht länger – *not any longer*
noch nie/nie – *never*
nichts – *nothing/not anything*
niemand – *nobody/no one*

Seit

In English, when we want to say we have been doing something for a certain length of time, we use the past tense. In German, when we wish to say that they have been doing it (for a year, etc.) and still are, we use the present tense.

Ich wohne hier seit sechs Jahren.	I have lived here for six years.
Er lernt Deutsch seit zwei Jahren.	He has been learning German for two years.

1.8 Word order

Word order is important in German sentences.

In English most sentences are made up of:

1 subject
2 verb
3 object

with no particular rules about where anything else has to go.

In German there are rules about where certain expressions should go in a sentence. Some rules are stricter than others.

Rule 1: Subject, verb, object

The verb **always** comes second in the sentence.

Most sentences begin with the subject, followed by the verb.

1 subject	2 verb	3 object + anything else
Mein Sohn	liebt	seine Freundin.
My son	loves	his girlfriend.
Meine Freundin	wohnt	mit ihrem Mann in Berlin.
My friend	lives	with her husband in Berlin.
Ihr Mann	arbeitet	für eine große internationale Firma.
Her husband	works	for a large international company.

For more practice, go to 1.8.1.

Rule 2: Time, manner, place

In longer sentences the word order is usually:

4 time
5 manner
6 place.

Expressions of **time** describe **when** something is done/happens: **gestern** – *yesterday*; **letztes Jahr** – *last year*; **jetzt** – *now*.

Expressions of **manner** describe **how** something is done/happens: **schnell** – *quickly*; **mit dem Flugzeug** – *by plane.*

Expressions of **place** describe **where** something is done/happens: **in Berlin** – *in* Berlin; **auf dem Land** – *in the country.*

1 subject	2 verb 1	3 time/ when?	4 manner/ how?	5 place/ where?	6 verb 2
Herr Schmidt	fährt	am Montag	mit dem Zug	nach Berlin.	
Mr. Smith takes the train on Monday to Berlin.					
Frau Schmidt	ist	am Montag	mit dem Auto	nach Berlin	gefahren.
Mrs. Smith went on Monday to Berlin by car.					
Frau Schmidt	kommt	nachmittags	sehr spät	in Berlin	an.
Mrs. Schmidt will arrive very late in the afternoon in Berlin.					
Sie	wollen	am Dienstag		nach Leipzig	fahren.
They want to go to Leipzig on Tuesday.					

Of course all sentences do not include all of these, but if they did, this is the order they should be in.

'Verb 2' includes past participles (**gelesen, gegessen**), prefixes of separable verbs (**auf, zurück**) and infinitives from sentences with modal verbs (**Ich möchte ein Eis essen**), all of which go to the very end.

For more practice, go to 1.8.2.

Rule 3: Inverted word order

If you begin the sentence with something other than the subject (for example, an expression of time, manner or place) the verb **must** still come second, followed by the subject. The rest of the order stays the same.

3 time	2 verb	1 subject	4 manner	5 place	6 past participle, etc.
Montag früh	**ist**	Herr Schmidt	mit einem Taxi	zum Bahnhof	gefahren.

On Monday morning Mr. Schmidt took a taxi to the train station.

Dienstag	**wollen**	sie	schnell	nach Leipzig	fahren.

On Tuesday they quickly want to go to Leipzig.

Freitag	**werden**	sie	spät	in Berlin	ankommen.

On Friday they will arrive late in Berlin.

 For more practice, go to 1.8.3.

Rule 4: Co-ordinating conjunctions: and – *und*, but – *aber*

And – **und** and *but* – **aber** join two **equal parts** of a sentence so you have to treat both parts the same and the word order in each part is the normal word order.

1 subject	2 verb	3 object	+ +	1 subject	2 verb	3 object
Ich	**esse**	Kuchen	und	ich	**trinke**	Tee.

I am eating cake and I am drinking tea.

Ich	**esse**	kein Fleisch	aber	ich	**esse**	Fisch.

I don't eat any meat but I eat fish.

Wir	**lesen**	die Zeitung	und	wir	**hören**	Musik.

We are reading the newspaper and we are listening to music.

For more practice, go to 1.8.4.

Rule 5: Subordinating conjunctions: because – *weil*, that – *dass*

Subordinating conjunctions add another clause to a sentence.

A clause is a part of a sentence which has a verb of its own.

A subordinate clause is a subsection of the sentence. It cannot stand on its own and its verb goes to the end of the subsection.

A subordinate clause is usually introduced by words like **weil** – *because*, **dass** – *that*, etc.

1 **subject**	**2** **verb**	**3** **object**	**+**	**1** **subject**	**3** **object**	**2** **verb**
Ich	besuche	meinen Freund,	weil	ich	ihn	**mag.**

I am visiting my friend because I like him.

Wir	glauben	ihm,	dass	er	das Geld	**bringt.**

We believe him, that he is going to bring the money. (literally)

Ich	treffe	meine Kollegin,	weil	wir	den Brief	**schreiben wollen.**

I am meeting my colleague because we want to write the letter.

For more practice, go to 1.8.5.

Rule 6: The indirect object *usually* comes before the direct object

In sentences with two objects the indirect object *usually* comes first followed by the direct object.

In English we can say either:

I gave my friend the video.

or

I gave the video to my friend.

In German you say to whom you are giving it first.

	indirect object	**direct object**
Ich habe	meinem Freund	das Video gegeben.
Ich sende	ihm	eine E-Mail.
I am sending	him	an e-mail.
Wir kaufen	meiner Nichte	ein Geschenk.
We are buying	my niece	a present.

 Although the rule exists you will hear Germans using both so don't worry about it, but you might want to use it as a guideline.

 If you are not sure what a direct object or indirect object is, go to 3.2 and 3.3.

 For more practice, go to 1.8.6.

1.8.1 Rule 1: Subject, verb, object

The most important rule is that the main verb has to be in second place (it is the second thought). Often the subject is the first idea in a sentence.

subject	**+verb**
Ich	esse.
I	eat.
I	am eating.

Subject	+verb	+object
Ich	esse	Kuchen.
I	eat	cake.
I	am eating	cake.

Subject	+verb	+object	+object
Ich	esse	Kuchen	mit meinem Kaffee.
I	eat	cake	with my coffee.
I	am eating	cake	with my coffee.

I What are these people doing? Put these words into the right order to form a sentence. Start with the subject.

a lernen wir Grammatik
b Bild Wolfgang malt ein
c Barbara E-Mails schreibt
d sein er Haus sauber macht
e sein Auto wäscht Ernie
f fährt Jackie mit dem Bus zur Arbeit
g schreibe einen Brief auf meinem ich Computer.
h Gras mähen das in Garten wir unserem
i besuchen unsere Kinder wir
j hört sie Musik

1.8.2 Rule 2: Time, manner, place

Although the rule 'time, manner, place' exists it is not a strict rule. You hear Germans changing the order depending on what they want to emphasise. So you might want to use it as a guideline only.

In longer sentences that describe when something is done, how something is done and/or where it is done, the word order is:

time	manner	place
When?	How?	Where?
Wann?	Wie?	Wo?

subject	verb	time	manner	place
Ich	fahre	mittwochs	mit meinem Auto	nach Dresden.
I	take	my car	on Wednesdays	to Dresden.
Die Züge	sind	meistens	pünktlich	in Deutschland.
The trains	are	usually	punctual	in Germany.
Wir	gehen	täglich	zusammen	spazieren.
We	go	daily	together	for a walk.
Wir	fahren	für zwei Stunden	mit dem Zug	durch die Berge.
We	travel	for two hours	by train	through the mountains.
Wir	gehen	morgens	zu Fuß	in die Stadt.
We	walk	in the morning		into town.

II Put these words into the right order, starting with the subject.

a bleibe am Wochenende ich lange meinem Bett in
b das Wochenende ich alleine meinem Haus in verbringe
c mit der Fähre Angelika fährt nach dieses Jahr Deutschland
d montags studieren im Deutschunterricht intensiv wir
e in Stadt die Klaus und Gabi am Montag schnell fahren
f fährt nächste Woche ihrem mit Freund nach meine Freundin Hamburg
g esse sonntags im Restaurant ich gerne
h gerne im Regen morgens den Park ich nicht so gehe durch
i liebt es mein Hund morgens im Park im Regen
j leider muss mein Auto die Werkstatt in am Mittwoch

1.8.3 Rule 3: Inverted word order

A sentence can start with an expression of time, manner or place, for example:

- time: *tomorrow* – **Morgen**, *in two weeks* – **in zwei Wochen**, *this evening* – **heute Abend**
- manner: *unfortunately* – **leider**, *maybe* – **vielleicht**, luckily – **glücklicherweise**
- place: *in Germany* – **in Deutschland**, *in the office* – **im Büro**.

Remember: The position of the verb *always* remains the same (second place) but it is followed by the subject. Subject and verb are inverted:

- time *verb* subject
- manner *verb* subject
- place *verb* subject.

Time/manner/place	verb	subject	other
a Am Montag	fahre	ich	nach Berlin.
b In Berlin	ist	es	sehr grün.
c Leider	ist	der Flug	teuer.
d Gestern	haben	wir	lange geschlafen.

 Translate these sentences literally. It sounds funny, but it is really effective as it will help you to remember.

Literal translation:

a *On Monday go I to Berlin.*
b *In Berlin is it very green.*
c *Unfortunately is the flight expensive.*
e *Yesterday have we long slept.*

III   Change the word order of the following sentences starting with the time, manner or place.

Example:

Ich komme leider erst Morgen. Leider komme ich erst Morgen.

a Ich habe glücklicherweise nächste Woche frei.
b Ich fahre am Sonntag nach London.
c Meine Freundin kommt nächstes Jahr nach Schottland.
d Wir treffen heute Abend unsere Freunde.
e Ich arbeite Morgen den ganzen Tag.
f Wir haben zum Glück noch Zeit.
g Es gibt leider Krieg in der Welt.
h Der Bus kommt dummerweise nicht.
i Meine Chefin ist komischerweise heute freundlich.
j Du bist endlich da.

1.8.4   Rule 4: And – *und*, but – *aber*

And and *but* are called co-ordinating conjunctions.

▶▶   **If you know what a co-ordinating conjunction is, go on to 1.8.5.**

A conjunction is a word that links words or groups of words, for example *and* – **und**, *but* – **aber**, etc.

Co-ordinating conjunctions do not change the word order of a sentence as they link words or clauses that are equal. If you removed the *and* or *but* you would have two sentences.

subject	verb	object	+	subject	verb	object
Ich	arbeite	in einer Kneipe,	**und**	ich	studiere	an der Universität.
I	am working	in a pub	and	I	am studying	at the university.
Er	wohnt	in Braunschweig,	**aber**	er	arbeitet	in Wolfsburg.
He	is living	in Braunschweig	but	he	is working	in Wolfsburg.

The most common co-ordinating conjunction words are:

and	und
but/on the contrary	sondern
or	oder
either ... or	entweder ... oder
but	aber
because	denn

 You use **sondern** in a negative sentence.

Ich lese nicht gerne Zeitschriften, sondern (ich lese) Zeitungen.

I don't like reading magazines, but I read newspapers.

You can drop the subject and verb after **sondern**.

Ich spreche kein Deutsch, sondern (ich spreche) Englisch.
Ich esse kein Fleisch, sondern (ich esse) Fisch.

 Choose some of these conjunctions to learn by heart, and remember that they don't change the structure of a sentence. It is also a good idea to memorise a simple sentence so that you remember the pattern.

Verbs

Subject	verb	object	+	subject	verb	object
Ich I	lerne am learning	Vokabeln, vocabulary	**und** and	ich I	lerne am learning	Grammatik. grammar.
Wir We	fahren are going	nach Deutschland, to Germany,	**oder** or	wir we	fahren are going	in die Schweiz. to Switzerland.
Er He	wohnt lives	in Braunschweig, in Braunschweig	**aber** but	er he	arbeitet works	in Wolfsburg. in Wolfsburg.
Ich I	fahre nicht am not going	nach Deutschland, to Germany	**sondern** but	(ich I	fahre) am going	nach Polen. to Poland.
Ich I	brauche need	einen Job, a job,	**denn** because	ich I	habe don't have	kein Geld. any money.
Wir We	fahren **entweder** are either	nach Hause, going home	**oder** or	wir we	gehen are going	in die Kneipe. to the pub.

Remember when you are using the perfect tense with an auxiliary verb *to have* – **haben** or *to be* – **sein** you use the same structure and rules.

Ich habe gestern Golf gespielt, und ich bin danach in die Kneipe gegangen. I played golf yesterday and after that I went to the pub.

Wir haben gestern eine Ausstellung besucht, aber wir sind auch ins Theater gegangen. We visited an exhibition yesterday, but we also went to the theatre.

Remember: When you use modal verbs, the modal verb comes second and the infinitive goes to the end. The same applies in sentences joined by co-ordinating conjunctions.

Ich **möchte** diesen Sommer gerne in Urlaub **fahren**, denn ich **konnte** letztes Jahr nicht **gehen**. Ich **kann** dir nicht **helfen**, aber ich **kann** dir jemanden **empfehlen**.

I would like to go on holiday this year because I could not go last year. I can't help you but I can recommend somebody to you.

For more practice on word structure in sentences with modal verbs go to 1.2.3 on modal verbs.

 Use a comma before the conjunction to separate the two parts of the sentence.

IV Which conjunction makes sense? Combine the sentences with an appropriate word: **denn, oder, aber, und, sondern, entweder ... oder.**

a Möchten Sie ein Stück Apfelkuchen, ___ möchten Sie lieber einen Käsekuchen?

b Ich möchte gerne einen Apfelkuchen, ___ ich mag Äpfel sehr gerne.

c Müssen Sie heute lange arbeiten, ___ könnnen Sie früh nach Hause gehen?

d Wir haben uns die Stadt angeguckt, ___ wir sind einkaufen gegangen.

e Gehst du gerne mit deinen Freunden ins Kino, ___ guckt ihr lieber Videos?

f Wir gucken ___ Videos, ___ wir gehen ins Kino.

g Sind Sie gestern ins Theater gegangen, ___ sind Sie zu Hause geblieben?

h Ich bin nicht ins Theater gegangen, ___ ich bin zu Hause geblieben.

i Sprechen Sie Englisch zu Hause, ___ sprechen Sie Deutsch?

j Wir sprechen Englisch, ___ es ist unsere Muttersprache.

Translate these sentences into English and go back later to translate them back into German.

V Which conjunction would you use? In some sentences more than one is possible. Choose from: **denn, aber, und, sondern, entweder ... oder.**

a Im Herbst regnet es oft, ___ es wird kälter.

b Im Winter ist es immer sehr früh dunkel, ___ es kann sehr kalt werden.

c Im Frühling kommen die ersten Blumen raus, ___ es sieht alles sehr farbenfroh aus.

d Im Sommer können wir länger im Garten sitzen, ___ es ist lange hell.

e Es regnet oft im Sommer in Schottland, ___ letztes Jahr hat es wenig geregnet.

f Die Wintertage in Schottland sind sehr kurz, ___ es ist früh dunkel.

g Wir gehen im Sommer nicht ins Hallenschwimmbad, ___ wir gehen ins Freischwimmbad.

h Meine Kinder fahren im Sommer ___ in die Schweiz, ___ nach Deutschland.

i Unsere Kollegin fährt im Sommer immer nach Spanien, ___ sie spricht kein Spanisch.

j Ich fahre im Winter in die Alpen, ___ ich mag den Schnee.

VI Complete these sentences by putting the words in brackets into the right order.

a Ich bin einkaufen gegangen, und ___ (habe gearbeitet ich).

b Es ist kalt im Haus, denn ___ (Heizung die kaputt ist).

c Die Erwachsenen mussten Eintritt bezahlen,aber (Kinder die mussten bezahlen nichts).

d Der Regen hat endlich aufgehört, aber (kalt es ist immer noch).

e Das Konzert fängt Morgen um 8 Uhr an, und (treffen wir uns um 7 Uhr).

f Wir kochen heute nicht, sondern (in gehen wir ein Restaurant).

g Die Besucher haben den Film sehr gemocht, denn (lustig sehr er war).

h Es gab sehr viele Autounfälle, denn (glatt es war auf der Straße).

i Die Wettervorhersage ist schlecht, aber (stimmt oft sie nicht).

j Klaus will nicht in Europa bleiben, sondern (USA er will in die ziehen).

1.8.5 Rule 5: Because – *weil*, that – *daß*

Because – **weil** is a subordinating conjunction because it joins a subordinate (or less important) part to the main sentence.

▶▶ **If you know about subordinating conjunctions, go on to 1.8.6.**

You can recognise the part of the sentence (or clause) introduced by the subordinating conjunction because it does not usually make sense on its own.

> A clause is a part of a sentence with its own verb:

- *because it was windy ___*
- *because I wanted to ___*
- *while I was there ___*
- *when he arrived ___*

You need the main part of the sentence to know what is being talked about.

The most common subordinating conjunctions are:

dass	that	bevor	before
seit	since	sobald	as soon as
seitdem	since then	während	while
damit	so that	obwohl	although
weil	because	ob	whether/if
wenn	when/if	als	when

These words all introduce a subordinate clause.

The English *when* can be expressed in German by **als** and **wenn**.

Als refers to a single action in the past or a period of time.

Wenn is used for the English *if, when* or *whenever.*

 Take a few minutes to learn the conjunctions by heart. It is a good idea to memorise a simple sentence to help you to remember the word order.

VII Without looking at the list on page 135 try to match up the German conjunction with its English meaning.

a dass	1 before
b seit	2 as soon as
c seitdem	3 although
d damit	4 since
e weil	5 whether/if
f wenn	6 that
g obwohl	7 when/if
h bevor	8 so that
i sobald wie	9 because
j während	10 since then
k ob	11 when (single event)
l als	12 while

In the main part of the sentence the words are in the usual order.

In a subordinate clause the verb goes to the end of the clause.

present tense and subordinate clause

1 subject	2 verb	3 other info	+ +	1 subject	3 other info	2 verb
Ich	habe	keine Zeit,	weil	ich		arbeite.

I don't have any time because I am working.

⫸

1 subject	2 verb	3 other info	+ +	1 subject	3 other info	2 verb
Ich	denke,		dass	ich	neue Schuhe	brauche.

I think that I need new shoes.

1 subject	2 verb	3 other info	+ +	1 subject	3 other info	2 verb
Ich	lebe	in England,	seit	ich	8 Jahre alt	bin.

I have been living in England since I was 8 years old.

1 subject	2 verb	3 other info	+ +	1 subject	3 other info	2 verb
Ich	koche	heute Abend,	wenn	ich	Hunger	habe.

I will cook this evening if I am hungry.

1 subject	2 verb	3 other info	+ +	1 subject	3 other info	2 verb
Ich	gehe	ins Kino,	obwohl	ich	müde	bin.

I will go to the cinema although I am tired.

> The same rule applies for the perfect tense but remember: the auxiliary verb **haben** – *to have* or **sein** – *to be* (as well as the modal verb) will now come at the end of the sentence. See 1.8.7.

VIII Complete the following sentences in the present tense by putting the words into the right order.

Example:
Ich bügele, weil ___ (niemand für es macht mich).
Ich bügele, weil es niemand für mich macht.
I am ironing, because nobody does it for me.

a Ich gehe spazieren, obwohl ___ (regnet es).
b Ich gehe in die Sauna, weil ___ (mag ich es).
c Ich gucke Fernsehen, weil ___ (sehen den Film will ich).
d Mein Vater ist sehr gesund, obwohl ___ (sehr er ist alt).
e Ich gehe zu einer Party, obwohl ___ (ich keine habe Lust).
f Ich glaube, dass ___ (Urlaub einen brauche ich).
g Ich befürchte, dass ___ (der Krieg noch zu ist Ende nicht).
h Ich mache den Kaffee, während ___ (telefonierst mit deiner Freundin du).
i Wir können entspannen, sobald ___ (sie sind weg).
j Wir meditieren, damit ___ (friedlich und sind ruhig wir).

IX Combine these sentences using **weil** or **denn**. (**Weil** sends the verb to the end, **denn** doesn't.)

a Ich gehe in die Sauna, ___ es mir Spaß macht.
b Wir gehen schwimmen, ___ ich brauche Bewegung.
c Das Geschäft ist heute geschlossen, ___ es Sonntag ist.
d Er kauft sich ein neues Auto, ___sein altes ist kaputt.
e Wir brauchen einen neuen Computer, ___ der alte zu langsam ist.
f Im Winter wollen wir mehr schlafen, ___ es so früh dunkel ist.
g Im Winter schlafen wir mehr, ___ wir haben weniger Energie.
h Wir wollen mit dem Bus fahren, ___ es ist billiger.
i Ich fahre gerne mit dem Zug, ___ es ist bequem.
j Mein Freund fährt lieber mit dem Auto, ___ es schneller ist.

X Which conjunction would you use: **damit** – *so that* or **aber** – *but*? (**Damit** sends the verb to the end, **aber** doesn't.)

a Die Blätter fallen von den Bäumen, ___ es sieht sehr schön aus.
b Wir bringen die Pflanzen in das Gewächshaus, ___ sie nicht erfrieren.
c Die meisten Vögel fliegen nach Süden, ___ einige bleiben hier.
d Die Kinder spielen im Schnee, ___ es ist sehr kalt.
e Wir brauchen Sonne, ___ wir Energie bekommen.
f Im Winter ist es früh dunkel, ___es ist sehr gemütlich im Haus.
g Ich stelle die Heizung an, ___ es dir warm wird.
h Ich mag Schnee, ___ ich hasse Eis auf der Strasse.
i Der Schneewagen kommt, ___ die Strasse wieder frei ist.
j Viele Leute haben eine Grippe, ___ ich bin gesund.

XI Combine the following sentences with the word in brackets by putting the second part into the right word order.

Example:

Viele Politiker machen Versprechen. Wir wählen sie.
(damit)

Viele Politiker machen Versprechen, damit wir sie wählen.

a Wir ernähren uns organisch. Das organische Essen ist teurer. (obwohl)
b Wir benutzen unser Handy nicht im Auto. Es ist verboten. (weil)
c Die Kinder lernen English. Sie sind in der Grundschule. (seit)
d Der Polizist regelt den Verkehr. Die Ampel ist kaput. (weil)
e Die Zuschauer im Kino sind ruhig. Der Film läuft. (während)
f Menschen sind ausgeglichener. Sie rauchen nicht. (wenn)

g Viele junge Leute trinken zu viel Alkohol. Es ist nicht gesund. (obwohl)
h Wir füllen den Tank mit Benzin. Wir haben genug Benzin für die Reise. (damit)
i Wir mögen unsere schönen Träume. Sie werden nicht immer wahr. (obwohl)
j Wir buchen ein Hotelzimmer. Wir fahren in Urlaub. (bevor)

1.8.6 Rule 6: Talking about the past using subordinate clauses

perfect tense and subordinate clause

subject	auxiliary verb	other info	past participle	+
Ich	bin	spät zur Arbeit	gegangen,	weil
I	went	to work late	because	I
Ich	bin	schnell aus dem	Zug gestiegen,	als
I	got	quickly off the train,	when	it
Ich	bin	nicht	skigefahren,	weil
I	didn't	go skiing	because	I

subject	other info	past participle	auxiliary verb
ich	erst um acht Uhr	aufgewacht	bin.
only	woke up	at 8 o' clock.	
er	auf dem	Bahnhof	angekommen ist.
arrived	at the station.		
ich	mein Bein	gebrochen	habe.
have	broken	my leg.	

XII Put the subordinate clause into the right order by rearranging the words in brackets.

a Ich bin in die Alpen in Urlaub gefahren, weil (ich lernen wollte Skifahren).
b Ich habe einen Anfängerkurs im Skifahren gemacht, weil (ich noch nie bin Ski gefahren).

c Es hat sehr viel Spaß gemacht, weil (sehr lustig gewesen sind die Leute).

d Ich habe mein Bein gebrochen, weil (beim hingefallen ich Skifahren bin).

e Ich musste ins Krankenhaus, als (ich habe mir das Bein gebrochen).

f Ich war sehr traurig, dass (ich fahren nicht mehr Ski konnte).

g Meine Freunde sind Ski gefahren, während (ich habe in gelegen der Sonne).

h Abends bin ich in die Skihütte gegangen, obwohl (mein Bein hat wehgetan).

i Wir hatten viel Sonne, obwohl (es gewesen sehr kalt ist).

j Ich hatte trotzdem noch einen schönen Urlaub, obwohl (ich Ski fahren nicht mehr konnte).

If you begin with the subordinate clause the main verb must come next, straight after the comma. This means you have two verbs beside each other – sometimes even one and the same verb. Translate the following sentences literally, to get a feeling for the structure.

1 subordinate clause	2 verb	3 subject	4 other	5 past participle, etc.
Obwohl ich spät aufgestanden bin,	bin	ich	pünktlich	zur Arbeit gekommen.
Als es stark geregnet hat,	bin	ich	mit dem Bus	gefahren
Weil ich spät aufgestanden bin,	habe	ich	den Bus	verpasst.

XIII Re-arrange these sentences so they begin with the subordinate clause.

Example:

Ich musste gestern lange arbeiten, weil ich am Montag frei hatte.

Weil ich am Montag frei hatte, musste ich gestern lange arbeiten.

a Ich habe dieses Wochenende viel Zeit gehabt, weil ich nicht gearbeitet habe.

    Weil ich nicht gearbeitet habe, ___

b Ich bin nicht in Urlaub gefahren, weil ich keine Zeit gehabt habe.

    Weil ich keine Zeit gehabt habe, ___

c Ich bin schwimmen gegangen, wenn die Sonne geschienen hat.

Wenn die Sonne geschienen hat, ___

d Wir haben unsere Verwandten in Hamburg besucht, als wir letzten Sommer in Hamburg waren.

Als wir letzten Sommer in Hamburg waren, ___

e Wir haben viel draußen gemacht, obwohl es oft geregnet hat.

Obwohl es oft geregnet hat, ___

f Ich habe viel Deutsch gelernt, während ich in Deutschland war.

Während ich in Deutschland war, ___

g Wir sind nach Belgien gefahren, bevor wir nach Holland gefahren sind.

Bevor wir nach Holland gefahren sind, ___

h Ich spreche besser Deutsch, seit ich in Deutschland gewesen bin.

Seit ich in Deutschland gewesen bin, ___

i Ich habe gestern Fernsehen geguckt obwohl ich studieren musste.

Obwohl ich studieren musste, ___

j Ich bin nacht nach New York geflogen, weil ich kein Geld gehabt habe.

Weil ich kein Geld gehabt habe, ___

1.8.7 Rule 7: The position of the direct and indirect object

In sentences with two objects the indirect object (dative) comes first followed by the direct object (accusative).

 If you are not sure about what a direct object or indirect object is, go to pages 156–157.

	dative **indirect object**	**accusative** **direct object**
Wir schicken	unserem Kunden	einen Brief.
We are sending	our customer	a letter.
Ich gebe	meinen Nachbarn	meine Schlüssel.
I am giving	my neighbours	my keys.

XIV Which object would you use first, using the indirect/direct object rule?

a Am Montag gebe ich ___ (meine Arbeit meiner Professorin).

b Wir empfehlen ___ (das kleine Hotel dem Fremden).

c Sie schicken ___ (Blumen der kranken Frau).

d Wir schenken (den Kindern Geld).

e Der Golflehrer empfielt (einen Golfschläger der Frau).

f Wir zeigen ___ (den Weg dem Fremden).

g Wir glauben ___ (dem Jungen die Lüge).

h Die Eltern verzeihen___ (die Verspätung der Tochter).

i Ich erzähle___ (meinem Enkelkind eine Geschichte).

j Wir geben ___ (das Buch dem Kind).

2 NOUNS AND DETERMINERS

How to recognise nouns

▶▶ **If you know what a noun is, go on to 2.2.**

Nouns are naming words. They tell you who somebody is (e.g. *he is a farmer, she is a dentist*) or what something is (e.g. *it is a table, it is a rainbow*).

> You can recognise nouns because you can say 'the' or 'a' in front of them, e.g. *a* pencil, *the* dog, *a* house, *the* postman.

A word can sometimes be a noun and sometimes a verb, e.g.

to drive (verb) – *the drive* (noun)

to cook (verb) – *the cook* (noun)

I   There are ten nouns in this text. Can you find them all?

My sister has her own restaurant. She goes to the market each morning to buy fresh vegetables to make soup for lunch. The other dishes she prepared the night before and left in the fridge ready to be cooked.

> It is easy to recognise a noun in German as they are ALL written with a capital letter.

How to recognise a determiner

▶▶ **If you know what a determiner is, go on to 2.1.**

A determiner is a word which comes in front of a noun to identify it, or determine which one it is: *the* coat, *a* coat, *my* coat, *your* coat, *this* coat, *which* coat, etc.

- *the* is also known as the definite article because it designates a definite object: *the* cat
- *a* is also known as the indefinite article as it does not specify which object it designates in particular: *a* cat

- *my/ his/ her*, etc. are also known as possessive pronouns as they indicate to whom something or somebody belongs, in other words who possesses them: *my* dog, *my* mother
- *which* is also known as an interrogative pronoun: *which* coat?
- *that/ this* are also known as demonstrative pronouns: *that* umbrella, *this* pen
- *Any* is also known as an indefinite pronoun: *any* mobile phone, *any* meeting.

II Which of these words are determiners?

a Have you got a car?
b I have lost my dog.
c Have you seen his photo?
d Where is their house?
e Have you got any good books?
f This is her bag.
g Which bag is his?
h I like this CD.
i Have you got a DVD player?
j Who is your favourite actor?

It is useful to be able to recognise determiners because in German they change according to whether the noun is masculine, feminine, neuter or plural. People will still understand you if you don't use the correct one(s) but it is better to try to get them right. They are not difficult to learn as they mostly follow the same pattern.

2.1 Nouns and gender

▶▶ **If you know about the gender of nouns, go on to 2.3.**

In German all nouns are either masculine, feminine or neuter.

The word for *flat* – **Wohnung** is a feminine word.

The word for *garden* – **Garten** is a masculine word.

The word for *house* – **Haus** is neuter.

Feminine words are usually indicated by (f) in the dictionary, masculine words by (m) and neuter words by (n).

The word for *the* changes in front of nouns in German according to whether they are masculine, feminine or neuter.

▶▶ **If you know about *der, die* and *das* and the gender of nouns, go on to 2.1.2.**

- The word for *the* in front of masculine nouns is **der**.
der Mann   the man   der Computer   the computer
- The word for *the* in front of feminine nouns is **die**.
die Frau   the women   die Tür   the door
- The word for *the* in front of neuter nouns is **das**.
das Baby   the baby   das Fenster   the window

> There is often no logic as to whether a noun is masculine, feminine or neuter. It is therefore best to learn a new word together with its gender: don't just learn **Besprechung** – *meeting*, learn **die Besprechung**. Still, there are a few helpful tips on how to identify a gender for some words (see 2.1.2).

When you look up a word in the dictionary, it usually tells you the gender of the word in brackets after it: **die** (f), **das** (n), **der** (m), **die** (pl). For example:

Wohnung (f) flat, **Haus (n)** house, **Bungalow (m)** bungalow

I   Put the correct word (**der, die, das**) in front of the following nouns.

     a ___ Auto (n)   car
     b ___ Koffer (m)   suitcase
     c ___ Tasche (f)   bag
     d ___ Laptop (m)   laptop
     e ___ Handy (n)   mobile phone
     f ___ Benzin (n)   petrol
     g ___ Kreditkarte (f)   credit card
     h ___ Reservierung (f)   reservation
     i ___ Sonne (f)   sun
     j ___ Stern (m)   star

II   Fill in the gaps with **der, die, das**.

     a ___ Wohnung (f)   flat
     b ___ Schloss (n)   castle
     c ___ Schule (f)   school
     d ___ Krankenhaus (n)   hospital
     e ___ Kirche (f)   church

f ___ Rathaus (n)	town hall
g ___ Wohnhaus (n)	block of flats
h ___ Hotel (n)	hotel
i ___ Allee (f)	avenue
j ___ Straße (f)	street

III Fill in the gaps with **der**, **die**, **das**.

a ___ Sackgasse (f)	cul-de-sac
b ___ Baum (m)	tree
c ___ Wasser (n)	water
d ___ Berg (m)	mountain
e ___ See (m)	lake
f ___ See (f)	sea
g ___ Fluss (m)	river
h ___ Bahnhof (m)	train station
i ___ Stadt (f)	town
j ___ Dorf (n)	village

2.1.2 Some useful ways to tell whether a noun is masculine, feminine or neuter

Masculine nouns (der)

All days, months, seasons, names for cars and trains, lakes and most alcoholic drinks are masculine.

der Wochentag	the day of the week	der Monat	the month
der Montag	Monday	der Januar	January
der Dienstag	Tuesday	der Juni	June
		der November	November

All names for cars and trains are masculine:

der BMW, der Mercedes, der VW, der Opel, der Audi

der Zug, der ICE, der Euro-City, der InterCity Express

Names of lakes and mountains tend to take the gender which describes them.

Der Berg (*mountain*) is masculine, therefore:

der Brocken, der Kahle Asten, der Harz, der Mount Everest, der Himalaya.

All names for lakes are masculine as the word for lake is **der See**:

der Tegernsee, der Bodensee,

as well as lakes outside Germany:

der Loch Lomond, der Lake Michigan.

Usually the names of alcoholic drinks are masculine:

der Vodka, der Schnaps, der Wein, der Whisky.

An exception is **das Bier**.

Nouns which end in **-el, -en, -er, -ig, -ich, -ling** are usually masculine.

- **-el**: der Apfel – *apple*, der Schlüssel – *key*, der Löffel – *spoon*
- **-en**: der Magen – *stomach*, der Wagen – *car*, der Kragen – *collar*, der Schaden – *damage*, der Faden – *thread*
- **-er**: der Teller – *the plate*, der Keller – *the cellar*, der Sommer – *summer*
- **-ig**: der Honig – *honey*, der Essig – *vinegar*
- **-ich**: der Kranich – *crane*, der Teppich – *carpet*
- **-ling**: der Feigling – *coward*, der Lehrling – *apprentice*

Feminine nouns (*die*)

Most trees, flowers and fruits are feminine:

- **die Fichte** – *spruce*, **die Tanne** – *pine*, **die Buche** – *beech*, **die Eiche** – *oak*; exception: **der Ahorn** – *maple*
- **die Osterglocke** – *daffodil*, **die Nelke** – *carnation*, **die Rose** – *rose*, **die Tulpe** – *tulip*; exception: **das Stiefmütterchen** – *pansy*
- **die Kirsche** – *cherry*, **die Banane** – *banana*, **die Zitrone** – *lemon*, **die Traube** – *grape*
- **die Apfelsine** – *orange*, **die Mango** – *mango*, **die Erdbeere** – *strawberry*; exception: **der Apfel** – *apple*

Nouns which end in **-e, -age, -ei, -heit, -keit, -schaft, -ie, -in, -ion, -tät, -ung** are almost always feminine.

- **-e**: die Sonne – *sun*, die Tasche – *bag*
- **-age**: die Garage – *(car) garage*, die Blamage – *disgrace*, die Courage – *courage*
- **-ei**: die Bäckerei – *bakery*, die Fleischerei – *butcher*, die Polizei – *police*
- **-heit**: die Frechheit – *cheekiness*, die Weisheit – *wisdom*, die Dummheit – *stupidity*
- **-keit**: die Einsamkeit – *loneliness*, die Kleinigkeit – *trifle*
- **-schaft**: die Freundschaft – *friendship*, die Eigenschaft – *characteristic*
- **-ie**: die Energie – *energy*, die Chemie – *chemistry*, die Melodie – *melody*
- **-ion**: die Infektion – *infection*, die Information – *information*, die Nation – *nation*

- **-ät: die Universität** – *university,* **die Fakultät** – *faculty,* **die Rarität** – *rarity*
- **-ung: die Verwaltung** – *administration,* **die Wohnung** – *flat,* **die Heizung** – *heating*

Neuter nouns (*das*)

Most names of hotels, cafés and theatres are neuter: **das Hotel zum Hang, das Hotel Kranz.**

Names of colours are neuter: **das Rot** – *red,* **das Gelb** – *yellow,* **das Grün** – *green,* **das Blau** – *blue,* **das Schwarz** – *black.*

Most metals are neuter: **das Kupfer** – *copper,* **das Blei** – *lead,* **das Gold** – *gold,* **das Silber** – *silver.*

Nouns which end in **-tum, -ment, -eum, -ium, -um, -ett** are usually neuter: **das Altertum** – *old age,* **das Instrument** – *instrument,* **das Duett** – *duo.*

Most nouns which end in **-chen** are also neuter: **das Mädchen** – *the girl,* **das Liebchen** – *the sweetheart.*

Most nouns with the prefix **ge-** are neuter: **das Gedächtnis** – *memory,* **das Gebäude** – *building,* **das Gebet** – *prayer*; exception: **die Geschichte** – *history.*

IV   What will they be: **der, die** or **das**?

a _____ Rotwein
b _____ Rose
c _____ Mercedes
d _____ Freitag
e _____ April
f _____ Lake Michigan
g _____ Tanne
h _____ Bodensee
i _____ Rosa
j _____ Adlon Hotel

V   And some more.

a _____ Sprache
b _____ Gehalt
c _____ Illusion
d _____ Hafen
e _____ Bücherei
f _____ Eigentum
g _____ Dummheit
h _____ Mantel
i _____ Liebling
j _____ Taufe

2.1.3 Different forms for the masculine and feminine

Some nouns have different forms for the masculine and feminine.

masculine	feminine
der Mann	die Frau
der Sohn	die Tochter
der Bruder	die Schwester
der Bulle	die Kuh
der Kater	die Katze

VI What is the feminine form for these words? If you are not sure, look them up – or guess them!

male		female
a	Vater	—— ——
b	Bruder	—— ——
c	Onkel	—— ——
d	Stiefvater	—— ——
e	Neffe	—— ——
f	Mann	—— ——
g	Opa	—— ——
h	Cousin	—— ——
i	Stiefbruder	—— ——
j	Sohn	—— ——

The word for baby and child is **das Baby** and **das Kind**. Remember some words with feminine meanings are also **das** words: **das Mädchen**.

VII What is the feminine form for these words? Try to match them up.

masculine		feminine
a	der Mann	die Zicke
b	der Putzmann	die Truthenne
c	der Krankenwärter	die Kuh
d	der Junge	das Huhn
e	der Ziegenbock	die Krankenschwester
f	der Bulle	die Frau
g	der Hirsch	die Putzfrau
h	der Truthahn	das Reh
i	der Hahn	das Mädchen

Most job titles have a masculine and a feminine form.

Most female job titles are made by adding **-in** to the masculine.

masculine	feminine
der Architekt	die Architektin – female architect
der Gärtner	die Gärtnerin – female gardener,

VIII What is the feminine of the following job titles?

male   female
a social worker – Sozialarbeiter   _____
b sales assistant – Verkäufer   _____
c doctor – Arzt   _____
d farmer – Bauer   _____
e teacher – Lehrer   _____
f lorry driver – Lastwagenfahrer   _____
g lawyer – Rechtsanwalt   _____
h vet – Tierarzt   _____
i engineer – Ingenieur   _____
j secretary – Sekretär   _____

2.2 Nouns in the plural: *die*

▶▶ **If you know about the plural, go on to 2.3.**

In the plural, the word for *the* becomes **die** for ALL nouns, whether masculine, feminine or neuter.

singular	plural
der Fernseher	die Fernseher
das Auto	die Autos
der Baum	die Bäume

To make the plural of the noun in English, we usually add an -*s*. There are various ways in German to form the plural. The main categories are:

- nouns which add **-s**
- nouns which add **-e** or **-̈e**
- nouns which add **-er** or **-̈er**
- feminine nouns which add **-en** or **-n**
- nouns which stay the same
- nouns which take an Umlaut

Some nouns change the vowel (add an Umlaut) before adding the ending.

In a dictionary the plural is usually shown in brackets after the noun:

Hund *m* (e) dog

m tells you it is masculine
(e) tells you that the plural ends in -**e**.

 When learning a new word for the first time it is a good idea to say it and the plural out loud so you get used to the sound: **der Hund – die Hunde**.

2.2.1 Nouns which add -s in the plural

The following nouns add an **-s** in German. They are mainly words of foreign origin or words that end in a vowel (other than **-e**).

singular	plural
der Job	die Jobs
der Laptop	die Laptops
der Clown	die Clowns
das Auto	die Autos
das Radio	die Radios
das Sofa	die Sofas

I Add the plural to the following words.

a der Park   die _____
b das Radio   die _____
c die Kamera   die _____
d das Foto   die _____
e die Oma   die _____
f der Opa   die _____
g das Taxi   die _____
h das Hotel   die _____
i die E-Mail   die _____
j das Restaurant   die _____

2.2.2 The plural of masculine nouns

Most masculine nouns form their plural by adding **-e** or **-̈e**.

Nouns which add **-e**:

der Tag → die Tage

der Monat → die Monate

Some nouns 'modify' the preceding vowel by putting an Umlaut on it. This is usually shown as ⸚e in the dictionary:

der Sohn → die Söhne

der Kuss → die Küsse

II   Write out the plural forms of these (-e) words.

singular   plural
a der Abend – evening   die ____
b der Schuh – shoe   die ____
c der Hund – dog   die ____
d der Schein – note   die ____
e der Film – film   die ____
g der Brief – letter   die ____
h der Ring – ring   die ____
i der Berg – mountain   die ____
j der Bildschirm – screen   die ____

III Write out the plural forms of these ⸚e words. (Where there are two or more vowels the Umlaut will always go on the last one.)

a der Betrag – amount   die ____
b der Umschlag – envelope   die ____
c der Zug – train   die ____
d der Golfplatz – golf course   die ____
e der Rucksack – rucksack   die ____
f der Kamm – comb   die ____
g der Pass – passport   die ____
h der Sturm – storm   die ____
i der Arzt – doctor   die ____
j der Kopf – head   die ____

2.2.3 The plural of neuter nouns

Most neuter nouns (approximately 75%) add **-e**:

das Pferd → die Pferd*e*

das Reh → die Reh*e*

das Schaf → die Schaf*e*

IV   What is the plural of the following words?

a das Telefon – telephone   die ____
b das Feuerzeug – lighter   die ____
c das Segelboot – sailing boat   die ____
d das Geschäft – business/shop   die ____
e das Fahrzeug – vehicle   die ____
f das Tor – goal   die ____

g das Tennisnetz – tennis net   die ____
h das Segelschiff – sailing ship   die ____
i das Haar – hair   die ____
j das Pfund – pound   die ____

Some nouns have a vowel change and add -er:

das Buch → die Bücher

das Haus → die Häuser

das Rathaus → die Rathäuser

das Fahrrad → die Fahrräder

V What is the plural of the following words?

a das Glas – glas   die ____
b das Gehalt – salary   die ____
c das Lamm – lamb   die ____
d das Clubhaus – club house   die ____
e das Schwimmbad – swimming pool   die ____
f das Krankenhaus – hospital   die ____
g das Fahrrad – bicycle   die ____
h das Dorf – village   die ____
i das Amt – office   die ____
j das Wort – word   die ____

Remember that the easiest way to learn nouns is to learn their gender and plural at the same time.

2.2.4 The plural of feminine nouns

Around 90% of all feminine nouns have the ending **-en** or **-n** in the plural.

singular	plural
die Rose	die Rosen
die Halskette	die Halsketten
die Hose	die Hosen
die Bank	die Banken
die Jacke	die Jacken

VI What is the plural of the following words?

a die Bürokratie – bureaucracy   die ____
b die Steuer – tax   die ____
c die Straße – street   die ____
d die Stufe – step   die ____

e die Strafe – punishment/penalty   die ____
f die Schule – school   die ____
g die Klasse – class   die ____
h die Feier – celebration/party   die ____
i die Inschrift – inscription   die ____
j die Industrie – industry   die ____

VII   What is the plural of the following words?

a die Versicherung – insurance   die ____
b die Genehmigung – permission   die ____
c die Feuerwehr – fire brigade   die ____
d die Verhandlung – negotiations   die ____
e die Verfassung – constitution/state of health   die ____
f die Rezeption – reception   die ____
g die Dummheit – stupidity   die ____
h die Frechheit – cheek   die ____
i die Information – information   die ____
j die Straftat – criminal offence   die ____

Feminine nouns for job titles which end in **-in** double the **n** in the plural:

die Lehrerin → die Lehrerin*n*en

die Studentin → die Studentin*n*en

2.2.5 Nouns which remain the same in both the singular and plural
Some nouns have identical singular and plural forms.

These are usually indicated by (-) in a dictionary.

singular	plural
das Messer – *knife*	die Messer
der Löffel – *spoon*	die Löffel

VIII   What is the plural of these (-) words?

a der Wagen – car/truck   die ____
b das Zimmer – room   die ____
c das Kissen – cushion   die ____
d der Sessel – armchair   die ____
e das Fenster – window   die ____
f der Teller – plate   die ____
g das Theater – theatre   die ____

Some nouns just change the vowel (add an Umlaut). Only the letters **o, a** and **u** can take an Umlaut:

der Vater → die Väter – the fathers

die Mutter → die Mütter – the mothers

der Bruder → die Brüder – the brothers

IX Now can you write out the plural of the following words?

a Buch (¨er)   die ____
b Zimmer (-)   die ____
c Rose (n)   die ____
d Kirsche (n)   die ____
e Regal (e)   die ____
f Kino (s)   die ____
g Architektin (nen)   die ____
h Tochter (¨)   die ____
i Hotel (s)   die ____
j Dorf (¨)   die ____

2.3 Determiners and cases

If you have forgotten what a determiner is – **der, ein, mein,** etc, – go back to 2.1.1 for more information.

The cases are: subject, direct object and indirect object.

You need to know about the cases because in German the determiners (*the, a, my, his, her*, etc.) can change according to whether the word is being used as the subject, direct object or indirect object of the sentence.

However, it doesn't matter too much because you will still be understood, but if you want to speak German correctly it is a good idea to know about cases. They all follow the same pattern so you only have to learn the pattern rather than each word.

▶▶ **If you know about cases, go on to 2.4.**

The subject of a sentence

The subject is the person or thing doing the action.

To find out which word is the subject of a sentence, ask yourself: Who or what is doing the action?

The subject of a sentence is in the nominative. You use **der, die, das, die** for the nominative.

nominative			
m	**f**	**n**	**pl**
der	die	das	die

The subject is shown here in italics.

Der Computer ist sehr alt.　　　*The computer* is very old.

What is very old? Answer: *the computer* – **der Computer**.

Der neue Kollege hat einen　　The new colleague has a
　modernen Computer.　　　　　modern computer.

Who has a new computer? Answer: *the colleague* – **der Kollege**.

 In English the subject always comes in front of the verb.

I　Now try for yourself. What is the subject of these sentences?

a Der Laptop ist neu.
b Die neue Studentin hat keinen Laptop.
c Das Fahrrad ist kaputt.
d Der Junge hat ein neues Fahrrad.
e Die Frau kauft ein Auto.
f Das Auto gehört der Frau.
g Das Mädchen spielt im Konzert.
h Das Konzert ist in der Konzerthalle.
i Die Schuhe sind im Schrank.
j Der Schrank ist voll von Schuhen.

The direct object

The direct object is the person or thing which is having the action done to it.

Its grammatical name is the accusative.

To find out which word in a sentence is the direct object, ask yourself who or what is having the action done to it.

You use **den**, **die**, **das**, **die** for the accusative. (In fact they all stay the same except the masculine which changes to **den**.)

The direct object is shown here in italics.

The dog chased *the cat*.　　Der Hund jagte *die Katze*.
The cat chased *the dog*.　　Die Katze jagte *den Hund*.

II　Now try for yourself. Which words are the direct object?

a Johnny was reading the　　Johnny hat die Zeitung
　newspaper.　　　　　　　gelesen.

b He was drinking a gin and tonic.

Er hat einen Gin Tonic getrunken.

c His wife had bought herself a new dress.

Seine Frau hatte sich ein neues Kleid gekauft.

d She was making dinner.

Sie hat Abendessen gemacht.

e She was cooking pasta.

Sie hat Nudeln gekocht.

f She made a bolognaise sauce.

Sie hat eine Bolognaise Soße gemacht.

g She dropped the plate on the floor.

Sie hat den Teller auf dem Boden fallengelassen.

h The sauce stained her new dress.

Die Soße hat ihr neues Kleid verfärbt.

i She had to throw the pasta away.

Sie mußte die Nudeln wegwerfen.

j Johnny preferred takeaways anyhow.

Johnny zieht sowieso Essen zum Mitnehmen vor.

The indirect object

The indirect object is the person or thing to whom you give/write/tell something. Its grammatical name is the dative.

You are only going to need it when you are talking about giving/sending/writing, etc. something to someone. If you find it confusing and are not going to need it yet, leave it and come back later. You can make yourself understood without it.

To find out what the indirect object is you can ask in English:

Who is *it* being given/sent/written *to?*

He sent his friend a letter. He sent a letter *to* his friend.

He gave his wife a present. He gave a present *to* his wife.

 See if the sentence still makes sense if you add the word *to.*

III Now try it yourself. Which words are the indirect object? (Ask: to whom was it happening?)

a Johnny was reading the children a story.

Johnny hat den Kindern eine Geschichte gelesen.

b His boss paged him to come at once.

Sein Boss hat ihm per Pager benachrichtigt, gleich zu kommen.

c He wanted to speak to his wife but her phone was off.

Er wollte mit seiner Frau sprechen, aber ihr Telefon war ausgestellt.

d He left her a message.

Er hat ihr eine Nachricht hinterlassen.

e He sent his boss a text message to say he would be late.

Er hat seinem Boss eine MSN geschickt um zu sagen, dass er zu spät kommen würde.

f	He texted the babysitter.	Er hat dem Babysitter eine MSN geschickt.
g	She texted Johnny back to say she would come straightaway.	Sie hat Johnny eine MSN zurückgeschickt, um ihm zu sagen, dass sie sofort kommen würde.
h	He gave the children some fish fingers and beans.	Er hat den Kindern Fish Fingers und Bohnen gegeben.
i	He sent his boss a message to say he was coming.	Er hat seinem Boss eine MSN geschickt, um zu sagen, dass er kommt.
j	He left the babysitter instructions on the back of an envelope.	Er hat dem Babysitter Instruktionen auf der Rückseite eines Umschlags hinterlassen.

2.3.1 The: *der, die, das* and cases

As you already know, in German nouns can be either masculine (**der**), feminine (**die**), neuter (**das**) or plural (**die**).

The **der/die/das** can change depending on whether the noun is being used as:

- the subject of a sentence (nominative)
- the direct object (accusative)
- the indirect object (dative).

 Always look for patterns to help you remember!

There is only one change in the accusative: **der** changes to **den**. The changes in the dative are **der → dem, die → der, das → dem, die → den**.

	masculine	**feminine**	**neuter**	**plural**
nominative	der	die	das	die
accusative	de**n**	die	das	die
dative	de**m**	de**r**	de**m**	de**n**

IV Which word is it?

a masc nom ___
b fem accus ___
c pl nom ___
d neut dat ___
e masc dat ___
f fem dat ___

g neut nom ___
h pl dat ___
i neut accus ___
j masc accus ___
k pl nom ___
l fem nom ___

V Which gender and case can they be: masculine, feminine, neuter or plural; nominative, accusative or dative?

a der ____
b die ____
c das ____
d dem ____
e den ____

2.3.2 A: *ein, eine, ein* and cases

▶▶ **If you know all about *ein, eine* and *einen*, go on to 2.3.3.**

The word *a* is also a determiner. It is also called the indefinite article because it refers to any item and not a specific one: *a* bottle of red wine, not *the* bottle that you have chosen specifically. If the noun is the subject of the sentence it is in the nominative.

> Remember these words for *a* are not very different from each other, so if you don't get it right people will still understand what you are saying, but if you want to get it right here are the rules.

Nominative

In the nominative the word for *a* in front of a:

- masculine noun is **ein**: **ein Mann** – *a man*, **ein Hund** – *a dog*, **ein Baum** – *a tree*
- feminine noun is **eine**: **eine Frau** – *a woman*, **eine Blume** – *a flower*, **eine Idee** – *an idea*
- neuter noun is **ein**: **ein Kind** – *a child*, **ein Eis** – *an ice cream*, **ein Pferd** – *a horse*.

	masculine	**feminine**	**neuter**
nominative	ein	eine	ein
accusative	eine**n**	eine	ein
dative	eine**m**	eine**r**	eine**m**

The pattern is nearly the same as the pattern for **der/die/das**; the only difference is that a does not have a plural.

If you have forgotten what the nominative, accusative and dative are, go back to 2.3.1.

Accusative

In the accusative the masculine form is the only one that changes.

VI Which words are in the accusative (the direct object) in the following sentences?

a Petra hat einen Bruder. — Peter has a brother.

b Ein Bruder von mir hat eine amerikanische Freundin. — One of my brothers has an American girlfriend.

c Ich treffe einen alten Freund. — I am meeting an old friend.

d Ein Freund von uns hat ein altes Auto. — One of our friends has an old car.

e Der alte Mann hat einen alten Hund. — The old man has an old dog.

f Ein Hund hat eine eigene Persönlichkeit. — A dog has its own personality.

g Die junge Frau hat ein kleines Kind. — The young lady has a small child.

h Ein Kind weint, wenn es einen neuen Zahn bekommt. — A child cries when it gets a new tooth.

i Ein Zahn hat ein großes Loch. — A tooth has a big hole.

VII Imagine you are talking about your family. How would you say you have one of all these?

Ich habe...

a ___ Bruder
b ___ Schwester
c ___ Oma
d ___ Opa
e ___ Kind

f ___ Sohn
g ___ Zwillingsbruder
h ___ Tante
i ___ Baby
j ___ Stiefmutter

VIII Complete the following sentences with the correct form of ein.

a Ich habe ___ netten Nachbarn. (m) — I have a nice neighbour.
b Ich habe ___ Geschäft. (n) — I have a shop.
c Ich habe ___ Baby. (n) — I have a baby.
d Wir kaufen ___ neue Brieftasche. (f) — We are buying a new wallet.
e Wir essen ___ Suppe. (f) — We are eating soup.
f Wir trinken ___ Tee. (m) — We are drinking tea.

g Sie liest ___ deutsches Buch. (n)   She is reading a German book.

h Er kauft ___ CD. (f)   He is buying a CD.

i Kaufst du dir ___ Fahrrad? (n)   Are you buying yourself a bicycle?

Dative

The dative (indirect object) form of *a* is mostly used with prepositions (see page 225).

The dative follows the usual dative pattern of **-m -r -m** (**einem**, **einer**, **einem**).

2.3.3 *Kein*: not a, not any, no and cases

In German there is a special word for *not a* or *not any*: **kein**. You can also use it for *no* in front of a noun, e.g. *No dogs!* – **Keine Hunde!**

If you are saying you haven't any, or you don't have a dog, etc. you use **kein/keine**.

The changes follow the usual pattern. It is just like **ein** with a **k-**, but it has a plural form.

	masculine	feminine	neuter	plural
nominative	kein	keine	kein	keine
accusative	kein**en**	keine	kein	keine
dative	kein**em**	kein**er**	kein**em**	kein**en**

Kein and the subject of the sentence (nominative)

	masculine	feminine	neuter	plural
nominative	kein	keine	kein	keine

 Look for similarities: masculine and neuter – **kein**; feminine and plural – **keine**.

IX Complete the following sentences with the correct form of **kein**.

a K ___ Tag ist wie der andere.   No one day is like the other.

b K ___ Problem ist unlösbar.   No problem is insurmountable.

c K ___ Urlauber sind am Strand.   No holiday makers are on the beach.

d K ___ Mensch ist perfekt.   No human being is perfect.
e K ___ Gäste sind gekommen.   No guests came.
f K ___ Tier sollte leiden.   No animal should suffer.
g K ___ Kinder sollten leiden.   No children should suffer.

Kein and the direct object of the sentence (accusative)

	masculine	feminine	neuter	plural
accusative	kein**en**	keine	kein	keine

Er hat keinen Laptop.   He hasn't got a laptop.
Sie hat keine E-Mail Adresse.   She doesn't have an e-mail
       address.
Er hat kein Geld.   He doesn't have any money.

X   Complete the following sentences with the correct form of
kein.

a Ich habe ___ Ahnung. (f)   I haven't got a clue.
b Ich habe ___ Idee. (f)   I've no idea.
c Ich habe ___ blassen   I haven't the slightest
Schimmer. (m)   idea.
d Ich habe ___ Interesse. (n)   I'm not interested.
e Ich habe ___ Fantasie. (f)   I have no imagination.
f Ich habe ___ Kontrolle   I have no control
darüber. (f)   over it.
g Ich habe ___ Angst. (f)   I am not scared.
h Ich habe ___ Sinn für   I have no sense of
Humor. (m)   humour.
i Ich habe ___ Erwartung. (f)   I've got no expectation.
j Ich habe ___ Handy. (n)   I haven't got a mobile phone.

Kein and the indirect object (dative)

	masculine	feminine	neuter	plural
dative	keinem	keiner	keinem	keinen

Sie sollten keinem Kind Zigaretten geben.   You should not give
       cigarettes to a child.

XI   Complete the following sentences with the correct form of
kein.

a Man sollte k_____ Kindern Alkohol   You should not give
geben.   alcohol to children.
b Er kann k_____ Menschen mehr   He cannot believe
glauben.   anybody any more.

c Kinder sollten mit k_____
Feuerzeugen spielen.

Children should
not play with lighters.

d Man sollte k_____ Alkoholiker
Alkohol geben.

You should not give
alcohol to an alcoholic.

e Man sollte k_____Kind Zigaretten
verkaufen.

You should not sell
cigarettes to a child.

2.4 My, your, his, her, etc.

 If you know all about these words, go on to 2.5.

These are words which tell you to whom something
belongs: *my coat*, **his** *umbrella*, **your** *briefcase*, **their** *house*, **our**
cat, etc.

The grammatical name is possessive adjectives, but they are
used as determiners and they follow the same pattern as
ein, **kein**, etc.

In English, we only have one form of each: *my, your, his, her,
our, their*. In German, it has to agree with the noun it is
describing.

		masculine	feminine	neuter	plural
I → my	ich	mein Hund	meine Freundin	mein Auto	meine Freunde
you → your	du	dein Hund	deine Freundin	dein Auto	deine Freunde
he → his	er	sein Hund	seine Freundin	sein Auto	seine Freunde
she → her	sie	ihr Hund	ihre Freundin	ihr Auto	ihre Freunde
it → its	es	sein Hund	seine Freundin	sein Auto	seine Freunde
we → our	wir	unser Hund	unsere Freundin	unser Auto	unsere Freunde
you → your	Ihr	euer Hund	eure Freundin	euer Auto	eure Freunde
you → your	Sie	Ihr Hund	Ihre Freundin	Ihr Auto	Ihre Freunde
they → their	ihr	ihr Hund	ihre Freundin	ihr Auto	ihre Freunde

mein, dein, sein, ihr, sein, unser, euer, Ihr, ihr all follow the
usual pattern.

	masculine	feminine	neuter	plural
nominative	mein	meine	mein	meine
accusative	mein**en**	meine	mein	meine
dative	mein**em**	mein**er**	mein**em**	mein**en**

2.4.1 My: *mein/meine*

The word for *my* agrees with the person or thing it is describing.

Don't worry – if you don't get the ending right you will still be understood!

Mein and the subject of a sentence (nominative)

	masculine	**feminine**	**neuter**	**plural**
nominative	mein	meine	mein	meine

I Imagine you are showing someone photographs of your family. What would you say?

Das ist/sind mein/meine ...

a ____ Kinder   **e** ____ Mutter   **i** ____ Kind
b ____ Mann   **f** ____ Schwester   **j** ____ Sohn
c ____ Frau   **g** ____ Brüder   **k** ____ Tochter
d ____ Bruder   **h** ____ Großeltern

Mein and the direct object of a sentence (accusative)

	masculine	**feminine**	**neuter**	**plural**
accusative	meinen	meine	mein	meine

 Remember only the masculine form changes.

II Kennen Sie ____ ?

a ____ Sohn   **f** ____ Nachbarin
b ____ Tochter   **g** ____ Kollegen
c ____ Mann   **h** ____ Freund
d ____ Frau   **i** ____ Nichte
e ____ Freundin   **j** ____ Neffen

Mein and the indirect object of a sentence (dative)

If you have forgotten what the indirect object is, go back to p.157.

You will probably only need to use the dative after certain prepositions, e.g. **zu**, **mit**, **von,** etc.

	masculine	feminine	neuter	plural
dative	meinem	meiner	meinem	meinen

III Imagine you are giving a letter to the following people. What would you say?

Wir geben einen Brief zu …

a _____ Tochter   **f** _____ Freundin
b _____ Mutter   **g** _____ Nachbarin
c _____ Vater   **h** _____ Postboten
d _____ Kollegen (pl)   **i** _____ Onkel
e _____ Kind   **j** _____ Tante

2.4.2 Your: dein/deine

You can only use **dein**, **deine**, **deinen** when speaking to a child or someone that you know very well and would address as **du**.

▶▶ **If you are not going to need this form, go on to 2.4.3.**

The words for *your* rhyme with the words for *my* (**mein**, **meine**, **meinen**) and behave in the same way.

Dein and the subject of a sentence (nominative)

	masculine	feminine	neuter	plural
nominative	dein	deine	dein	deine

IV Put the correct form of **dein/deine** in front of these words.

Das ist/sind dein/deine …

a ___ Bruder   **e** ___ Freund   **i** ___ Hund
b ___ Vater   **f** ___ Großeltern   **j** ___ Katze
c ___ Mutter   **g** ___ Tochter
d ___ Schwestern   **h** ___ Sohn

V How would you ask what they are called?

Wie heissen/heisst …?

a ___ Freunde   **e** ___ Kollegin   **i** ___ Chefs
b ___ Freundin   **f** ___ Kollegen   **j** ___ Liebhaber
c ___ Freund   **g** ___ Chef
d ___ Kollege   **h** ___ Chefin

Dein and the direct object of a sentence (accusative)

 Remember that, as usual, the masculine form is the only one to change.

	masculine	feminine	neuter	plural
accusative	dein*en*	deine	dein	deine

Können wir dein**en** Freund kennenlernen?   Can we meet your (male) friend?

VI Fill in the missing part of **dein**.

a Können wir _____ Architekten kennenlernen (m)?
b Können wir _____ Architektin kennenlernen?
c Können wir _____ Partner kennnenlernen?
d Können wir _____ Partnerin kennenlernen?
e Können wir _____ Mann kennenlernen?
f Können wir _____ Frau kennenlernen?
g Können wir _____ Kind kennenlernen?
h Können wir _____ Gärtner kennenlernen?
i Können wir _____ Freund kennenlernen?
j Können wir _____ Freundin kennenlernen?

Dein and the indirect object of a sentence (dative)
Remember the dative is mostly used after certain prepositions like **mit** – *with*.

Ich treffe mich morgen mit deinem Onkel.   I am meeting your uncle tomorrow.

	masculine	feminine	neuter	plural
dative	dein*em*	deiner	dein*em*	dein*en*

VII Put in the correct form of **dein**.

a Ich treffe mich morgen mit _____ Lehrer.
b Ich treffe mich morgen mit _____ Lehrerin.
c Ich treffe mich morgen mit _____ Lehrern.
d Ich treffe mich morgen mit _____ Lehrerinnen.
e Ich treffe mich morgen mit _____ Rechtsanwalt.
f Ich treffe mich morgen mit _____ Rechtsanwältin.
g Ich treffe mich morgen mit _____ Rechtsanwälten.
h Ich treffe mich morgen mit _____ Freundin.
i Ich treffe mich morgen mit _____ Freunden.
j Ich treffe mich morgen mit _____ Freundinnen.

His: *sein/seine/seinen* and her: *ihr/ihre/ihren*

The words for *his/her* also rhyme with the words for *my* (**sein**, **seine**, **seinen**), and **ihr**, **ihre**, **ihren** are used in the same way.

▶▶ **If you know all about *sein*, *seine*, *seinen*, go on to 2.4.4.**

Remember:

- nominative – subject of the sentence
- accusative – direct object of the sentence
- dative – indirect object of the sentence

If you don't know what the subject, direct object or indirect object is, go back to p.155.

	masculine	**feminine**	**neuter**	**plural**
nominative	sein/ihr	seine/ihre	sein/ihr	seine/ihre
accusative	seinen/ihren	seine/ihre	sein/ihr	seine/ihre
dative	seinem/ihrem	seiner/ihrer	seinem/ihrem	seinen/ihren

Sein/ihr and the subject of a sentence (nominative)

VIII Erzählen Sie mir über Thomas. **Tell me about Thomas by filling in the right words: sein, seine.**

a ___ Freundin heißt Susanne.
b ___ Schwägerin heißt Anne.
c ___ Bruder ist älter als er.
d ___ Mutter ist eine Schauspielerin.
e ___ Vater arbeitet bei der Deutschen Bank.
f ___ Schwester ist eine Opersängerin.
g ___ Lieblingssport ist Golf.
h ___ Lieblingsmusik ist Rock & Roll.
i ___ Lieblingsspeise ist Spagetti.
j ___ Hobby ist Musik hören.

Sein/ihr and the direct object of a sentence (accusative)

IX Which form of **ihr** or **sein** would you use?

Wen treffen Anne und Paul? **Who do Anne and Paul meet?**

Anne trifft ihren/ihre/ihr …

Paul trifft seinen/seine/sein …

Nouns and Determiners

a Anne trifft _____ Freund in der Stadt.
b Paul trifft _____ Freund im Kino.
c Anne trifft _____ Mutter zu Hause.
d Paul trifft _____ Freundin im Park.
e Anne trifft _____ Trainer im Sportzentrum.
f Paul trifft _____ Kollegen in der Kantine. (male colleague)
g Anne trifft _____ Golfpartner auf dem Golfplatz.
h Paul trifft _____ Gitarrenlehrer im College.
i Anne trifft _____ Kind vor dem Kindergarten.

Sein/ihr and the indirect object of a sentence (dative)

Helfen – _to help_ takes the dative. In German you (give) help to someone.

X Ulrike and Jens like to help everybody. Which form of **ihr** or **sein** would you use?

a Ulrike hilft _____ Schwester beim Aufräumen.
b Jens hilft _____ Bruder beim Lernen.
c Ulrike hilft _____ Mutter beim Kochen.
d Jens hilft _____ Vater bei der Hausarbeit.
e Ulrike hilft _____ Chefin beim Fotografieren.
f Jens hilft _____ Nichte bei den Hausaufgaben.
g Ulrike hilft _____ beiden Brüdern beim Studieren.
h Jens hilft _____ Patienten im Krankenhaus.
i Ulrike hilft _____ Kind beim Englisch lernen.
j Jens hilft _____ Oma beim Einkaufen.

2.4.4 Our: _unser/unsere/unseren_

The word for _our_ is **unser**.

▶▶ **If you know all about _unser_, go on to 2.4.5.**

Unser behaves in exactly the same way as the **ein/mein/kein**, etc.

	masculine	**feminine**	**neuter**	**plural**
nominative	uns**er**	uns**ere**	uns**er**	uns**ere**
accusative	uns**eren**	uns**ere**	uns**er**	uns**ere**
dative	uns**erem**	uns**erer**	uns**erem**	uns**eren**

Unser and the subject of a sentence (nominative)

XI How would you say these are *our* things?

Das ist unser/unsere …

a ___ Haus (m)   **e** ___ Balkon (m)   **h** ___ Rasen (m)
b ___ Wohnung (f)   **f** ___ Garage (f)   **i** ___ Flur (m)
c ___ Bungalow (m)   **g** ___ Garten (m)   **j** ___ Küche (f)
d ___ Keller (m)

Unser and the direct object of a sentence (accusative)

XII Anne und Timo zeigen ihr neues Haus. Anne and Timo are showing their new house.

a Hier haben wir _____ Flur.
b Hier haben wir _____ Küche.
c Hier haben wir _____ Schlafzimmer.
d Hier haben wir _____ Balkon.
e Hier haben wir _____ Keller.
f Hier haben wir _____ Bad.
g Hier haben wir _____ Sauna.
h Hier haben wir _____ Toilette.
i Hier haben wir _____ Garten.
j Hier haben wir _____ Garage.

Unser and the indirect object of a sentence (dative)

XIII Anne und Timo erklären, was sie in ihrem Haus machen. Anne and Timo tell us what they do in which room. **In** and **auf** are both prepositions which can take the accusative or the dative. Here they are followed by the dative.

a In _____ Wohnzimmer hören wir Musik.
b In _____ Garage parken wir unser Auto.
c In _____ Küche kochen und backen wir.
d In _____ Schlafzimmer schlafen wir.
e In _____ Badezimmer duschen und baden wir.
f In _____ Garten pflanzen wir Blumen.
g Auf _____ Balkon sonnen wir uns.
h Auf _____ Terasse grillen wir.
i In _____ Kinderzimmer spielen und schlafen die Kinder.
j In _____ Flur hängen wir unsere Mäntel auf.

2.4.5 Your: *Ihr* (polite form)

The word for *your* is **Ihr/Ihren/Ihrem/Ihre.** You use it when you are using the **Sie** (polite) form, i.e. when speaking to an adult or more than one adult.

This is exactly the same as the word for *her* but it is written with a capital letter.

	masculine	feminine	neuter	plural
nominative	Ihr	Ihre	Ihr	Ihre
accusative	Ihre**n**	Ihre	Ihr	Ihre
dative	Ihre**m**	Ihre**r**	Ihre**m**	Ihre**n**

Ihr and the subject of a sentence (nominative)

XIV Ask if these are *your* things.

Ist das Ihr/Ihre …?

a ___ Stuhl? **d** ___ Schirm? **g** ___ Schlüssel **j** ___ Auto
b ___ Tasche? **e** ___ Essen? **h** ___ Brieftasche
c ___ Glas? **f** ___ Mantel? **i** ___ Zeitung

XV Talking to the owner of a garden. Fill in the correct form of **Ihr.**

a _____ Rosen (pl) sind wunderschön.
b _____ Erdbeeren (pl) sind reif zum pflücken.
c _____ Rasen (m) sieht sehr gepflegt aus.
d _____ Apfelbäume (pl) sind voller Äpfel.
e _____ Gärtner (m) ist sehr gut.
f _____ Rasenmäher (m) ist sehr ruhig.
g _____ Gemüse (n) sieht sehr gesund aus.
h _____ Treibhaus (n) sieht interessant aus.
i _____ Misthaufen (m) ist halbvoll.
j _____ Robert hat einen wunderschönen Garten kreiert.

Ihr and the direct object of a sentence (accusative)

XVI Fill in the correct form of **Ihr.**

a Ich gebe Ihnen _____ Schlüssel.
b Ich gebe Ihnen _____ Post.
c Ich gebe Ihnen _____ Zeitung.
d Ich gebe Ihnen _____ Zimmerschlüssel.
e Ich gebe Ihnen _____ Kaffee.
f Geben Sie mir bitte _____ Telefonnummer.
g Geben Sie mir bitte _____ Adresse.
h Geben Sie mir bitte _____ E-Mail Adresse.
i Geben Sie mir bitte _____ Handynummer.
j Geben Sie mir bitte _____ Mantel.

Ihr and the indirect object of a sentence (dative)
The dative is used after prepositions such as **mit**.

XVII Fill in the correct form of **Ihr.**

  a Ich helfe Ihnen mit _____ Gepäck. (n) luggage
  b Ich helfe Ihnen mit _____ Auto. (n) car
  c Ich helfe Ihnen mit _____ Deutsch. (n) German
  d Ich helfe Ihnen mit _____ Grammatik. (f) grammar
  e Ich helfe Ihnen mit _____ Vokabeln. (pl) vocabulary
  f Ich helfe Ihnen mit _____ Übersetzung. (f) translation
  g Ich helfe Ihnen mit _____ Aussprache. (f) pronunciation
  h Ich helfe Ihnen mit _____ Intonation. (f) intonation
  i Ich helfe Ihnen mit _____ Computer. (m) computer

2.4.6 Your: *euer*

This is the plural form of **du.** You only use it with more than one person that you know really well.

▶▶ **If you are not going to need *euer*, go on to 2.4.7.**

Euer behaves in exactly the same way as the others: **ein, mein, kein,** etc.

	masculine	feminine	neuter	plural
nominative	euer	eure	euer	eure
accusative	euren	eure	euer	eure
dative	eurem	eurer	eurem	euren

Euer and the subject of a sentence (nominative)

XVIII Say these are *your* things.

Das ist/sind euer/eure _____

  a ___ Koffer   **f** ___ Disko
  b ___ Kaffee   **g** ___ Rathaus
  c ___ Essen   **h** ___ Tempel
  d ___ Getränk   **i** ___ Schwimmbad
  e ___ Kellnerin   **j** ___ Fußballstadium

Euer and the direct object of a sentence (accusative)

XIX Say where we are going.

Wir gehen in euer/eure/euren …

  a ___ Kino   **f** ___ Schule
  b ___ Disko   **g** ___ Universität
  c ___ Club   **h** ___ Büro
  d ___ Tempel   **i** ___ Kirche
  e ___ Restaurant   **j** ___ Atelier

2.4.7 Their: *ihr*

 This is just the same as the word for *her* and behaves in exactly the same way.

XX Say these are *their* things.

Das ist/sind ihr/ihre ...

a _____ Plätze (seats)
b _____ Gepäck (luggage)
c _____ Pässe (passports)
d _____ Fahrkarten (tickets)
e _____ Koffer (suitcase)
f _____ Rucksack (rucksack)
g _____ Regenschirm (umbrella)
h _____ Skier (skis)
i _____ Skateboard (skateboard)
j _____ Skipass (ski pass)

2.5 More determiners

These are also determiners as they determine which noun is being referred to:

Welcher Mann?	Which man?
dieser Mann	this man
jeder Mann	each/every man

 They all follow the same pattern as **der**, **die**, **das**, **die**.

	masculine	**feminine**	**neuter**	**plural**
nominative	dieser	diese	dieses	diese
accusative	diesen	diese	dieses	diese
dative	diesem	dieser	diesem	diesen

2.5.1 Which?: *Welche?*

This is also called an interrogative adjective because **welche** agrees with the noun.

Asking about the subject of the sentence

I Add the correct ending to **Welch**.

Welcher Mantel gehört Ihnen? **Which coat belongs to you?**

a Welch____ Jacke gehört Ihnen?
b Welch____ Mantel gehört Ihnen?
c Welch____ Tasche gehört Ihnen?
d Welch____ Hut gehört Ihnen?
e Welch____ Schirm gehört Ihnen?

Asking about the direct object

II Put in the correct form: **welchen, welche or welches**.

a Which hotel would you prefer?   ____ Hotel ziehen Sie vor?
b Which room would you prefer?   ____ Zimmer ziehen Sie vor?
c Which table do you prefer?   ____ Tisch ziehen Sie vor?
d Which flowers do you prefer?   ____ Blumen ziehen Sie vor?
e Which wine do you prefer?   ____ Wein ziehen Sie vor?

Asking about the indirect object

III Put in the correct form: **welchem, welcher or welchen**.

a Which address should I send it to?   Zu _____ Adresse soll
ich es schicken?

b Which floor should I send it to?   Zu _____ Etage soll
ich es schicken?

c Which house should I send it to?   Zu _____ Haus soll
ich es schicken?

d Which hotel should I send it to?   Zu _____ Hotel soll
ich es schicken?

e Which shop should I send it to?   Zu _____ Geschäft soll
ich es schicken?

2.5.2 Each/every: *jeder*

Jeder has the same endings as **welcher** and **dieser**.

Jeder Tag (m) bringt etwas Neues.   Each day brings
something new.

Jede Woche (f) bringt etwas Neues.   Each week brings
something new.

Jedes Jahr (n) bringt etwas Neues.   Each year brings
something new.

IV Fill in the missing form of **jeder**.

a Wir kommen ___ Tag.
b Wir kommen ___ Woche.
c Wir kommen ___ Jahr.
d Wir begrüßen ___ Gast persönlich.
e Wir begrüßen ___ Kind persönlich.
f Wir begrüßen ___ Besucher persönlich.
g Wir begrüßen ___ Gewinner persönlich.
h Wir begrüßen ___ Kandidatin persönlich.

2.5.3 Other determiners

 Some are only used in the plural so they end in **-e**.

alle	all
beide	both
einige	some
jene	those
manche	some, a number of
mehrere	several
sämtliche	many, a great number of
viele	many
wenige	few

2.6 ▶**Fast track:** nouns and determiners

All nouns in German fit into the following categories: masculine, feminine or neuter.

The word for *the* in front of masculine nouns is **der**.

The word for *the* in front of feminine nouns is **die**.

The word for *the* in front of neuter nouns is **das**.

The word for *the* in front of plural nouns is **die**.

Although there is no logic to whether a noun is masculine, feminine or neuter, there are some ways to help you remember the gender of a noun (see 2.1.2).

Der/die/das can change depending on whether the noun is being used as:

- the subject in a sentence (nominative)
- the direct object (accusative)
- the indirect object (dative).

Nouns and Determiners

There is only one change in the accusative: **der** changes to **den**.

The changes in the dative are **der** → **dem**, **die** → **der**, **das** → **dem**, **die** → **den**.

	masculine	feminine	neuter	plural
nominative	der	die	das	die
accusative	de**n**	die	das	die
dative	de**m**	de**r**	de**m**	d**en**

The words for *a* – **ein** and *not a* – **kein** follow the same pattern.

	masculine	feminine	neuter
nominative	ein	eine	ein
accusative	eine**n**	eine	ein
dative	eine**m**	eine**r**	eine**m**

Possessive adjectives are determiners that tell you to whom something belongs:

my	mein
your	dein
his	sein
her	ihr
our	unser
your	euer
your (polite form)	Ihr
their	ihr

All these determiners follow the same pattern:

	masculine	feminine	neuter	plural
nominative	mein	meine	mein	meine
accusative	meinen	meine	mein	meine
dative	meinem	meiner	meinem	meinen

Other determiners:

 Some are only used in the plural so they end in **-e**.

alle	all
beide	both
dieser	these
einige	some
jene	those
manche	some, a number of
mehrere	several
sämtliche	many, a great number of
viele	many
wenige	few

3 PRONOUNS

A pronoun is a word which stands for a noun. Instead of saying:

- *Mr Jones*, you can say *he* – **er**
- *the lady*, you can say *she* – **sie**
- *my husband/wife and I*, you can say *we* – **wir**
- *the children*, you can say *they* – **sie**

In English we say *it* instead of *table*.

In German everything is either masculine, feminine or neuter:

- **der Tisch** – *the table* is masculine so it is **er** – *he*
- **die Lampe** – *the lamp* is feminine so it is **sie** – *she*
- **das Buch** – *the book* is neuter so it is **es** – *it*.

3.1 Ich, du, er, sie, es – I, you, he, she, it: subject pronouns

▶▶ **If you know what a subject pronoun is, go on to 3.2.**

The subject is the person or thing who does the action: *I* run, *you* play, *he* eats, *she* drinks, *it* shuts, *we* live, *you* swim, *they* talk.

The subject pronouns in German are as follows:

singular		plural	
ich	I	wir	we
du	you (informal)	ihr	you
Sie	you (formal)	Sie	you (formal)
er/sie/es	he/she/it	sie	they

I Which pronoun are you going to use?

a You are talking about Herr Braun.   —
b You are talking about Frau Braun.   —
c You are talking about yourself.   —

d You are talking to a child. _____

e You are taking to a group of children. _____

f You are talking to your business acquaintance. _____

g You are talking about yourself and someone else. _____

h You are talking about your parents. _____

3.1.1 *Ich – I*: the first person singular

You use the first person when you are talking about yourself.

Ich lese	I am reading
Ich schlafe	I am sleeping
Ich bin	I am
Ich heiße Frau Smith und ich lebe …	I am called Mrs Smith and I live …

Ich (*I*) is only written with a capital letter at the beginning of a sentence.

Sie (*you* formal) is always written with a capital letter.

After **ich** the verb ends in **-e** in the present tense.

3.1.2 *Du – you*: the second person singular

You use **du** when you are talking to someone you know very well – a relative, close friend or someone who has invited you to do so, or a child.

There is a special verb which means *to call someone du* – **duzen**.

Hast du einen Hund?	Have you got a dog?
Bist du traurig?	Are you sad?

After **du** the verb ends in **-st** in the present tense.

3.1.3 *Er/sie/es – he/she/it*: the third person singular

You use er/sie/es when you are talking about someone or something else.

It translates: *he, she* and *it*.

Remember that in German everything is either masculine, feminine or neuter.

The bus is *he* – **er**, the soup is *she* – sie, and the baby is *it* – **es**.

Der Bus hat eine Panne.	The bus is not working.
Er ist liegengeblieben.	It has broken down.
Die Suppe kommt. Sie ist kalt.	The soup is coming. It is cold.
Das Baby weint. Es ist hungrig.	The baby is crying. It is hungry.

After **er/sie/es** the verb ends in -t in the present tense.

II Which would you use: **er**, **sie** or **es**?

a der Bus – the bus ___
b die Suppe – the soup ___
c das Baby – the baby ___
d der Brief – the letter ___
e das Mädchen – the girl ___
f der Tisch – the table ___
g das Buch – the book ___
h der Computer – the computer ___
i die Reise – the journey ___
j die Kirche – the church ___

III Which would you use: **er**, **sie** or **es**?

a der Bahnhof – the station ___
b der Parkplatz – the car park ___
c das Restaurant – the restaurant ___
d die Brücke – the bridge ___
e das Hotel – the hotel ___
f die Kreuzung – the crossing ___
g der Fluss – the river ___
h die Stadt – the town ___
i der Park – the park ___
j die Bushaltestelle – the bus stop ___

IV Which pronoun would you use to talk about them: **er**, **sie**, **es**, **wir**?

a Meine Freundin ___
b Ihr Freund ___
c Dein Hund ___
d Dein Kind ___
e Sein Haus ___
f Mein Bruder ___
g Ihre Katze ___
h Mein Wagen ___
i Ihre Freundin ___
j Mein Garten ___

3.1.4 *Wir* – we: the first person plural

You use **wir** to talk about yourself and someone else.

You use it when you would use *we* in English.

Wir ziehen es vor, früh zu gehen.	We prefer to leave early.
Mein Mann und ich gehen Morgen ins Theater.	My husband and I are going to the theatre tomorrow.

After **wir** the verb ends in -**en** in the present tense.

> **Man** (one) is often used in conversation instead of **wir**. It is followed by the third person singular of the verb (the *he/she/it* form).
> After **man** the verb usually ends in -**t** in the present tense. **Man** can be translated as *one*.

Man kann das tun.	One/we can do that.
Man sollte das nicht machen.	One/we should not do that.

3.1.5 *Ihr* – you

You use **ihr** to talk to a group of young people, relatives or friends.

You only use this form when speaking to one, two or more people you know very well or children.

▶▶ **If you are not going to need ihr, go on to 3.1.6.**

Wohin geht ihr?	Where are you going?
Geht ihr heute ins Kino?	Are you going to the cinema today?

After **ihr** the verb ends in -**t**.

3.1.6 *Sie* – you (polite form)

This is the form of *you* you will need most.

You use **Sie** when you are talking to someone else. It translates *you*.

Sie is often referred to as the 'polite' form, as it is used not only in the plural but also when talking to someone older than you or to a stranger, even if there is only one person. There is a special verb which means *to call someone Sie* – **Siezen**.

After **Sie** the verb ends in -**en** in the present tense.

Sie is written with a capital letter (in the singular and in the **181**
plural).

Pronouns

3.1.7 *Sie* – they: the third person plural

You use **sie** (with a small letter) when you are talking about
more than one person or thing.

It translates *they*.

You use **sie** to refer to two or more people.

Die Bücher sind sehr interessant.	The books are very interesting.
Sie kosten nicht viel.	They don't cost much.
Paula und Martin kommen	Paula and Martin are coming
mit. Sie haben Zeit.	with us. They have time.

After **sie** the verb ends in **-en** in the present tense.

V Which German pronoun should you use?

a I am going to the cinema tonight.
b After the cinema we are going to a restaurant.
c My girlfriends will be there.
d The boys are going to a football match.
e Klaus is playing.
f Susanne is going to watch.
g Where are you going? (asking a group of young people)
h Where are you going? (asking a child)
i Where are you going? (asking an adult)
j Where are you going? (asking more than one adult)

VI Which pronoun would you use in these sentences?

a Andreas wohnt in Norddeutschland. ___ wohnt in Hamburg.
b Barbara und Timo wohnen im Süden. ___ wohnen in München.
c ___ wohne in Berlin.
d Wo wohnen ___? ___ wohne in London.
e Ich wohne mit meinem Mann. ___ wohnen in einem großen Haus auf
dem Land.
f Tobias wohnt in einer schönen Wohnung. ___ ist glücklich.
g Meine Schwester wohnt in Aachen. ___ studiert in Aachen.
h Meine Freunde wohnen in Bremen. ___ wohnen bei ihren Eltern.
i Wo wohnen ___ Frau Krüger?
j Wohnt ___ bei euren Eltern?

VII What does the verb usually end with?

a ich ___
b du ___
c er ___
d sie ___
e es ___

f wir ___
g ihr ___
h sie ___
i Sie ___

3.2 Me, you, him, her, it, us, them

These are called direct object pronouns.

►► **If you know what a direct object pronoun is and how to use it, go on to 3.3.**

This is the person or object which has the action done to him/her/it.

I saw John/*him.*

John saw Karen/*her.*

I bought the watch/*it.*

I like Paul/*him.*

He likes Isabelle/*her.*

She doesn't like the boys/*them.*

> An easy way to find the direct object pronoun is to ask the question: Who did I ___? Who does he ___? (including the verb in the question) or what did I/he/she/we ___ do (including the verb in the question).

I see John/*him.* Who do I see? *him* (direct object pronoun)

I bought a rose/*it.* What did I buy? *it* (direct object pronoun)

He likes Isabelle/her. Who does he like? *her* (direct object pronoun)

In English it is easy to recognise the direct object as it always comes straight after the verb.

I Which is the direct object?

a I bought a new car.
b My husband drove it home for me.
c A dog chased a cat across the road.
d He swerved and hit a tree.
e He broke the wing mirror.

f He bought me a bunch of flowers.
g He took the car to the garage to be repaired.

3.2.1 Personal pronouns in the accusative (direct object)

Ich treffe **sie** Morgen.   I am going to meet her tomorrow.
Sie hat **mich** besucht.   She visited me.

singular		plural	
ich – mich	me	wir – uns	us
du – dich	you (informal)	ihr – euch	you (informal)
Sie – Sie	you (formal)	Sie – Sie	you (formal)
er – ihn	him	sie – sie	them
sie – sie	her		
es – es	it		

There are four pronouns called **sie**. Two are written with a capital letter **Sie** (formal singular) and **Sie** (formal plural). The other two are **sie** – *her* and **sie** – *them*. You sometimes won't know who is meant by **sie**: it can mean: *they, she* or *you*, but don't worry. You will be able to work it out from the context.

II   Which is the accusative (object) personal pronoun in the following sentences?

a Ich treffe ihn am Montag in der Stadt.
b Wir werden dich nicht vergessen.
c Tobias sieht sie in der Pause.
d Ich mag sie sehr.
e Wir sehen euch einmal in der Woche.
f Er mag mich, weil ich ehrlich bin.
g Sie mag ihn, weil er Humor hat.
h Wir werden ihn vom Zug abholen.
i Wir respektieren Sie, weil Sie uns geholfen haben.
j Susi manipuliert ihn, weil er sich manipulieren läßt.

III   Replace the word(s) in bold with the appropriate accusative pronoun.

a Wir haben **einen guten Film** im Kino gesehen.   Ich habe ___ schon einmal gesehen.
b Ich habe den Film mit **meiner Tochter** gesehen.   Der Film hat ___ begeistert.
c Im Film gab es **gute Musik der 60iger Jahre**.   Ich fand ___ damals richtig super.

d Ich liebe **die Musik der 60iger Jahre**.	Wir haben ___ stundenlang gehört.
e Ich habe mir auch **die Mode von damals** angeguckt.	Ich habe ___ sehr gemocht.
f Ich habe damals **meinen Mann** kennengelernt.	Ich habe ___ dann geheiratet.
g Wir haben viel Zeit in **Kneipen** verbracht.	Ich habe ___ sehr gemütlich gefunden.
h Wir haben uns auch für **Politik** interessiert.	Wir fanden ___ sehr wichtig.
i Wir fanden **die Emanzipation** der Frauen sehr wichtig.	Wir haben ___ sehr unterstützt.
j Ich denke, wir hatten einen Einfluss auf **die Gesellschaft.**	Wir haben ___ etwas verändert.

3.3 *Mir* – to me, *ihm* – to him, *ihr* – to her

These are called indirect object pronouns.

▶▶ **If you know what an indirect object pronoun is and how to use it, go on to 3.4.**

In English, an indirect object pronoun is the same as a direct object pronoun but has (or can have) *to* or *for* in front of it.

I bought her it. I bought it (direct object – it is the thing that you bought) *for her* (indirect object).

Give me it. Give it (direct object – the thing which is being given) *to me* (indirect object).

They showed him it. They showed it (direct object – the thing which is being shown) *to him* (indirect object).

 Indirect pronouns are used with verbs like: give, send, write, show, buy, offer, tell, lend, etc. where you do *something to/for someone/something.*

I Identify the indirect object pronouns in these sentences.

 Try saying *to/for* in front of the pronoun to see if it is indirect.

a Hans sent me a text message in German.
b I could not read it. My friend could. I showed it to her.

c She translated it for me.
d I wrote him a reply.
e She sent it for me.
f He sent her a new message.
g She did not show it to me.
h She sent him a photo of herself.
i He sent her another message.
j She sent him a reply.
k He texted her.
l She did not tell me what he said.
m She gave me my phone back and went.

3.3.1 Personal pronouns in the dative (indirect object)

The indirect object is replaced by the indirect object pronoun:

I am giving the flowers to my girlfriend.	Ich gebe ihr die Blumen.
I am sending you an e-mail.	Ich schicke dir eine E-Mail.
He is sending her a text message.	Er schickt ihr eine MSM.

indirect object pronouns singular	plural
ich – mir (to) me	wir – uns (to) us
du – dir (to) you	ihr – euch (to) you
er – ihm (to) him	sie – ihnen (to) them
sie – ihr (to) her	
es – ihm (to) it	
Sie – Ihnen (to) you (formal)	Sie – Ihnen (to) you (formal)

Note: **ihm** means *(to) him* and *(to) it*.

In German indirect pronouns are used with verbs like:
geben – *to give*, **schicken** – *to send*, **schreiben** – *to write*,
zeigen – *to show*, **kaufen** – *to buy*, **anbieten** – *to offer*, **sagen** –
to tell, **leihen** – *to lend*, etc. where you do *something to/for
someone/something*.

II Which indirect pronoun would you use?

a We are going to
Anne and Günther
for Christmas.

Wir fahren Weihnachten zu Anne
und Günther. Wir fahren
Weihnachten zu ___.

b We are buying some
things for them.

Wir kaufen ein paar Sachen für
sie. Wir kaufen ___ ein paar
Sachen.

c We are giving Thomas a bottle of wine as a thank you.

Wir geben Thomas eine Flasche Wein, als Danke schön. Wir geben ___ eine Flasche Wein.

d We are sending some flowers to Anne.

Wir schicken Anne ein paar Blumen. Wir schicken ___ ein paar Blumen.

e We are sending a Christmas card to both of them.

Wir schicken den Beiden eine Weihnachtskarte. Wir schicken ___ eine Weihnachtskarte.

f We told Anne's mother about our holiday.

Wir haben Annes Mutter über unseren Urlaub erzählt. Wir haben ___ über unseren Urlaub erzählt.

g We bought a nice present for her son.

Wir haben ihrem Sohn ein schönes Geschenk gekauft. Wir haben ___ ein schönes Geschenk gekauft.

h They invited Klaus and me to stay overnight.

Sie haben Klaus und mir angeboten, über Nacht zu bleiben. Sie haben ___ angeboten, über Nacht zu bleiben.

i We thanked Anne and Günther for it.

Wir haben Anne und Günther dafür gedankt. Wir haben ___ dafür gedankt.

III More practice. Which indirect pronoun would you use?

a Hans sent me a text message in German.

Hans hat ___ eine SMS in Deutsch geschickt.

b I could not read it. My friend could. I showed her it.

Ich konnte ___ nicht lesen. Meine Freundin konnte. Ich habe es ___ gezeigt.

c I wrote him a reply.

Ich habe ___ geantwortet.

d She sent it to him.

Sie hat es ___ geschickt.

e He sent her a new message.

Er hat ___ eine neue Nachricht geschickt.

f She did not show it to me.

Sie hat es ___ nicht gezeigt.

g She sent him a photo of herself.

Sie hat ___ eine Foto von ___ geschickt.

h He sent her another message.

Er hat ___ eine andere Nachricht geschickt.

i She sent him a reply.

Sie hat ___ eine Antwort geschickt.

j He replied to her.

Er hat ___ geantwortet.

k She did not tell me what he said.	Sie hat ___ nicht gesagt, was er geschrieben hat.		
l She gave me my phone back and went off to meet him.	Sie hat ___ das Telefon wieder gegeben und ist gegangen um ihn zu treffen.		

3.3.2 Verbs which are followed by the dative

In German some verbs are followed by the dative. Here are some of the most common ones.

 To help you learn them, remember them with *to*: **antworten** – *to answer (to) someone*, **begegnen** – *to meet (to) someone*, **danken** – *to thank (to) someone*.

to answer (to) someone	antworten + dative	Ich antworte ihm.	I am answering him.
to meet (to) somebody	begegnen + dative	Ich bin ihr begegnet.	I met her.
to thank (to) somebody	danken + dative	Ich danke dir.	I thank you.
to allow (to) somebody	erlauben + dative	Ich erlaube euch zu telefonieren.	I allow you to phone (informal plural).
to follow (to) somebody	folgen + dative	Ich folge Ihnen.	I follow you (formal singular).
to belong to someone	gehören + dative	Es gehört mir.	It belongs to me.
to believe (to) somebody	glauben + dative	Sie glaubt ihm.	She believes him.
to help (to) someone	helfen + dative	Ich helfe dir.	I'll help you.
to forgive (to) somebody	vergeben + dative	Wir vergeben ihr.	We forgive her.
to forbid (to) somebody	verbieten + dative	Ich verbiete ihnen zu laufen.	I forbid them to run.

IV Which indirect object pronoun would you use to answer these questions?

a Kannst du mir bitte helfen?   Ja, ich helfe ___.
b Kannst du den Kindern helfen?   Ja, ich helfe ___.
c Willst du Klaus einen Brief schreiben?   Ja ich will ___ einen Brief schreiben.
d Glauben Sie ihrem Freund?   Ja, ich glaube ___.

e Verbietet er den Kindern laut zu sein?   Ja, er verbietet ___ laut zu sein.

f Verzeihst du mir?   Ja, ich verzeihe ___.

g Verzeihst du Wolfgang?   Ja, ich verzeihe ___.

h Gehört der Hund zu Ihnen?   Ja, er gehört ___.

i Helfen die Kinder der Mutter?   Ja, sie helfen ___.

j Sind Sie Ihrem neuen Boss schon begegnet?   Ja, ich bin ___ schon begegnet.

3.3.3   Word order of pronouns: direct + indirect

▶▶ **If you don't want to know about this yet, go on to 3.4.**

If you have more than one pronoun in front of the verb, they usually go in the following order:

nominative + accusative + dative

This is the same order as in English! **Wunderbar**!

Haben Sie es ihnen schon geschickt?   Have you sent it to them already?

Wann haben Sie sie (die Blumen) ihm gegeben?   When did you give them (the flowers) to him?

Warum hast du mich ihr nicht vorgestellt?   Why did you not introduce me to her?

Kannst du es mir vorlesen?   Can you read it to me?

V   How would you say the following?

In the following sentences, *it* stands for *your telephone number* (**die Telefonnummer**).

a He gave it to me.
b I gave it to her.
c She gave it to them.
d They gave it to you (formal).
e You gave it to us.

In the following sentences, *it* stands for *the book* (**das Buch**).

f She bought it for him.
g He read it to them.
h He gave it to us.
i We gave it to you (informal).
j They read it to him.
k She lent it to me.
l We gave it to her.

3.4 Reflexive pronouns

Reflexive pronouns are used with reflexive verbs.

For more on reflexive pronouns and verbs, go back to 1.2.1.

A pronoun sometimes refers back to the subject of the sentence, for example:

Ich wasche mich.   I wash myself/I am washing myself.
Ich stelle mich vor.   I introduce myself.

These are called reflexive pronouns. There are reflexive pronouns in the accusative and the dative.

Accusative reflexive pronoun

singular		plural	
mich	myself	uns	ourselves
dich	yourself (informal)	euch	yourselves
sich	yourself (formal)	sich	yourselves
sich	him-/her-/itself	sich	themselves

to sit down – **sich hinsetzen**
Sit yourself down!   **Setzen Sie sich!**

to hurry up – **sich beeilen**
Hurry up!   **Beeilen Sie sich!**

Ich setze mich.	Wir setzen uns.
Du setzt dich.	Sie setzten sich.
Sie setzen sich.	Ihr setzt euch.
Er setzt sich.	Sie setzen sich.
Sie setzt sich.	
Es setzt sich.	

I   Which reflexive pronoun would you use?

a Ich habe ___ geduscht.   I had a shower.
b Hast du ___ gewaschen?   Have you washed yourself?
c Er hat ___ gekämmt.   He combed his hair.
d Petra hat ___ gestritten.   Petra quarrelled.
e Ute hat ___ geärgert.   Ute got angry.
f Wir haben ___ gefreut.   We were pleased.
g Er hat ___ vorgestellt.   He introduced himself.
h Ich habe ___ geirrt.   I made a mistake.
i Ihr habt ___ getäuscht.   You were wrong.
j Ich habe ___ gestritten.   I argued.

Dative reflexive pronoun

singular		plural	
mir	myself	uns	ourselves
dir	yourself	euch	yourselves
sich	yourself	sich	yourselves
sich	himself	sich	themselves
sich	herself		
sich	itself		

II Fill in the missing pronoun.

a Ich habe ___ eine Pizza bestellt.   I ordered myself a pizza.

b Wir haben ___ eine Flasche Wein bestellt.   We ordered ourselves a bottle of wine.

c Hast du ___ ein Eis bestellt?   Did you order an ice cream for yourself?

d Er hat ___ eine Tasse Kaffee bestellt.   He ordered himself a cup of coffee.

e Sie hat ___ einen Tee bestellt.   She ordered herself a tea.

f Sie haben ___ Suppe bestellt.   They ordered themselves some soup.

g Habt ihr ___ etwas bestellt?   Did you order yourself something?

h Haben Sie ___ ein Bier bestellt?   Did you order a beer for yourself?

i Wir haben ___ Kuchen bestellt.   We ordered ourselves some cake.

j Der Kellner hat ___ die falsche Pizza gebracht.   The waiter brought me the wrong pizza.

3.5 Pronouns and the imperative

You probably already know the imperative. Check that it sounds familiar and then move on.

Talking to an adult:

singular		plural	
Warten Sie auf mich!	Wait for me!	Warten Sie auf uns!	Wait for us!
Warten Sie auf ihn!	Wait for him!	Warten Sie auf sie!	Wait for them!
Warten Sie auf sie!	Wait for her!		

Talking to a child/relative or friend:

singular		plural	
Warte auf mich!	Wait for me!	Warte auf uns!	Wait for us!
Warte auf ihn!	Wait for him!	Warte auf sie!	Wait for them!
Warte auf sie!	Wait for her!		

Talking to an adult:

Hören Sie auf mich!   Listen to me!

I   How do you say the following to an adult?

a Listen to him!
b Listen to her!
c Listen to them!
d Listen to us!
e Listen to yourself!

How do you say to a child:

f Listen to him!
g Listen to her!
h Listen to them!
i Listen to us!
j Listen to yourself!

You may need to use two pronouns.

 If you are not going to be telling people what to do, leave this out and go on to 3.6.

To tell an adult what to do, the order of the pronouns is:

nominative – accusative – dative

	nominative	accusative	dative	
Vergessen	Sie	es!		Forget it!
Halten	Sie	es	ihm!	Hold it for him!
Holen	Sie	es	mir!	Get it for me!
Geben	Sie	es	mir!	Give it to me!
Kaufen	Sie	es	uns!	Buy it for us!
Holen	Sie	es	ihm!	Get it for him!

II   Put the following sentences into the right order!

a Sie mich küssen
b Sie mit tanzen mir
c es mir kaufen Sie
d es mir geben Sie
e holen ihr Sie es

f ihm geben Sie es
g Sie es bestellen sich
h bestellen wir uns es
i kaufen sich Sie es
j geben mir Sie es

To tell a child, relative or friend what to do (**du** form):

verb	accusative	dative	
Vergiss	es!		Forget it!
Wähl	es!		Choose it!
Kauf	es	dir!	Buy it for yourself!
Hol	es	uns!	Get it for us!
Gib	es	mir!	Give it to me!

3.6 The one who, which, whose: relative pronouns

These are called relative pronouns because they 'relate' back to 'the one' who/which has already been mentioned.

▶▶ **If you know about relative pronouns, go on to 3.7.**

If you are not sure just read the next few lines as relative pronouns are relatively easy!

They are just like **der/die/das**. In German you only translate the *the*.

Die Frau, die nebenan wohnt.	The lady, the (one *who*) lives next door.
Der Hund, der die ganze Nacht bellt.	The dog, the (one *which*) barks all night.
Mein Handy, das nicht mehr geht.	My mobile, the (one *which*) doesn't work any more.
Das Buch, das wir gerade gekauft haben.	The book, the (one *which*) we have just bought.
Der Mann, dessen Auto immer gewaschen ist.	The man, the (one *whose*) car is always washed.

The following is the more difficult bit:

▶▶ **If you are not ready for it yet, leave it and come back later.**

Remember if you do not get it right you will still be understood!

While in English relative pronouns are often omitted, you cannot drop them in German.

This is the film (the one) which I saw yesterday.

Das ist der Film, den ich gestern gesehen habe.

Because the film is the object of the sentence, **der** has become **den**.

 As you can see from the table below, the relative pronoun is the same as the definite article, *except* for the plural dative, and it is therefore easy to remember.

Relative pronoun:

	masculine	**feminine**	**neuter**	**plural**
nominative	der	die	das	die
accusative	den	die	das	die
dative	dem	der	dem	den**en**

3.6.1 Relative pronoun replacing the subject (nominative)

Siehst du die Frau in dem Bus, *die* einen roten Hut trägt?

Do you see the woman in the bus, the (one who) is wearing a red hat?

She is wearing the hat so *she* is the subject – nominative.

I Which relative pronoun would you use to complete these sentences?

a Magst du die Schuhe, ___ in dem Schaufenster sind?

Do you like the shoes that are in the shop window?

b Magst du den Mantel, ___ in dem Schaufenster ist?

Do you like the coat that is in the shop window?

c Magst du die Tasche, ___ in dem Schaufenster ist?

Do you like the bag that is in the shop window?

d Magst du das T-Shirt, ___ in dem Schaufenster ist?

Do you like the t-shirt that is in the shop window?

e Kennen Sie den Song, ___ im Radio war?

Do you know the song that was on the radio?

f Kennen Sie das Buch, ___ Grammatik einfach erklärt?

Do you know the book that explains grammar in an easy way?

g Kennen Sie die Komödie, ___   Do you know the comedy
im Fernsehen war?   which was on the TV?

h Kennen Sie die R&B Songs, ___ es   Do you know the R&B
im MTV zu sehen gibt?   songs that are going to be
                                         on MTV?

3.6.2 Relative pronoun replacing the direct object (accusative)

Remember: **der** changes to **den**, the others stay the same.

Das ist *der* Mann, *den* ich   That is the man, the (one
gestern getroffen habe.   who) I saw yesterday.

II   Which relative pronoun would you use?

a Wir holen den Wagen, ___ wir gestern gekauft haben.

b Wir holen das Auto, ___ wir gestern gekauft haben.

c Wir holen die Jacke, ___ wir gestern gekauft haben.

d Wir holen die Jeans, ___ wir gestern gekauft haben.

e Wir essen die Schokolade, ___ wir gestern gekauft haben.

f Wir essen den Kuchen, ___ wir gestern gekauft haben.

g Wir essen das Brot, ___ wir gestern gekauft haben.

h Wir essen die Kekse, ___ wir gestern gekauft haben.

i Wir holen die Schuhe, ___ wir gestern gekauft haben.

j Wir trinken den Wein, ___ wir gestern gekauft haben.

3.6.3 Relative pronoun replacing the indirect object (dative)

Sehen Sie den Mann, *dem* ich   Do you see the man, the
die Fahrkarte gegeben habe?   (one to whom) I gave the
                                    ticket?

Remember the plural form is **denen**!

III   Which relative pronoun would you use?

a Kennen Sie die Frau, ___ ich das Geld gegeben habe?

b Ich warte auf die Kollegin, von ___ ich eine Akte bekomme.

c Er trifft den Kunden, ___ er einen Brief geschrieben hat.

d Der Kunde telefoniert mit dem Mann, ___ er eine E-Mail geschickt hat.

e Ich spreche mit dem Kind, ___ ich zum Geburtstag gratuliert habe.

f Wir treffen die Leute wieder, ___ du uns vorgestellt hast.

g Ich spreche mit der Zeitungsfrau, ___ ich das Geld für die Zeitung gegeben habe.

h Sie trifft den Briefträger, ___ sie ein Paket gegeben hat.

i Sie sucht einen Menschen, ___ sie vertrauen kann.

3.6.4 Relative pronouns: *deren* and *dessen* (whose)

This is the genitive case. The genitive is another case which used to be used a lot in German but is no longer used much except as a relative pronoun.

	masculine	feminine	neuter	plural
genitive	dessen	deren	dessen	deren

If you do not want to learn to use it just now, listen to the sentences and remember what **dessen** and **deren** mean.

| Ich treffe den Vermieter in dessen Haus ich wohne. | I am meeting the landlord in whose house I am living. |
| Ich treffe die Vermieterin in deren Haus ich wohne. | I am meeting the landlady in whose house I am living. |

IV Fill in the missing word: **dessen** or **deren**.

a Ich habe mit dem Autor gesprochen, ___ Buch ich eben gelesen habe.

b Wir haben mit der Autorin gesprochen, ___ Buch ich noch nicht gelesen habe.

c Ich habe mich bei dem Mädchen bedankt, ___ Fahrrad ich geliehen hatte.

d Wir sind zu meinen Verwandten gefahren, ___ Haus am See liegt.

e Wir bleiben bei meinem Bruder, ___ Haus sehr groß ist.

f Ich spreche mit Angela, ___ Mutter krank ist.

g Wir denken an die Menschen, ___ Häuser überflutet sind.

h Der Junge träumt von dem Mädchen, ___ Hand er gehalten hat.

i Der Rechtsanwalt vertritt den Angeklagten, ___ Alibi falsch war.

j Der Richter verurteilt die Angeklagte, ___ Alibi falsch war.

3.7 Who? whom? – *Wer? wen? wem? wessen?*

These are called interrogative pronouns.

▶▶ **If you have had enough of pronouns for the moment, go on to 4.1 and come back later.**

An interrogative pronoun is used to ask a question.

Subject:

Who is Mrs Meier?   Wer ist Frau Meier?

Direct object:

Whom do you know here?   Wen kennen Sie hier?

Indirect object:

To whom are you giving the book?   Wem geben Sie das Buch?

Genitive:

Whose car is that?   Wessen Auto ist das?

Was (*what*) refers to a thing. It has no case form. **Isn't it wunderbar!**

Was ist das?   What is that?
Was machst du?   What are you doing?

You can avoid having to use **wessen** by using **gehören** – *to belong to*:

Wem gehört das Radio?   Whose radio is it?/To whom does the radio belong?
Das Radio gehört mir.   The radio belongs to me.

I Which interrogative pronoun would you use?

a ___ ist das?   What's that?
b ___ ist Frau Meier?   Who is Mrs. Meier?
c ___ geben Sie das Geld?   To whom are you giving the money?
d ___ Buch ist das?   Whose book is that?
e ___ helfen Sie?   Who(m) are you helping?
f ___ kennt den Fußballspieler?   Who knows the football player?
g ___ kennst du?   Who do you know?
h ___ Uhr ist das?   Whose watch is that?
i ___ besuchst du heute?   Who are you visiting today?
j ___ kommt mit ihm?   Who is coming with him?

3.8 *Das ist meiner* – it's mine, it's yours

These are called possessive pronouns.

They translate *mine, yours, his, hers, ours, yours, theirs.* They have to agree with the noun they are replacing.

	masculine	**feminine**	**neuter**	**plural**
nominative	meiner	meine	*mein(e)s	meine

*It is very common to drop the **e** of **meines/deines**, etc. and say **meins**, etc.

Look at the coat! To whom does it belong?	Gehört dir den Mantel? Wem gehört der?
It's mine.	Das ist meiner.
It's yours (informal).	Das ist deiner.
It's his.	Das ist seiner.
It's hers.	Das ist ihrer.
It's its.	Das ist seiner.
It's ours.	Das ist unserer.
It's yours (informal).	Das ist eurer.
It's theirs.	Das ist ihrer.
It's yours (formal).	Das ist Ihrer.

 You can avoid having to use it by repeating the noun: **Das ist mein Mantel!**

I Replace the nouns in italics with the correct form of the pronoun **meiner**.

a Das ist *mein Bier* (n)   Das ist ___.
b Das ist *mein Eis* (n)   Das ist ___.
c Das ist *meine Pizza* (f)   Das ist ___.
d Das ist *mein Mantel* (m)   Das ist ___.
e Wem gehört *der Schirm?* (m)   Das ist ___.
f Wem gehört *die Tasche?* (f)   Das ist ___.
g Wem gehört *das Photo?* (n)   Das ist ___.
h Wem gehört *das Adressbuch?* (n)   Das ist ___.
i Wem gehört *der Ausweis?* (m)   Das ist ___.
j Wem gehört *die Eintrittskarte?* (f)   Das ist ___.

 The other pronouns follow the same pattern as **meiner**.

3.9 ▶Fast track: pronouns

A pronoun is a word that stands for a noun: *I* run, *you* play, *he* eats, *she* drinks, *it* shuts, *we* live, *you* swim, *they* talk.

The subject is the person or thing who does the action. You use the nominative if the pronoun is the subject of the sentence.

You use the accusative if the pronoun is the direct object or after certain prepositions (see 6.2.1).

You use the dative if the pronoun is the indirect object or after certain prepositions (see 6.2.2).

Table of pronouns:

nominative	accusative	dative	reflexive (acc)	reflexive (dat)
ich	mich	mir	mich	mir
du	dich	dir	dich	dir
er	ihn	ihm	sich	sich
sie	sie	ihr	sich	sich
es	es	ihm	sich	sich
wir	uns	uns	uns	uns
ihr	euch	euch	euch	euch
sie	sie	ihnen	sich	sich
Sie	Sie	Ihnen	sich	sich

4 ADJECTIVES

4.1 What is an adjective?

▶▶ **If you know what an adjective is, go on to 4.2.**

Adjectives are 'describing' words; you use them to say what something or someone is like.

I Highlight the adjectives in these sentences.

a Jack is tall and good-looking.
b He has short, dark hair and blue-grey eyes.
c He has just bought a new car.
d He likes to wear smart clothes when he goes to work and casual clothes at the weekend.
e His house is quite modern and has a big garden.
f His girlfriend is small and bubbly.
g She manages a large bank.
h He has an older brother and a younger sister.
i His favourite dish is tagliatelle alla carbonara.
j He likes his coffee very hot and very black.

4.1.1 How to use adjectives

Adjectives can be used in two main ways:

• Adjectives may be separated from the noun by the verb *to be* – **sein** or *to become* – **werden**.

Das Wetter *ist* heute *schrecklich*.   The weather is terrible today.

These adjectives do not change.

• Adjectives may come before the noun they are describing:

The terrible weather gets   Das *schreckliche* Wetter geht mir
on my nerves.   auf die Nerven.

These adjectives have to agree with the nouns.

II Underline the adjectives in the following sentences.

a Susanne ist eine attraktive, junge Frau, und sie ist sehr klug.
b Susanne ist groß und schlank.
c Sie hat blonde Haare.
d Sie ist intelligent, und sie hat immer gute Laune und viel Humor.
e Sie hat viele, interessante Freunde.

f Sie wohnt in einer kleinen Wohnung in einer ruhigen Gegend.
g Die Wohnung ist billig und schön.
h Susanne studiert zur Zeit Philosophie an einer deutschen Universität.
i Das Studium ist anstrengend, aber es ist auch interessant.
j Nächstes Jahr wird sie in den langen Semesterferien nach Tibet reisen.

4.1.2 Adjectives placed after the noun they are describing

Adjectives which are used to describe a noun and are placed *after* the verb *to be* – **sein** or *to become* – **werden** don't take an ending.

Das Rathaus ist *alt*.	The town hall is old.
Die Stadt ist *schön*.	The city is nice.
Das Wetter wird *schön*.	The weather is going to be nice.

III Replace the English adjective with the correct German adjective: **alt, freundlich, höflich, laut, schmutzig, schüchtern, schwach, selbstbewusst, unehrlich, wunderbar**

a Meine Beine sind ___ .	My legs are weak.
b Mein Computer ist ___ .	My computer is old.
c Meine Kollegin ist ___ .	My colleague is friendly.
d Die junge Frau ist ___ .	The young woman is self-confident.
e Der junge Mann war ___ .	The young man was dishonest.
f Die Kinder sind ___ .	The children are loud.
g Die Straße ist ___ .	The street is dirty.
h Das junge Mädchen ist ___ .	The young girl is shy.
i Die Verkäuferin ist ___ .	The sales assistant is polite.
j Das Wetter wird ___ .	The weather is wonderful.

IV Now add the opposites: **arm, billig, dünn, faul, kalt, klein, neu, schnell, traurig, voll**

Das Auto ist *laut* und das Fahrrad ist *leise*.

a Die Flasche ist leer, aber das Glas ist ___ .
b Der Mann ist groß, und die Frau ist ___ .
c Helga ist lustig, und Klaus ist ___ .
d Gabi ist dick, und Susanne ist ___ .
e Viele Menschen in Europa sind reich, während viele Menschen in Asien ___ sind.
f Der Tee ist warm, aber der Kaffee ist ___ .
g Gabi ist fleißig, aber Susanne ist ___ .
h Der Pullover ist teuer, aber der Rock ist ___ .
i Mein Auto ist alt, aber mein Fahrrad ist ___ .
j Mein Fahrrad ist langsam, aber mein Auto ist ___ .

4.1.3 Adjectives which come in front of the noun

Adjectives placed in front of a noun take different endings. They must agree with the noun in gender and number.

Der rote Hut kostet viel Geld.	The red hat costs a lot of money.
Ein roter Hut ist selten.	A red hat is rare.
Rote Hüte gibt es in der Hutabteilung.	There are red hats in the hat department.
Die Frau hat einen roten Hut.	The woman has a red hat.

 As adjective endings differ only slightly, don't worry too much about using the correct ending. People will still understand you. Remember, you can always mumble the endings – most people do!

Do the exercises in any case, and perhaps you will remember some of the endings and learn other things in the process.

If you want to get it right, or if you will be writing a lot in German, find out the article, the gender, the number and the case of the noun which follows the adjective.

A good way to go about it is by asking yourself the following questions:

- Is there a definite article (**der**, **die**, **das**), an indefinite article (**ein**, **kein**, **mein**) or no article?
- Is the noun masculine, feminine or neuter?
- Is the noun singular or plural?
- Is the noun the subject of the sentence (nominative case), the direct object of the sentence (accusative case), the indirect object of the sentence (dative case) or the genitive (showing possession)?
- Had enough? Don't give up, it is easier than it sounds!

4.1.4 Adjectives after *der, die, das, die* and *dieser* (this)

	singular masculine	feminine	neuter	plural
Nominative	-e	-e	-e	**-en**
Accusative	**-en**	-e	-e	**-en**
Dative	**-en**	**-en**	**-en**	**-en**

As you can see from the table above there are only two different endings for adjectives following the definite articles, **der**, **die**, **das**, **die** and **dieser**, **-e** and **-en**.

Adjectives describing the subject of the sentence (nominative)

The adjective endings after *the* + nominative (subject) are as follows.

	masculine	feminine	neuter	plural
nominative	-e	-e	-e	-en

Der/dieser interessante Mann ist mein Bruder. (m)
This interesting man is my brother.

Die/diese interessante Frau ist meine Freundin. (f)
This interesting woman is my friend.

Das/dieses interessante Kind ist meine Nichte. (n)
This interesting child is my niece.

Die/diese interessanten Leute sind meine Verwandten. (pl)
These interesting people are my relatives.

Der Mann/die Frau, etc. is the subject of the sentence and is therefore used in the nominative case. As you can see from the sentences above, the adjective describing the subject in the sentences all end in **-e** apart from the plural which ends in **-en**. So that is easy to remember.

V Which form of the adjective in brackets would you use to complete these sentences?

a Der ___ Junge ist mein Neffe. (klein)
The small boy is my nephew.

b Die ___ Frau ist meine Tante. (groß)
The tall woman is my aunt.

c Die ___ Babys haben Hunger. (schreiend).
The screaming babies are hungry.

d Die ___ Kinder sind meine Enkelkinder. (fröhlich)
The cheerful children are my grandchildren.

e Die ___ Dame ist meine Oma. (alt)
The old lady is my granny.

f Das ___ Auto gehört mir. (schwarz)
The black car belongs to me.

g Dieser ___ Hund heißt Benno. (groß).
This big dog is called Benno.

h Die ___ Kleider sehen sehr schön aus. (lang)
The long dresses look very pretty.

i Dieser ___ Abend ist bald vorbei. (wunderschön).	This wonderful evening will soon be over.	
j Der ___ Kaffee schmeckt nicht gut. (kalt)	The cold coffee does not taste good.	

Adjectives describing the direct object of a sentence (accusative case)

The adjective endings after *the* + accusative (direct object) are as follows.

	masculine	feminine	neuter	plural
accusative	**-en**	-e	-e	-en

Ich treffe den neu*en* Kollegen.	I am meeting the new (male) colleague.
Ich treffe die neu*e* Kollegin.	I am meeting the new (female) colleague.
Ich treffe das neu*e* Kindermädchen.	I am meeting the new au-pair girl.
Ich treffe die neu*en* Nachbarn.	I am meeting the new neighbours.
Ich treffe diese neu*en* Nachbarn.	I am meeting these new neighbours.

As you can see from the sentences above, **Kollege**, **Kindermädchen**, **Nachbar** are the direct object of the sentence and therefore accusative. The masculine article ends in **-n**, the other adjectives are the same as the nominative.

VI Which form of the adjective in brackets would you use to complete these sentences?

a Ich sehe den ___ Jungen. (klein)
b Ich kenne die ___ Frau. (jung)
c Ich mag das ___ Baby. (schreiend)
d Ich sehe die ___ Kinder. (fröhlich)
e Ich mag die ___ Oma. (alt)
f Ich sehe das ___ Auto. (schwarz)
g Ich kenne den ___ Hund. (groß)
h Ich trage das ___ Kleid. (lang)
i Ich genieße diesen ___ Abend. (wunderschön)
j Ich mag den ___ Kaffee nicht. (kalt)

Adjectives describing the indirect object (the dative)

The adjective endings after *the* + dative (indirect object) are as follows.

	masculine	feminine	neuter	plural
dative	**-en**	**-en**	**-en**	**-en**

Ich gebe den Schlüssel dem/ diesem neuen Gast.

I am giving the key to the new guest.

Ich gebe den Schlüssel der/ dieser neuen Kollegin.

I am giving the key to the new (female) colleague.

Ich gebe den Schlüssel dem/ diesem neuen Kindermädchen.

I am giving the key to the new au-pair girl.

Ich gebe den Schlüssel den/ diesen neuen Angestellten.

I am giving the key to the new employees.

The dative is really easy to remember – all adjectives end in **-en**.

VII Which form of the adjectives in brackets would you use to complete these sentences?

a Ich spreche mit dem ___ Jungen. (klein)
b Ich helfe dem ___ Mädchen. (nett)
c Peter hilft dem ___ Mann über die Straße. (alt)
d Frau Schmidt gibt der ___ Frau das Geld. (freundlich)
e Wir helfen den ___ Menschen in der Welt. (hungernd)
f Das Geschäft gehört dem ___ Nachbarn. (geizig)
g Das Geld kommt von der ___ Frau. (großzügig)
h Die Wohltätigkeitsorganisation gibt den ___ Wohnungslosen etwas zu essen. (arm)
i Die Sozialarbeiter helfen dem ___ Mann. (verwirrt)
j Die Krankenschwestern helfen den ___ Menschen. (krank)

4.1.5 Adjectives after the indirect article

The adjective endings after the indefinite article *a* – *ein*, *no/not any* – **kein** and the possessives *my* – **mein**, *your* – **dein**, etc. are as follows:

	masculine	feminine	neuter	plural
Nominative	-er	-e	-es	**-en**
Accusative	**-en**	-e	-es	**-en**
Dative	**-en**	**-en**	**-en**	**-en**

There are four different endings (**-e**, **-er**, **-en**, **-es**) but **-en** is used most.

Adjective endings after *ein, mein, kein,* etc. + nominative

	masculine	**feminine**	**neuter**	**plural**
nominative	-er	-e	-es	-en

Ein *guter* Tee schmeckt herrlich.	A good tea tastes great.
Eine *gute* Tasse Kaffee schmeckt wunderbar.	A good cup of coffee tastes wonderful.
Ein *gutes* Eis schmeckt lecker.	A good ice cream tastes delicious.
Keine hochprozentigen Getränke, bitte.	No high-proof drinks, please.

VIII Which form of the adjective in brackets would you use to complete these sentences?

a Ihr ___ Sofa (n) ist sehr bequem. (klein)
b Mein ___ Handy (n) ist sehr gut. (neue)
c Ihre ___ Gardinen (pl) sehen schick aus. (grün)
d Eine ___ Küche (f) sehr viel. (modern)
e Ein ___ Drucker (m) nützt mir nichts. (kaputt)
f Sein ___ Radio (n) ist noch sehr gut. (alt)
g Dein ___ Pullover (m) gefällt mir nicht. (hässlich)
h Ihre ___ Laune (f) steckt an. (schlecht)
i Eine ___ Dokumentation (f) kann interessant sein. (gut)
j Mein ___ Studierzimmer (n) ist sehr groß. (neu)

Endings for adjectives describing a direct object (the accusative) after *ein, mein, kein,* etc.

	masculine	**feminine**	**neuter**	**plural**
accusative	-en	-e	-es	-en

Ich trinke gerne einen leckeren Tee.	I like drinking a delicious cup of tea.
Ich trinke gerne eine leckere Tasse Kaffee.	I like drinking a delicious cup of coffee.
Ich esse gerne ein leckeres Eis.	I like eating a delicious ice cream.
Ich trinke keine hochprozentigen Getränke.	I don't drink any high-proof drinks.

IX Which form of the adjective in brackets would you use to complete these sentences?

a Ich kaufe mir eine ___ Wohnung. (neu)
b Ich treffe meinen ___ Kollegen. (neu)
c Ich kaufe mir ein ___ Haus. (klein)
d Die Kinder bekommen einen ___ Ball. (klein)
e Die Touristen besuchen eine ___ Ausstellung. (interessant)
f Wir haben gestern einen ___ Film gesehen. (interessant)
g Wir holen uns einen ___ Stadtplan. (groß)
h Wir lesen ein ___ Buch. (spannend)
i Das Schwimmbad hat einen ___ Bademeister. (neu)
j Der Vater liest den Kindern eine ___ Geschichte vor. (neu)

Endings for adjectives describing the indirect object (dative) after *ein, mein, kein,* etc.

	masculine	**feminine**	**neuter**	**plural**
dative	-en	-en	-en	-en

The dative is easy as all adjectives end in **-en**.

Zu einem *guten* Wein esse ich gerne Salzgebäck.	I like eating savoury biscuits with a good wine.
Zu einer *guten* Tasse Kaffee esse ich gerne Kuchen.	I like eating cake with a good cup of coffee.
Zu einem *schönen* Essen trinke ich gerne eine Flasche Wein.	I like drinking a bottle of wine with a nice meal.
Zu ein paar *leckeren* Keksen trinke ich gerne eine Tasse Kaffee.	I like drinking a cup of coffee with a few tasty biscuits.

X Which form of the adjective in brackets would you use to complete these sentences?

a Meine Freunde kommen zu meiner ___ Geburtstagsparty. (groß)
b Der Nikolaus gibt die Geschenke zu unseren ___ Kindern. (lieb)
c Zu ihrem ___ Hochzeitstag wünscht Susi sich einen neuen Ring. (erst)
d Wir geben unserer ___ Vermieterin einen Blumenstrauß. (nett)
e Ich schenke meinem ___ Nachbarn ein Buch. (hilfsbereit)
f Zu seinem ___ Geburtstag wünscht sich Paul eine CD. (sieben)
g Seine Freunde kommen alle zu seiner ___ Party. (groß)
h Sie fährt regelmäßig zu ihrem ___ Großvater. (alt)
i Ich trinke Bier zu meinem ___ Essen. (scharf)
j Die Kinder fahren nicht gerne zu ihrer ___ Tante. (arrogant)

4.1.6 Adjectives describing a noun which has no article

This is not used very much in conversation except in certain expressions.

The endings are the same as the endings for the definite article (*the*).

	singular masculine	**feminine**	**neuter**	**plural**
Nominative	-er	-e	-es	-e
Accusative	**-en**	-e	-es	-e
Dative	-em	-er	-em	-en

Nominative

Frische Luft macht hungrig. (f)   Fresh air makes you hungry.

XI Which form of the adjectives in brackets would you use to complete these sentences?

a ___ Wetter macht gute Laune. (schön)   Good weather makes you feel good.

b ___ Kaffee macht wach. (stark)   Strong coffee keeps you awake.

c ___ Kinder brauchen viel Schlaf. (klein)   Little children need a lot of sleep.

d ___ Menschen brauchen mehr Ruhe. (alt)   Old people need more rest.

e ___ Menschen sind sehr angenehm. (freundlich)   Friendly people are very pleasant.

f ___ Menschen sind selten zu finden. (ehrlich)   Honest people are seldom found.

g ___ Hunde sind sehr verspielt. (jung)   Young dogs are very playful.

h ___ Computerspiele sind nicht gut. (agressiv)   Agressive computer games are not good.

i ___ Gespräche bringen nichts. (sinnlos)   Useless conversations don't lead to anything.

Accusative

Ich höre gerne klassische Musik.   I like listening to classical music.

Ich mag treue Freunde.   I like loyal friends.

XII Which form of the adjectives in brackets would you use to complete these sentences?

a Ich mag ___ Sonne. (warm)   I like hot sun.

b Kinder mögen ___ Nebel. (dicht)   Children like thick fog.

c Ich mache mir ___ Schokolade. (heiß)   I am making myself hot cocoa.

d Meine Freundin mag ___ Gewitter. (laut)   My friend likes loud thunderstorms.

e Ich finde ___ Abende wunderbar. (entspannend)   I find relaxing evenings wonderful.

f Susanne schaut gerne ___ Filme. (spannend)   Susanne likes watching exciting films.

g Ich treffe gerne ___ Leute. (neu)   I like meeting new people.

h Im Fernsehen zeigen sie oft ___ Nachrichten. (schrecklich)   They often show horrible news on TV.

i Wir würden gerne ___ Dinge hören. (positiv)   We would like to hear positive things.

j Wir treffen oft ___ Leute im Urlaub. (nett)   We often meet nice people on holiday.

Dative

Ich benutze einen Regenschirm bei *starkem* Regen. (m)   I use an umbrella in heavy rain.

Ich hasse Regen mit *starkem* Wind. (m)   I hate rain with a strong wind.

Ich benutze einen Sonnenhut bei *warmer* Sonne. (f)   I wear a sunhat when the sun is warm.

Ich benutze keinen Mantel bei *gutem* Wetter. (n)   I don't use a coat in good weather.

Ich fahre gerne Ski im *tiefen* Schnee. (m)   I like to ski in deep snow.

Ich benutze einen Regenschirm bei *starken* Hagelstürmen. (pl)   I use an umbrella in heavy hailstorms.

XIII Which form of the adjectives in brackets would you use to complete these sentences?

a Ich fahre nicht gerne Fahrrad bei ___ Wetter. (schlecht)

b Mein Sohn surft gerne bei ___ Wind. (stark)

c Gabi joggt nicht gerne bei ___ Hitze. (groß)

d Ich benutze einen Sonnenhut bei ___ Sonne. (stark)

e Die Straßen sind glatt bei ___ Wetter. (kalt)

f Man muss vorsichtig fahren bei ___ Verkehr. (stark)

g Man muss langsam fahren bei ___ Schnee. (tief)

h Man kann gut entspannen bei ___ Musik. (klassisch)

i Die Jugendlichen tanzen bei ___ Musik. (laut)

4.2 Big, bigger, biggest: the comparative and superlative

The comparative is the form you use when comparing two things: something is *bigger, smaller, newer, older,* etc.

The superlative is the form you use when comparing more than two things: *biggest, best, newest, oldest,* etc.

4.2.1 The comparative

In English the comparative is formed either by adding *-er* to the end of the adjective (large → larger) or by inserting the word *more* (expensive → more expensive).

In German there is only one way. The comparative is formed by adding **-er** to the adjective. The English *than* is translated by **als** in German.

Ich bin kleiner *als* meine Schwester.	I am smaller *than* my sister.
Dieser Film ist interessanter *als* der andere.	This film is more interesting than the other.

active	aktiv	→	more active than	aktiver als
bad	schlecht	→	worse than	schlechter als
cheerful	fröhlich	→	more cheerful than	fröhlicher als
conservative	konservativ	→	more conservative than	konservativer als
honest	ehrlich	→	more honest than	ehrlicher als
loud	laut	→	louder than	lauter als
modern	modern	→	more modern than	moderner als
selfless	selbstlos	→	more selfless than	selbstloser als
small	klein	→	smaller than	kleiner als
stressed	gestresst	→	more stressed than	gestresster als

Exception:

good	gut	→	better than	besser als

I Say that the second thing/person is taller, higher, etc. than the first, using the adjective in brackets.

Example: Susi ist klein, aber Peter ist kleiner.

a Klaus ist ___, aber Susanne ist ___ (laut).
b Wir sind ___, aber meine Chefin ist ___ (gestresst).
c Mein Auto ist ___, aber mein Fahrrad ist ___ (rostig).
d Sein Hemd ist ___, aber seine Hose ist ___ (schmutzig).
e Mein Wohnzimmer ist ___, aber mein Schlafzimmer ist ___ (sauber).
f Mein Handy ist ___, aber deins ist ___ (cool).

g Die Erwachsenen sind ___, aber die Kinder sind ___ (fröhlich).
h Der Stuhl ist ___, aber das Sofa ist ___ (bequem).
i Der Zug ist ___, aber das Flugzeug ist ___ (schnell).
j Die alte Dame ist ___, aber der alte Mann ist ___ (hilfsbereit).

Some adjectives take an umlaut in the comparative and the superlative, for example:

long	lang → länger → am längsten
old	alt → älter → am ältesten
poor	arm → ärmer → am ärmsten
warm	warm → wärmer → am wärmsten
strong	stark → stärker → am stärksten
stupid	dumm → dümmer → am dümmsten
young	jung → jünger → am jüngsten
clever	klug → klüger → am klügsten
short	kurz → kürzer → am kürzesten
tall	groß → größer → am größten
cold	kalt → kälter → am kältesten

II Say that the second thing is taller, higher, etc. than the first.

a Das Hemd ist kurz, aber die Hose ist ___.
b Der Kirche ist alt, aber der Tempel ist ___.
c Einige Menschen sind arm in Europa, aber die Menschen in Afrika sind ___.
d Es ist warm im Sommer in Deutschland, aber es ist ___ in Spanien.
e Der Baum ist grün, aber das Gras ist ___.
f Der Junge ist klug, aber das Mädchen ist ___.
g Die Osterferien sind lang, aber die Sommerferien sind ___.
h Der Bus ist spät, aber der Zug ist ___.
i Die Suppe ist scharf, aber der Pfeffer ist ___.

4.2.2 The superlative

The superlative is the form you use to say that something is *the best, the biggest, the smallest, the best of all.* In English we either use *-est* or the word *most* or *least* (for the lowest degree). In German we add **-st**: **der klein*ste* Junge, das klein*ste* Mädchen**. If the superlative is placed in front of a noun it is usually used with the direct article – ***der/die/das*** – and needs the correct adjective endings.

Superlatives separated from the noun they are describing

If the superlative is separated from the person or thing it is describing by the verb to be (*is/was*) it is usually used with am ___-sten; e.g. **am schnellsten** – *the fastest* and this doesn't change.

Er ist am schnellsten.	He is the fastest.
Sie ist am ältesten.	She is the oldest.
Wir sind am größten.	We are the tallest.
Du bist am kleinsten.	You are the smallest.

An exception is **gut** → **am besten**.

Du bist am besten.	You are the best.

Some superlatives add an extra **-e** to make them easier to pronounce.

interesting	interessant → am interessantesten, das interessanteste
nice	nett → am nettesten, das netteste
bad	schlecht → am schlechtesten, das schlechteste

III   How do you make it the biggest, the largest, etc.?

a Das Rathaus ist am ___ (groß).
b Das Modegeschäft ist am ___ (teuer).
c Der Bus ist am ___ (billig).
d Die U-Bahn ist am ___ (schnell).
e Das Restaurant ist am ___(bequem).
f Das Stadium ist am ___ (voll).
g Die Autobahn ist am ___ (gefährlich).
h Der Tempel ist am ___ (interessant).
i Die Kirche ist am ___ (alt).
j Die Hauptstrasse ist am ___ (lang).

Superlatives placed in front of the noun

If the superlative is placed in front of a noun it behaves like any other adjective and changes its ending accordingly (see 4.1.3).

 Remember most endings are **-ste or -sten**.

After **der**, **die** or **das** the ending will be either -ste or -sten.

Adjectives describing the subject of the sentence (nominative):

Er ist der schnell**ste** Junge in seinem Tennisverein. (m)	He is the fastest boy in his tennis club.
Sie ist die kleins**te** Frau in ihrem Fußball Team. (f)	She is the smallest woman in her football team.
Sie ist das klein**ste** Mädchen in ihrem Fußball Team. (n)	She is the smallest girl in her football team.
Wir sind die älte**sten** in der Kneipe. (pl)	We are the oldest in the pub.

Adjectives describing the direct object of a sentence (accusative) after the direct article *the* – **den**, **die**, **das**, **die**:

Er klettert auf den höch**sten** Baum. (m)	He is climbing the highest tree.
Das Zimmer hat die schön**ste** Aussicht. (f)	The room has the best view.
Das Zimmer hat das bequem**ste** Bett. (n)	The room has the most comfortable bed.
Er beobachtet die selten**sten** Vögel. (pl)	He is watching the rarest birds.

Adjectives describing the indirect object of the sentence (dative):

Ich wohne in dem Zimmer mit dem schön**sten** Balkon. (m)	I live in the room with the most beautiful balcony.
Ich wohne in dem Zimmer mit der schön**sten** Aussicht. (f)	I live in the room with the most beautiful view.
Ich wohne in dem Zimmer mit dem schön**sten** Bad. (n)	I live in the room with the most beautiful bath.
Ich wohne in dem Zimmer mit den schön**sten** Pflanzen. (pl)	I live in the room with the most beautiful plants.

IV Fill the gaps using the superlative of the adjectives in brackets.

a Er möchte das ___ Stück Kuchen. (klein)
b Sie möchte das ___ Stück Kuchen. (groß)
c Die Jugendlichen hören immer die ___ Musik. (laut)
d Wir hatten gestern den ___ Tag. (kalt)
e Heute ist der ___ Wind. (stark)
f Die Weihnachtsferien sind die ___ Ferien. (kurz)
g Sie ist die ___ Läuferin. (schnell)
h Die ___ Läufer kommen am Ende. (langsam)
i Heute haben wir das ___ Wetter. (herrlich)
j Die Sommerferien sind die ___ Ferien. (lang)

The superlative with the indefinite article – nominative

When you use the superlative with the indefinite article **ein**, **mein**, **sein**, **kein** to describe the subject of the sentence, the adjective takes the following endings:

masculine	feminine	neuter	plural
-ster	-ste	-stes	-sten

Das ist ihr be**ster** Freund. (m)	This is her best male friend.
Das ist seine be**ste** Freundin. (f)	This is his best female friend.

Das ist ihr interessante**stes** Ferienerlebnis. (n)

This is her most interesting holiday experience.

Das sind meine billig**sten** Ferien. (pl)

This are my cheapest holidays.

V Fill the gaps using the superlative of the adjectives in brackets.

a Das ist mein ___ Buch. (n) (interessant)
b Das ist sein ___ Film. (m) (langweilig)
c Das ist ihr ___ Traum. (m) (groß)
d Das ist dein ___ Ergebnis. (n) (schlecht)
e Das war unser ___ Urlaub. (m) (schön)
f Das war sein ___ Erlebnis. (n) (schrecklich)
g Das ist unser ___ Essen. (n) (schmackhaft)
h Das war sein ___ Erlebnis. (n) (fantastisch)
i Das war unser ___ Abend. (m) (lustig)
j Das war mein ___ Tag. (m) (langweilig)

The superlative with the indefinite article – accusative

The superlative with the indefinite article **ein, mein, sein, kein** is used to describe the direct object of the sentence as follows.

Ich habe meinen bes*ten* Mantel angezogen. (m)

I put on my best coat.

Ich habe meine bes*te* Hose angezogen. (f)

I put on my best trousers.

Ich habe mein bes*tes* Kleid angezogen. (n)

I put on my best dress.

Ich habe meine bes*ten* Schuhe angezogen. (pl)

I put on my best shoes.

If you have forgotten how the adjective behaves after **ein**, etc., go back to 4.1.5 and check.

Reminder: gut: besser, beste, besten, bestes.

VI Fill the gaps using the superlative of the adjectives in brackets.

a Er liest ihren ___ Roman. (m) (neu)
b Er trägt sein ___ Hemd. (n) (alt)
c Er ruft seine ___ Freundin an. (f) (neu)
d Er gießt seine ___ Blumen. (pl) (schön)
e Er trägt seinen ___ Mantel. (m) (hässlich)
f Sie benutzt ihr ___ Geschirr. (n) (gut)
g Wir kaufen die ___ Lebensmittel. (pl) (gut)
h Du brauchst den ___ Rechtsanwalt. (m) (gut)
i Sie hat die ___ Ärztin. (f) (gut)

The superlative with the indefinite article – dative

The superlative with the indefinite article **ein**, **mein**, **sein**, **kein** is used to describe the indirect object of the sentence as follows:

Sie haben mir bei meinem schwierigsten Fall geholfen. (m)	They helped me with my most difficult case.
Sie haben mir bei meiner schwierigsten Aktion geholfen. (f)	They helped me with my most difficult campaign.
Sie haben mir bei meinem schwierigsten Problem geholfen. (n)	They helped me with my most difficult problem.
Sie haben mir bei meinen schwierigsten Aufgaben geholfen. (pl)	They helped me with my most difficult tasks.

If you have forgotten how the adjective behaves after **ein**, etc., go back to 4.1.5 and check.

VII Which adjective ending would you use?

a Sie hat das Buch ihrem best ___ Freund gegeben. (m)
b Sie hat das Buch ihrer best ___ Freundin gegeben. (f)
c Sie hat das Buch ihrem best ___ Kindermädchen gegeben. (n)
d Sie hat das Buch ihren best ___ Freundinnen gegeben. (pl)
e Sie hat ihrem best ___ Freund geholfen. (m)
f Sie hilft seiner best ___ Freundin. (f)
g Sie kauft ihrem best ___ Freund eine neue CD. (m)
h Sie kauft ihrer best ___ Freundin ein Buch. (f)
i Sie hilft ihren best ___ Freunden. (pl)
j Sie hat ihrem best ___ Kollegen ein Buch gekauft. (m)

VIII Which adjective endings would you add to show that it was your longest, best, etc.? The case is given in brackets.

a Mein schönst ___ Urlaub war dieses Jahr im Dezember. (m. nom.)
b Das war mein best ___ Ferienerlebnis. (n. nom.)
c Ich bin mit meinem best ___ Freund in Urlaub gefahren. (m. dat.)
d In meinen nächsten Ferien besuche ich meine best ___ Freundin Emmanuelle in Paris. (f. acc.)
e Mein längst ___ Urlaub ist im Sommer. (m. nom.)
f Ich habe mein best ___ Essen in Wien gegessen. (n. acc.)
g Mein teuerst ___ Urlaub war vor zwei Jahren. (m. nom.)
h Meine billigst ___ Ferien hatte ich in einem Zelt. (pl. acc.)
i Ich habe immer die tollst ___ Leute im Urlaub getroffen. (pl. acc.)
j Mein schlechtest ___ Ferienerlebnis war letztes Jahr im Sommer. (n. nom.)

4.2.3 Saying as (big) as

If you are comparing two things which are similar, you use the expression **so ___ wie** – *as ___ as: as tall as* – **so groß wie**.

Er ist *so* groß *wie* sein Vater.   He is as tall as his father.
Er ist *so* komisch *wie* sein Bruder.   He is as strange as his brother.

IX Say these places/things/people are as big/tall as ___:

a Das Kind ist ___ freundlich ___ ihre Mutter.
b Die Kinder sind ___ unordentlich ___ ihre Eltern.
c Der Junge ist ___ unhöflich ___ sein Vater.
d Dieser Stuhl ist ___ unbequem ___ der andere.
e Dieses grüne Sofa ist ___ teuer ___ das rote.
f Die Waschmaschine ist ___ gut ___ die andere.
g Das Wetter hier ist ___ schön ___ in Spanien.
h Die Erwachsenen lernen nicht ___ schnell ___ die Kinder.
i Der Schnee ist ___ hoch ___ in den Alpen.
j Du sprichst ___ gut Deutsch ___ ein Deutscher.

4.2.4 ▶**Fast track:** adjectives

In German you can use adjectives in two main ways:

• Adjectives may be separated from the noun. These don't change.
• Adjectives may come directly in front of the noun. These change to agree with the noun in gender, number and case. This sounds more complicated than it is.

Adjectives placed *in front of* the noun have three different patterns of endings according to whether they are:

1 preceded by *the* (**der**, **die**, **das**) or *this* (**dieser**).
2 preceded by *a*, etc. (**ein**, **kein**, **mein**, etc.)
3 used without a determiner.

In group 1 the endings are **-e** and **-en**.

In group 2 the endings in the nominative are **-er**, **-es**, **-e**, **-en**. The rest of the endings are like the group 1 endings except for neuter nouns which stay **-es** in the accusative (but you aren't likely to need the neuter ending much).

In group 3 the endings are like the endings for **der**, **die**, **das** except the nominative and accusative neuter endings which are **-es**, but you aren't likely to use adjectives without a determiner.

And the one that you are likely to use most is **-en**. So when in doubt mumble **-en** at the end of the adjective!

The comparative and superlative

The comparative is made by adding **-er** to the adjective.

• Comparative adjectives which are separated from the noun don't agree.

- Comparative adjectives which come direcly in front of the noun behave like ordinary adjectives, i.e. they agree in gender, number and case according to whether they are following *the* or *a*, or there is no determiner.
- The most common ending is **-en**.

The superlative is made by adding **-ste** to the adjective.

- Superlative adjectives separated from the noun take the form **am (schnell)sten**.
- Superlative adjectives which come directly in front of the noun behave like other adjectives and agree in gender, number and case according to whether they are following *the* or a, or there is no determiner.
- The most common ending is **-en**.

5 ADVERBS

Adverbs are words which describe *how* you do something.

 Ask the question *'How do you/they do it?'* to check if a word is an adverb.

	verb	**adverb**	
She	drives	*fast.*	How does she drive? Fast!

	verb	**adverb**	
He	speaks	*loudly.*	How does he speak? Loudly! (describing a verb)

And the good news is adverbs don't change.

5.1 Formation of adverbs

In English most adverbs are made by adding *-ly* to an adjective: *quick → quickly; slow → slowly.*

German adverbs don't change. **Wunderbar!**

Er singt *wunderschön.*	He sings *beautifully.*
Sie spricht *langsam.*	She speaks *slowly.*
Wir fahren *schnell.*	We drive *quickly.*

I Complete the following sentences using the adverbs in brackets.

a Wir sprechen sehr ___. (fast)
b Sprechen Sie bitte ___. (slowly)
c Sprechen Sie es bitte ___ aus. (clearly)
d Ich buchstabiere es ___. (correctly)
e Sprechen Sie bitte nicht so ___. (quickly)
f Wiederholen Sie es bitte noch einmal ___. (slowly)
g Sie sprechen es sehr ___ aus. (well)
h Er spricht sehr ___. (precisely)
i Sie spricht ___. (strangely)
j Sie sprechen ___. (constantly)

II How would you translate the words in brackets?

a Sie kommt ___ bald. (hopefully)
b Er joggt ___. (regularly)
c Sie wohnt ___ um die Ecke. (left)
d Ich übe ___ Klavier spielen. (often)
e Wir wohnen ___ in der Stadt. (fortunately)
f Er kann ___ nicht kommen. (unfortunately)
g Sie ist ___ krank. (really)
h Er joggt immer ___. (in the morning)
i Der Zug kommt ___ spät. (seldom)
j Der Bus kommt ___ pünktlich. (never)

III Match the German adverbs with the correct English counterpart.

a langsam	1 soon
b gut	2 often
c sofort	3 slowly
d plötzlich	4 approximately
e ungefähr	5 probably
f regelmäßig	6 quickly
g oft	7 suddenly
h bald	8 immediately
i wahrscheinlich	9 regularly
j schnell	10 well

IV How would you say the following in German?

a It rains regularly.
b He speaks loudly.
c The woman speaks quickly.
d They speak fast.
e She speaks slowly.
f They speak clearly.
g You speak very well.
h She does that well.
i He dances badly.
j She drinks quickly.

5.1.1 Some more useful adverbs

These are used with an adjective or another adverb:

sehr	very
ganz	quite
zu	too

Expressions of time: *When?*

bald	soon
oft	often

endlich	finally
dann	then
jetzt	now
selten	seldom
immer	always
täglich	daily

Expressions of manner: *How?*

schnell	fast
gern	gladly, like to
hoffentlich	hopefully
leider	unfortunately
schon	already
wirklich	really

Some adverbs can be formed by adding **–erweise** to an adjective.

adjective	adverb	meaning
dumm	dummerweise	stupidly/unfortunately
glücklich	glücklicherweise	fortunately

V How would you form adverbs from the following adjectives?

a komisch
b interessant
c möglich
d erstaunlich
e normal
f natürlich
g vernünftig
h notwendig
i kompliziert
j unglücklich

5.1.2 Structure of a sentence beginning with an adverb

Sentences can start with the adverbs or adverbial phrase. Remember that the verb has to come second in the sentence so the subject will be sent to third place.

Wir fahren Montags immer mit dem Auto nach Bremen.	→	Montags fahren wir mit dem Auto nach Bremen.
Ich gehe gelegentlich zum Einkaufen in die Stadt.	→	Gelegentlich gehe ich zum Einkaufen in die Stadt.
Wir haben bald Ferien.	→	Bald haben wir Ferien.

Wir haben den neuen Kollegen   →   Gestern haben wir den
gestern kurz im Büro kennengelernt.   neuen Kollegen kurz im
                                                           Büro kennengelernt.

VI   How would you structure the following sentences starting
with an adverb?

a   ich bin nach Dumfries gefahren gestern mit dem Zug
b   Verspätung hatte der Zug allerdings viel
c   musste warten ich unglücklicherweise eine halbe Stunde
d   ich warten konnte in dem Warteraum glücklicherweise
e   zu spät er neulich eine Stunde ist gekommen
f   umsteigen ich nicht musste glücklicherweise
g   fahre ich mit dem Zug sehr gerne am Wochenende
h   ich auch das Auto nehme gelegentlich
i   fahren die Züge bald pünktlich hoffentlich wieder
j   fahre ich genau so lange normalerweise mit dem Auto

6 PREPOSITIONS

6.1 Recognising prepositions

▶▶ **If you know what a preposition is, go on to 6.3.**

Prepositions are words like *in, on* and *under*. Unlike adjectives, they do not change. They are usually used in conjunction with a noun or pronoun, e.g. *in the cupboard, near the station, for her, with me.*

Prepositions can tell you:

* where a person or thing is, i.e. its position
  auf dem Tisch   on the table
  unter der Brücke   under the bridge
* how something is done, i.e. manner
  mit Butter   with butter
  ohne Wasser   without water
* when something happens, i.e. time
  in einer Minute   in a minute
  nach dem Abendessen   after dinner
* for whom something is done
  für mich   for me
  für ihn   for him

6.2 German prepositions

In German the prepositions are mainly followed by the accusative or dative of the pronoun or determiner.

Prepositions may be followed by:

* the accusative
* the dative
* either the accusative or the dative – these are referred to as two-way prepositions.

If you have forgotten what the accusative and dative are, go back to 2.3 (determiners) and 3.2 (pronouns).

6.2.1 Prepositions followed by the accusative case

If you have forgotten about the accusative, go back to p.156.

Reminder:

	masculine	**feminine**	**neuter**	**plural**
nominative	der	die	das	die
accusative	**den**	**die**	**das**	**die**
dative	dem	der	dem	den

These prepositions are followed by the accusative:

bis	by/until/(up) to/as far as
durch	through
für	for/on behalf of
gegen	against/around/towards
ohne	without
um	around/about
entlang	along

I Match the English to the German.

a bis	1 against
b durch	2 without
c für	3 by/until/(up) to
d gegen	4 for/on behalf of
e ohne	5 along
f um	6 around/about
g entlang	7 through

When **bis** refers to a place it means *as far as/(up) to.*

Ich fahre bis München.	I am going as far as Munich.
Ich fliege bis Hamburg.	I am flying to Hamburg.

When **bis** refers to a time it means *until* or *by.*

Bis nächsten Montag.	Until next Monday.
Ich habe es bis Montag fertig.	It will be ready by Monday.

> Bis is also used for expressions like: **Bis bald!** – See you soon!
> **Bis nächste Woche!** – Until next week! **Bis zum nächsten**
> **Mal!** – Until next time!

When **durch** refers to a place it means *through.*

Wir gehen durch den Park.	We are walking through the park.
Gehen Sie durch den Eingang.	Go through the entrance.

When **durch** refers to a cause or means it means *by/through.*

| Der Baum wurde durch den Wind zerstört. | The tree was destroyed by the wind. |
| Es ist durch ihre eigene Schuld passiert. | It happened through her own fault. |

When **für** refers to time it means *for*.

| Ich arbeite für zwei Monate. | I am going to work for two months. |
| Kann ich Ihr Handy für zwei Minuten benutzen? | Can I use your mobile phone for two minutes? |

Für can be used in the sense of *on behalf of/for*.

| Bitte machen Sie das für mich. | Please do it on my behalf. |
| Ich arbeite für eine Firma. | I work for a company. |

II   Which preposition would you use: **durch**, **bis**, **für**, **um**, **entlang**?

a Gehen Sie ___ die Tür!
b Mein Freund joggt ___ den Park. (around)
c Ich fahre ___ Nürnberg. (as far as)
d Ich warte ___ 10 Minuten.
e Ich warte ___ sie kommt.
f Ich kenne Peter ___ meine Freundin.
g ___ Morgen!
h Es ist ___ ihren Geburtstag.
i Herr Braun geht die Straße ___.
j ___ wen ist der Kaffee?

When **gegen** refers to a place or direction it means *against/into*.

| Das Fahrrad ist gegen einen Baum gelehnt. | The bicycle is leaning against a tree. |
| Sie fuhr gegen eine Mauer. | She drove into a wall. |

When **gegen** refers to a time it means *around/towards*.

| Ich komme so gegen 5 Uhr nach Hause. | I am coming home around 5 o'clock. |
| Wir werden gegen Abend ankommen. | We are going to arrive towards evening. |

Gegen can also mean *against*.

| Ich bin gegen Atomwaffen. | I am against nuclear weapons. |
| Ich bin gegen den Krieg. | I am against (the) war. |

Ohne is used the same way as *without* in English.

| Du kannst das ohne mich machen. | You can do that without me. |
| Er verlässt das Haus nicht ohne seinen Regenschirm. | He does not leave the house without his umbrella. |

When **um** refers to a time it means *around/towards*. **So um** means *around*.

Die Gäste kamen um 6 Uhr an.	The guests arrived at 6 o'clock.
Wir kommen so um 5 Uhr an.	We are going to arrive about 5 o'clock.

When **um** refers to a place it means *around*.

Sie wohnt um die Ecke.	She lives around the corner.
Wir sitzen um den Tisch.	We are sitting around the table.

Um in the sense of *about* means *in respect of/regarding*.

Es geht um deinen Vater.	It is regarding your father.
Es geht um deinen Unfall.	It is about your accident.

Entlang follows the noun.

Er fuhr den Fahrradweg entlang.	He drove along the cycle path.
Fahren Sie die Straße entlang.	Drive along the street.

Cover up the English and see if you can translate the sentences.

III Match the English to the German.

a Ich bin gegen den Krieg. It is about your accident.
b Du kannst das ohne mich machen. I am coming home around 5 o'clock.
c Wir kommen so um 5 Uhr an. Paul is coming without his girlfriend.
d Sie wohnt um die Ecke. She drove into a wall.
e Es geht um deinen Unfall. Drive along the street.
f Fahren Sie die Straße entlang. She lives around the corner.
g Sie fuhr gegen eine Mauer. You can do that without me.
h Ich komme so gegen 5 Uhr nach Hause. I am against the war.
i Paul kommt ohne seine Freundin. We are going to arrive around 5 o'clock.

IV Which preposition would you use: **um, gegen, ohne, entlang**?

a Er kommt ___ Mittag an. (around)
b Ich bin ___ 9 Uhr im Büro. (at)
c Wir gehen den Weg ___. (along)
d Wir kommen so ___ 19 Uhr im Hotel an
e Ich trinke Tee ___ Zucker. (without)
f Wir haben Winter ___ Schnee. (without)

g Gehen Sie ___ die Ecke. (around)
h Fahren Sie die Straße ___. (along)
i Es geht in der Besprechung ___ die Finanzierung. (about)
j Ich muß es ___ seine Zustimmung machen. (without)

V Which preposition would you use?

a Wir kommen ____ 18 Uhr an. (around)
b Sie kommen ____ 15 Uhr an. (at)
c Es geht auch ____ Ihre Hilfe. (without)
d Fahren Sie ____ den Tunnel. (through)
e Das Auto fuhr ____ den Baum. (into)
f Viele Menschen sind ____ Gewalt. (against)
g Fahren Sie ____ das Haus herum. (around)
h Gehen Sie die Hauptstrasse ____. (along)
i Wir machen das ____ die älteren Menschen. (for)
j Es geht ____ Ihre Bewerbung. (about)

6.2.2 Prepositions followed by the dative

If you have forgotten about the dative, go back to p.157.

Reminder:

	masculine	**feminine**	**neuter**	**plural**
nominative	der	die	das	die
accusative	den	die	das	die
dative	dem	der	dem	den

These prepositions are followed by the dative:

aus	out of/from/made of
außer	apart from/except for
bei	at/near/with
gegenüber	across from
mit	with/by
nach	after/to/according to
seit	since/for
von	from/by/of
zu/zum/zur	to/at/for

When **aus** refers to a direction it means *from*.

Ich bin aus dem hohen Norden.   I am from the far North.

When **aus** refers to material it means *made of.*

Das Brot ist aus Roggenmehl.   The bread is made of rye flour.

Aus can also mean *out of.*

Er kommt aus seinem Haus raus.   He is coming out of his house.

Außer means *except for/ apart from.*

Außer mir tut das keiner.	Apart from me nobody does it.
Außer Ihnen kommt niemand.	Apart from you nobody else is coming.

When **bei** refers to a place it means where somebody lives.

Sie wohnt bei ihren Eltern.	She lives with her parents.
Er wohnt bei der Universität.	He lives near the university.

When **gegenüber** refers to a place it means *opposite/ across.*

Das Kino ist gegenüber der Kirche.	The cinema is across from the church.

Gegenüber can also mean *in respect of/ towards.*

Er ist mir gegenüber nicht sehr freundlich.	He is not very friendly towards me.

VI Which preposition would you use: **außer**, **aus**, **bei**, **gegenüber**?

a Ich komme ____ Berlin, und Sie?
b Die Tasse ist ____ Keramik gemacht.
c Sie wohnt ____ ihrer Oma.
d Kommt ____ mir noch jemand?
e ____ dir kommen noch drei Leute.
f Der Kuchen kommt ____ dem Schwarzwald.
g Sie wohnen ____ der Uni.
h Du kannst ____ mir bleiben.
i ____ uns im Haus ist es sehr warm.
j Benimm dich ____ ihr.

Mit is used the same way as *with* in English.

Ich komme mit dir.	I am coming with you.
Er nimmt die Blumen mit ihm mit.	He is taking the flowers with him.

Mit can also mean *by* when referring to travelling.

Ich fliege mit dem Flugzeug.	I am going by plane.
Ich fahre mit der Fähre.	I am going by ferry.

When **nach** refers to a place it means *to.*

Ich fahre nach Bayern in Urlaub.	I am going to Bavaria on holiday.
Ich gehe nach Hause.	I am going (to my) home.

When **nach** refers to time it means *after.*

Wir haben uns nach der Schule getroffen.	We met after school.
Er trifft sie nach der Arbeit.	He is going to meet her after work.

Nach can also mean *according to.*

Meiner Meinung nach ist das richtig.	In (according to) my opinion that is correct.
Nach dem Fahrplan kommt der Zug in drei Minuten.	According to the time table the train is arriving in three minutes.

When **seit** refers to time it means *since* or *for.*

Ich mache es seit August.	I have been doing it since August.
Ich wohne seit einem Monat in Schottland.	I have been living in Scotland for a month.
Er wohnt seit einem Jahr in Deutschland.	He has been living in Germany for a year.
Ich lerne Deutsch seit drei Monaten.	I have been learning German for three months.

Note that you use the present tense after **seit** (*since/for*) in German because you have been learning German for/since three months *and still are*; you have been living in Berlin for a year *and still are.*

Von means *from.*

Ich habe das von meinen Eltern.	I have got that from my parents.

VII Which preposition would you use: **seit, mit, nach, von**?

a Fahren Sie ____ dem Bus.
b Ich kenne ihn ____ 2003.
c Wir fahren im Sommer ____ Italien.
d ____ wo kommen Sie?
e Ich habe die Broschüre ____ dem Verkehrsverein.
f Die Postkarte ist ____ meinem deutschen Freund.
g Wir können ____ dem Essen telefonieren.
h Ich gehe ____ ihr ins Kino.
i Das ist das Auto ____ meiner Mutter.
j Ich wohne ____ vier Jahren in Spanien.

When **von** refers to a place it means *from.*

Er ist von hier.	He is from here.
Sie ist von einem Dorf.	She is from a village.

Von can also mean *by.*

Das ist eine Komposition von Mozart.	This is a composition by Mozart.
Das ist ein Film von Wim Wenders.	That is a film by Wim Wenders.

When **zu** refers to a place it means *to*.

Die Studenten gehen zu der neuen Bibliothek.	The students go to the new library.
Viele Leute sind zu der neuen Ausstellung gegangen.	Many people went to the new exhibition.

VIII Which preposition would you use: **von, zu**?

a Das Buch ist ____ einer Deutschen geschrieben.
b Ich habe das Buch ____ einem Buchladen in der Stadt.
c Sie schicken die Briefe ____ vielen Kunden.
d Wir fahren ____ dem neuen Einkaufszentrum.
e Der Film ist ____ dem Videogeschäft.
f Das neue Lied ____ der britischen Sängerin ist sehr gut.
g Die Muscheln kommen ____ einem Strand von der Nordsee.
h Der Artikel ist ____ einem Amerikaner geschrieben.
i Paula kommt ____ einem kleinem Ort in Schwaben.
j Gehen Sie ____ der nächsten Ampel!

Zu is often changed to **zum** and **zur** when it is used with *the*:

- with masculine nouns: **zu + dem → zum**
- with neuter nouns: **zu + dem → zum**
- with feminine nouns: **zu + der → zur**.

Ich gehe zum Theater. (n)	I am going to the theatre.
Ich fahre zum Bahnhof. (m)	I am going to the station.
Ich gehe zur Bank. (f)	I am going to the bank.

IX How would you say you were going to these places?

Ich gehe __

a Strand (m)
b Hotel (n)
c Schule (f)
d U-Bahn Station (f)
e Museum (n)
f Kino (n)
g Theater (n)
h Universität (f)
i Büro (n)
j Bankautomaten (m)

X Which preposition would you use: **zum** or **zur**?

a Die Fußballfans gehen ____ Fußballstadium. (n)
b Die Kinder gehen ____ Zoo. (m)
c Die Schüler gehen ____ Schule. (f)
d Der Opernsänger geht ____ Theater. (n)
e Wir fahren mit dem Auto ____ Tankstelle. (f)
f Wir müssen ____ Autobahn fahren. (f)

g Die Studenten gehen ____ Universität. (f)
h Die Astronauten fliegen ____ Mond. (m)
i Die jungen Leute gehen ____ Disko. (f)
j Die Golfer gehen ____ Golfclub. (m)

XI How would you ask the way to these places in Berlin?

Entschuldigen Sie bitte, wie komme ich zum/zur ____?

a Funkturm (m)
b Charlottenburger Schloß (n)
c Brandenburger Tor (n)
d Hotel Adlon (n)
e Kurfürstendamm (m)
f Ruine der Künste (f)
g Wannsee (m)
h Hauptstraße (f)
i Potsdamer Platz (m)
j Bushaltestelle (f)

 You use **nach** for *to* when you are talking about going to cities and countries: **Wie komme ich nach Berlin? Ich fliege nach Deutschland**.

6.2.3 Two-way prepositions

Two-way prepositions are used as follows:

- to say where somebody or something is they are followed by the dative
- to say where somebody or something is going they are followed by the accusative.

If the preposition expresses movement it is followed by the accusative. If it expresses a position it is followed by the dative.

 To find out if it is followed by the accusative ask: Where are you going?
Ich gehe in die Bar. – *I am going (in)to the bar.*

 To find out if it is followed by the dative ask: Where are you?
Ich bin in der Bar. – *I am in the bar.*

These are the two-way prepositions:

accusative asking where to? wohin?		dative asking where? wo?
an to	Ich gehe an **die** Tür. I am going to the door.	Ich bin an **der** Tür. I am at the door.
auf on/onto	Sie klettern auf **den** Baum. They climb onto the tree.	Sie sind auf **dem** Baum. They are in the tree.
hinter behind	Ich fahre das Auto hinter **das** Haus. I drive the car behind the house.	Der Parkplatz ist hinter **dem** Haus. The car park is behind the house.
in in/ into	Ich springe in **das** Wasser. I jump into the water.	Ich bin in **dem** Wasser. I am in the water.
neben next to/beside	Ich lege das Buch neben **das** Telefon. I put the book beside the telephone.	Das Buch liegt neben **dem** Telefon. The book is lying beside the telephone.
über over	Das Flugzeug fliegt über **das** Meer. The plane flies over the sea.	Das Flugzeug ist über **dem** Meer. The plane is over the sea.
unter under	Das Boot fährt unter **die** Brücke. The boat goes underneath the bridge.	Das Boot ist unter **der** Brücke. The boat is under the bridge.
vor in front of	Das Taxi fährt vor **das** Haus. The taxi is driving in front of the house.	Das Taxi wartet vor **dem** Haus. The taxi is waiting in front of the house.
zwischen between	Ich setze mich zwischen **meine** Freunde. I am going to sit between my friends.	Ich sitze zwischen **meinen** Freunden. I am sitting between my friends.

Reminder:

	masculine	feminine	neuter	plural
nominative	der	die	das	die
accusative	den	die	das	die
dative	dem	der	dem	den

XII Do you recognise which case is being used? Look for clues: -**e** or -**n** endings indicate the accusative; -**m** or -**r** endings indicate the dative.

a mit meinem Freund
b durch den Wald
c in der Stadt
d zu der Tankstelle
e mit meiner Freundin

f in den Kindergarten
g für meine Freundin
h ohne meine Frau
i um den Park
j von dem Blumengeschäft

XIII And some more. Which case is being used?

a nach meinem Geburtstag
b seit meiner letzten Party
c Ich gehe in den Wald
d über die Straße
e neben dem Rathaus

f unter der Brücke
g vor dem Haus
h auf der Bank.
i hinter der Tür
j Ich schreibe an die Familie.

XIV Üben Sie! Complete the sentences.

Ask yourself *in* or *into; on* or *onto?*

a Wir steigen in d___ Zug ein.
b Wir bleiben in d___ Zug.
c Der Ball liegt auf d___ Dach.
d Das Kind wirft den Ball auf d___ Dach.
e Ich gehe an d___ Fenster.
f Ich sitze an d___ Fenster.
g Wir wohnen neben d___ Theater.
h Wir fahren das Auto neben d___ Theater.
i Das Kind kriecht unter d___ Bettdecke.
j Das Kind schläft unter d___ Bettdecke.

XV Wo ist Robert? Match the picture with the sentence.

a Er ist unter der Dusche.

b Er ist hinter der Badezimmertür.

c Er steht vor dem Spiegel.

d Er ist zwischen den beiden Türen.

e Er sitzt im Bett.

f Er sitzt vor dem Fernsehen.

Did you notice? In English you say 'He is **in** the shower', while in German you say 'Er ist unter der Dusche.'

XVI   What would you say to tell someone where the telephone is?

Das Telefon ist:

a _____ dem Tisch

b _____ der Ablage

c _____ dem Nachtschrank

d _____ der Schublade

e _____ dem Vorhang

6.3 Useful prepositional phrases

These tell you where something or someone is. They are called phrases because they are made up of more than one word, e.g. *in front of* is a prepositional phrase in English because it is made up of three words.

gegenüber von	opposite from
in der Nähe von	near
weit von	far from
nicht weit von	not far from

6.3.1 Useful expressions to tell you where someone or something is in a building

im oberen Stockwerk	upstairs
im unteren Stockwerk	downstairs
im Erdgeschoss	on the ground floor
in der ersten/zweiten Etage	on the first/second floor
im ersten/zweiten Stock	on the first/second floor
im Untergeschoss	in the basement

 Etage and **Stock** are interchangeable.

6.3.2 Saying where you live

There are two ways of expressing in German where you live with *bei/mit*.

Bei is a special preposition which means *at the house of*. It is followed by the person's name or the relevant pronoun.

Die Party ist __	The party is __
bei Peter.	at Peter's house.
bei mir.	at my house.
bei ihm/ihr.	at his/her house.
bei meinen Eltern.	at my parents' house.

You can also use *mit*.

Ich wohne __	I live __
mit meinen Eltern.	with my parents.
mit meinem Mann.	with my husband.
mit meiner Frau.	with my wife.
mit meinem Kind.	with my child.

6.3.3 Expressions of time

These tell you when something happened.

um	at
um 10 Uhr	at ten o'clock
nach	after
nach dem Frühstück	after breakfast
vor	before
vor dem Büro	before going to the office
während	during
während des Tages	during the day
für	for
für eine Woche	for a week
gegen	about/around
gegen 10 Uhr	about/towards ten o'clock
seit	since/for
Ich warte auf Sie seit heute Morgen.	I've been waiting for you since this morning.
Ich wohne hier seit drei Jahren.	I have been living here for three years.
Wie lange studieren Sie schon?	How long have you been studying? I have been studying (and I still am) for two years.
Ich studiere seit zwei Jahren.	

I   Match the German with the English.

a seit einem Jahr	1	for one second
b seit einem Monat	2	for two days
c seit einer Stunde	3	for one year
d seit einem Tag	4	for many years
e seit einer Sekunde	5	for exactly two hours
f seit zwei Monaten	6	for a month
g seit vielen Jahren	7	for one minute
h seit genau zwei Stunden	8	for two months
i seit einer Minute	9	for an hour
j seit zwei Tagen	10	for one day

COMMON IRREGULAR VERBS

Verbs with prefixes are not included but they are irregular in the same way.

 Look up the verb without the prefix and add it back on, e.g **umfallen**. Look up **fallen**: third person **er fiel um**, past participle **gefallen** → **umgefallen**. **Er ist umgefallen.**

 Verbs with *use **sein**. **Ich bin gefallen**. – *I fell*.

Reminder:

Present tense: ich backe, du backst, er/sie/es backt, wir backen, ihr backt, Sie backen, sie backen

Imperfect tense/simple past: ich backte, du backtest, er/sie/es backte, wir backten, ihr backtet, Sie backten, sie backten

Past tense: Ich habe gebacken, du hast gebacken, er/sie/es hat gebacken, wir haben gebacken, ihr habt gebacken, Sie haben gebacken, sie haben gebackt

*Ich bin geflogen, du bist geflogen, er/sie/es ist geflogen, wir sind geflogen, ihr seid geflogen, Sie sind geflogen, sie sind geflogen

Infinitive	3rd person singular present tense	Imperfect	past participle	English meaning
backen	bäckt	backte	gebacken	to bake
befehlen	befiehl	befahl	befohlen	to command/order
beginnen	beginnt	begann	begonnen	to begin
beißen	beißt	biss	gebissen	to bite
bergen	birgt	barg	geborgen	to rescue

IIII➡

Infinitive	3rd person singular present tense	Imperfect	past participle	English meaning
biegen	biegt	bog	*gebogen	to bend, turn
bieten	bietet	bot	geboten	to offer
binden	bindet	band	gebunden	to tie, bind
bitten	bittet	bat	gebeten	to ask, request
bleiben	bleibt	blieb	*geblieben	to stay, remain
braten	brät	briet	gebraten	to roast
brechen	bricht	brach	gebrochen	to break
brennen	brennt	brannte	gebrannt	to burn
bringen	bringt	brachte	gebracht	to bring/take
denken	denkt	dachte	gedacht	to think
dringen	dringt	drang	*gedrungen	to force/push/ penetrate
dürfen	darf	durfte	gedurft	to be allowed to/ may
empfehlen	empfiehlt	empfahl	empfohlen	to recommend
erschrecken	erschrickt	erschrak	erschrocken	to frighten
essen	isst	aß	gegessen	to eat
fahren	fährt	fuhr	*gefahren	to drive
fallen	fällt	fiel	*gefallen	to fall
fangen	fängt	fing	gefangen	to catch
finden	findet	fand	gefunden	to find
fliegen	fliegt	flog	*geflogen	to fly
fliehen	flieht	floh	*geflohen	to flee
fließen	fließt	floss	*geflossen	to flow
fressen	frisst	fraß	gefressen	to eat (animals)
frieren	friert	fror	gefroren	to freeze (feel cold)
geben	gibt	gab	gegeben	to give
gehen	geht	ging	*gegangen	to go/walk
gelingen	gelingt	gelang	*gelungen	to succeed, manage
gelten	gilt	galt	gegolten	to be valid
genießen	genießt	genoss	genossen	to enjoy
geschehen	geschieht	geschah	geschehen	to happen
gewinnen	gewinnt	gewann	gewonnen	to win/gain
gießen	gießt	goß	gegossen	to pour
gleichen	gleicht	glich	geglichen	to resemble
gleiten	gleitet	glitt	*geglitten	to glide/slide
graben	gräbt	grub	gegraben	to dig
greifen	greift	griff	gegriffen	to grasp/seize
haben	hat	hatte	gehabt	to have
halten	hält	hielt	gehalten	to hold/stop
hängen	hängt	hing	gehangen	to hang
heben	hebt	hob	gehoben	to lift/raise

⫸

Infinitive	3rd person singular present tense	Imperfect	past participle	English meaning
heißen	heißt	hieß	geheißen	to be called
helfen	hilft	half	geholfen	to help
kennen	kennt	kannte	gekannt	to know/to be familiar with
klingen	klingt	klang	geklungen	to sound
kommen	kommt	kam	*gekommen	to come
können	kann	konnte	gekonnt	to be able to
kriechen	kriecht	kroch	*gekrochen	to creep, crawl
laden	lädt	lud	geladen	to load
lassen	lässt	ließ	gelassen	to let, allow, leave
laufen	läuft	lief	*gelaufen	to run
leiden	leidet	litt	gelitten	to suffer
leihen	leiht	lieh	geliehen	to lend
lesen	liest	las	gelesen	to read
liegen	liegt	lag	gelegen	to lie
lügen	lügt	log	gelogen	to tell a lie
messen	misst	maß	gemessen	to measure
mögen	mag	mochte	gemocht	to like
müssen	muss	musste	gemusst	to have to, must
nehmen	nimmt	nahm	genommen	to take
nennen	nennt	nannte	genannt	to name
pfeifen	pfeift	pfiff	gepfiffen	to whistle
raten	rät	riet	geraten	to advise
reiben	reibt	rieb	gerieben	to rub
reißen	reißt	riss	gerissen	to tear
reiten	reitet	ritt	(*)geritten	to ride
rennen	rennt	rannte	*gerannt	to run, race
riechen	riecht	roch	gerochen	to smell
rufen	ruft	rief	gerufen	to call
saufen	säuft	soff	gesoffen	to drink heavily (animal)
saugen	saugt	saugte/sog	gesaugt/ gesogen	to suck
schaffen	schafft	schuf	geschaffen	to create
scheiden	scheidet	schied	geschieden	to separate
scheinen	scheint	schien	geschienen	to shine, seem
schieben	schiebt	schob	geschoben	to push, shove
schießen	schießt	schoss	geschossen	to shoot
schlafen	schläft	schlief	geschlafen	to sleep
schlagen	schlägt	schlug	geschlagen	to hit, strike, beat
schleichen	schleicht	schlich	*geschlichen	to creep
schmeißen	schmeißt	schmiss	geschmissen	to fling, throw

Infinitive	3rd person singular present tense	Imperfect	past participle	English meaning
schmelzen	schmilzt	schmolz	*geschmolzen	to melt
schneiden	schneidet	schnitt	geschnitten	to cut
schreiben	schreibt	schrieb	geschrieben	to write
schreien	schreit	schrie	geschrie(e)n	to cry
schreiten	schreitet	schritt	*geschritten	to stride
schweigen	schweigt	schwieg	geschwiegen	to be silent
schwimmen	schwimmt	schwamm	*geschwommen	to swim
schwören	schwört	schwor	geschworen	to swear(an oath)
sehen	sieht	sah	gesehen	to see
sein	ist	war	*gewesen	to be
senden	sendet	sendete/sandte	gesendet	to send
singen	singt	sang	gesungen	to sing
sinken	sinkt	sank	*gesunken	to sink
sitzen	sitzt	saß	gesessen	to sit
sollen	soll	sollte	gesollt	to be supposed to
sprechen	spricht	sprach	gesprochen	to speak
springen	springt	sprang	gesprungen	to jump, leap
stechen	sticht	stach	gestochen	to sting, prick
stehen	steht	stand	gestanden	to stand
stehlen	stiehlt	stahl	gestohlen	to steal
sterben	stirbt	starb	gestorben	to die
stinken	stinkt	stank	gestunken	to stink, smell bad
stoßen	stößt	stieß	gestoßen	to push
streichen	streicht	strich	gestrichen	to stroke
streiten	streitet	stritt	gestritten	to argue, quarrel
tragen	trägt	trug	getragen	to carry, wear
treffen	trifft	traf	getroffen	to meet, hit
treiben	treibt	trieb	(*) getrieben	to drift/drive
treten	tritt	trat	(*) getreten	to step/kick
trinken	trinkt	trank	getrunken	to drink
tun	tut	tat	getan	to do
verderben	verdirbt	verdarb	(*) verdorben	to spoil, ruin, go bad
vergessen	vergisst	vergaß	vergessen	to forget
verlieren	verliert	verlor	verloren	to lose
vermeiden	vermeidet	vermied	vermieden	to avoid
verschwinden	verschwindet	verschwand	*verschwunden	to disappear
verzeihen	verzeiht	verzieh	verziehen	to pardon, excuse
wachsen	wächst	wuchs	*gewachsen	to grow
waschen	wäscht	wusch	gewaschen	to wash
weisen	weist	wies	gewiesen	to point, show

||||➡

Infinitive	3rd person singular present tense	Imperfect	past participle	English meaning
wenden	wendet	wendete	gewendet	to turn
werben	wirbt	warb	geworben	to advertise
werden	wird	wurde	*geworden	to become
werfen	wirft	warf	geworfen	to throw
wiegen	wiegt	wog	gewogen	to weigh
wissen	weiß	wusste	gewußt	to know (a fact)
wollen	will	wollte	gewollt	to want to, wish
ziehen	zieht	zog	*gezogen	to pull
zwingen	zwingt	zwang	gezwungen	to force, compel

Common Irregular Verbs

PRONUNCIATION

Pronunciation of the alphabet

a	ah
b	beh
c	tseh
d	deh
e	eh
f	eff
g	geh
h	hah
i	ee
j	yot
k	kah
l	ell
m	em
n	en
o	oh
p	peh
q	kuh
r	err
s	ess
t	teh
u	uh
v	fow
w	veh
x	iks
y	üppsilon

z	tsett
ä	äh (a- umlaut)
ö	öh (o- umlaut)
ü	üh (u- umlaut)
ß	ess-tsett

If you wish to speak German with a good accent, the following tips will be useful. However it is always easier to listen to the pronunciation of a native German speaker.

Vowels

German vowels are pronounced long or short depending on the consonants that follow.

They are pronounced *short* if they are followed by:

- two or more consonants, e.g. **alt**, **Geld**
- a double consonant, e.g. **Fett**, **Ball**.

They are pronounced *long*

- if they are followed by one consonant, e.g. **Tag**, **Bus**
- usually before a single consonant, e.g. **fragen**, **sagen**, **leben**
- if they are followed by **h** and one consonant, e.g. **Jahr**, **ihr**, **ohne**.

vowel	examples
long **a**	ja, Paar, mag, Tag
short **a**	Mann, wann, bald
long **e**	Tee, sehen, Regen
short **e**	Bett, Welt, Geld
long **i**	wie, ihn, Knie
short **i**	Kind, ich, mit
long **o**	Dom, so, Tod
short **o**	Morgen, Obst, offen
long **u**	du, tun, Stuhl
short **u**	Hund, und, Butter

Note that the letter **e** is always pronounced at the end of the word, e.g. **Name, Schule, ich gehe**.

The vowels **a, o, u** sound different when they have dots (called Umlauts) over them:

ä, ö, ü. They are best practised with a word. You might have heard them in names like **Müller**, **Jörg** and the word **Mädchen**.

Consonants

Most consonants are easy to pronounce for English learners.

The consonants **b**, **d**, **g**, are pronounced the same as in English at the beginning of a word: *bed* – **Bett**, *blue* – **blau**, *date* – **Datum**, *go* – **gehen**.

Note : The consonants **t**, **k** and **p** must be pronounced at the end of the word: **nich*t*, kapu*tt*, kran*k*, schlan*k*, schla*pp***. At the end of a word **b** is pronounced **p**: **Kal*b***; and **d** is pronounced **t**: **Han*d*, Wan*d***.

C is not often used on its own apart from in foreign words: **Café, Camping**. It is more often found in the combination **ch**, which sounds like **k** at the beginning of a word: **Chaos, Charakter**.

Ch after **a**, **au**, **o** and **u** is pronounced as in the Scottish word *loch*: **Dach, Bach, Strauch, Loch, doch, Buch, suchen**. After **e**, **ei**, **eu**, **i**, **äu**, **ü**, **ch** sounds softer: **Teich, weich, euch, ich, Dächer, Bräuche**.

G is the same as in English when it precedes a vowel: **Wege, sagen**. When it is at the end of a word **g** is pronounced like a **k**: **Tag, mag**.

You don't pronounce the **h** after a vowel; it just shows you that the vowel is long: **gehen, fehlen, Sohn, wohnen, Sahne**.

J at the beginning of a word is pronounced as **y** in English: **Jugend, jodeln**.

K is pronounced at the beginning and the end of a word: **krank, Kneipe**.

The pronunciation of **l** is much lighter than in English.

R before a vowel is pronounced by gargling slightly or it is spoken gutturally: **Rad fahren, regnen**. With another consonant or a single **r** at the end of the word it is however much weaker and is pronounced like the **r** in the English *here*: **lieber, wieder**.

S is pronounced in two different ways: as in the English *house* before consonants and at the end of words: **das, Haus, Eis**; as in the English *busy* when it precedes a vowel: **Rose, Saft**.

Sch is pronounced like the English *sh* in *sheep*: **schön, Fisch**.

Th is pronounced **t**: **Theorie, Theologie**.

V sounds like the English *f* as in *for, from*.

W sounds like the English *v* as in *very*.

ß is pronounced **s, ss**.

Two vowels together:

- **Au** is pronounced like *ow/ou* in the English *how* or *house*: **Aufzug, Tauben, Frau**.
- **Äu** and **eu** are pronounced as in the English *boy*: **Mäuse, Gebäude, Freude, Eule**.
- **Ei** sounds like the English *eye*: **frei, drei, mein**.
- **Ie** sounds like the English *ee*: **Brief, Liebe, Bier**.

ANSWERS

1.1.1

I   **a**   **c**   **d**   **f**   **i**

II   **a**   **b**   **f**   **h**   **i**

III   **a** 9   **b** 10   **c** 7   **d** 6   **e** 8   **f** 1   **g** 4   **h** 3   **i** 5   **j** 2

IV   **a** 9   **b** 3   **c** 7   **d** 6   **e** 4   **f** 5   **g** 10   **h** 2   **i** 1   **j** 8

1.1.2

V   **a** renn   **b** mach   **c** frag   **d** telefonier   **e** informier   **f** kommunizier   **g** veränder   **h** fütter   **i** behandel

VI   **a** kauf   **b** hör   **c** wein   **d** lächel   **e** sing   **f** ruf   **g** treff   **h** lach   **i** sag   **j** versteh

VII   **a** essen   **b** akzeptieren   **c** laufen   **d** fahren   **e** wandern   **f** suchen   **g** machen   **h** lächeln   **i** genießen   **j** tun

1.1.3

VIII   **a** ich   **b** sie   **c** er   **d** wir   **e** du   **f** Sie   **g** ihr   **h** Sie   **i** er   **j** sie

IX   **a** er   **b** sie   **c** er   **d** sie   **e** ich   **f** sie   **g** wir

1.1.4

X   **a** wohne   **b** wohnst   **c** wohnen   **d** wohnt   **e** wohnt   **f** wohnt   **g** wohnen   **h** wohnt   **i** wohnen   **j** wohnen

XI   **a** singe   **b** singst   **c** singt   **d** singen   **e** singt   **f** singen   **g** singt   **h** singt   **i** singen   **j** singen

XII   **a** wir   **b** er   **c** ich   **d** du   **e** er   **f** wir   **g** wir   **h** du   **i** er   **j** ich

1.1.5

XIII   **a** du bäckst, er bäckt   **b** du brätst, sie brät   **c** du gräbst, sie gräbt   **d** du säufst, sie säuft   **e** du empfängst, sie empfängt   **f** du fängst, er fängt   **g** du hältst, es hält   **h** du trägst, sie trägt   **i** du wächst, er wächst   **j** du wäschst, er wäscht

XIV   **a** du gibst, er gibt   **b** du nimmst, sie nimmt   **c** du misst, es misst   **d** du stiehlst, er stiehlt   **e** du stirbst, sie stirbt   **f** du sprichst, er spricht   **g** du befiehlst, sie befiehlt   **h** du empfiehlst, er empfiehlt   **i** du wirfst, er wirft   **j** du brichst, er bricht

1.1.6

XV   **a** haben   **b** habe   **c** hast   **d** habe   **e** hat   **f** hat   **g** habe   **h** haben   **i** habe   **j** hat

XVI   **a** habe   **b** haben   **c** hat   **d** habt   **e** hast   **f** hat   **g** haben   **h** hat   **i** hat   **j** haben

XVII   **a** ich bin   **b** ihr seid   **c** er ist   **d** wir sind   **e** du bist

XVIII   **a** Are you German?   **b** Yes, I am German.   **c** Are you married?

d Yes, I am married. **e** Is he a student? **f** Yes, he is a student. **g** Is she a nurse? **h** Yes, she is a nurse. **i** Are you in a good mood? **j** Yes, we are in a good mood.

XIX **a** sind **b** bin **c** ist **d** ist **e** seid **f** sind **g** sind **h** bin **i** ist **j** ist

XX **a** bin **b** ist **c** sind **d** ist **e** ist **f** ist **g** ist **h** sind **i** ist **j** sind

1.2.1

I **a** mich **b** dich **c** sich **d** sich **e** sich **f** sich **g** uns **h** euch **i** sich **j** sich

II **a** 7 **b** 10 **c** 5 **d** 8 **e** 3 **f** 9 **g** 1 **h** 4 **i** 6 **j** 2

III **a** beeile mich **b** benimmt sich **c** entscheidet sich **d** erholen sich **e** erkältet, sich **f** dich verabschieden **g** weigere mich **h** stellt sich **i** bedanke mich **j** verstecken sich

IV **a** verstehst, dich **b** verstehe mich **c** versteht sich **d** versteht sich **e** verstehen uns **f** streitet sich **g** streiten sich **h** streiten, sich **i** streite mich **j** streitet sich

V **a** mich **b** mir **c** dich **d** mich **e** dir **f** dir **g** mir **h** mir **i** mir **j** mich

VI **a** mir **b** dir **c** mir **d** dir **e** uns **f** sich **g** mir **h** mir **i** sich **j** mir

VII **a** 8 **b** 10 **c** 5 **d** 9 **e** 6 **f** 7 **g** 4 **h** 3 **i** 2 **j** 1

VIII **a** 8 **b** 9 **c** 1 **d** 6 **e** 5 **f** 2 **g** 7 **h** 10 **i** 3 **j** 4

1.2.2

IX **a** to give out **b** to help out **c** to run out **d** to try out

X **a** to drive back **b** to go back **c** to hold back **d** to call back

XI **a** to grow up **b** to give up **c** to hang up **d** to lift up

XII **a** an **b** auf **c** ein **d** an **e** aus **f** zurück **g** herein **h** aus **i** zurück **j** ab

XIII **a** abfahren *to leave* **b** aufmachen *to open* **c** abschicken *to send off* **d** einsteigen *to get on* **e** abheben *to withdraw* **f** ankommen *to arrive* **g** stattfinden *to take place* **h** einkaufen *to buy* **i** abholen *to collect* **j** zurückrufen *to phone back*

XIV **a** Sie kommt zurück. **b** Sie kommt bald an. **c** Machen Sie die Tür auf! **d** Machen Sie die Tür zu! **e** Steigen Sie ein! **f** Steigen Sie aus! **g** Er will/möchte einschlafen. **h** Er will/möchte ausschlafen. **i** Hören Sie auf! **j** Hören Sie zu!

XV **a** **b** **c** **e** **h** **i** **j**

1.2.3

XVII **a** können **b** kann **c** kannst **d** können **e** kann **f** kann **g** können **h** kann **i** können **j** kann

English sentences: **a-i** can **j** is allowed

XVIII **a** kannst **d** kann **c** können **d** kann **e** können **f** kann **g** kann **h** können **i** kannst **j** können

XIX **a** *allowed* darf **b** *allowed* dürfen **c** *may* darf **d** *allowed* dürfen **e** *must* must

XXII **a** wollen **b** willst **c** will **d** wollt **e** will **f** will **g** will **h** wollen **i** will **j** willst

XXIV **a** muss **b** musst **c** müssen **d** muss **e** müsst **f** muss **g** muss **h** müssen **i** muss **j** muss

XXVI **a** soll **b** sollen **c** sollst
d soll **e** soll **f** sollen **g** soll
h sollen **i** soll **j** sollen

XXVII **a** mag **b** mögen
c mögen **d** mag **e** magst
f mögen **g** mögen **h** mag
i mögt **j** mögen

XXIX **a** möchten **b** möchten
c möchtest **d** möchtet **e** möchte
f möchtest **g** möchten
h möchten **i** möchten **j** möchtest

XXX **a** kann **b** müssen **c** muss
d kannst **e** wollt **f** soll **g** willst
h können **i** müsst **j** mögen

XXXI **a** Kann er mir helfen? **b** Sie
kann mir bei der Grammatik helfen.
c Wie soll ich das wissen? **d** Wir
können verstehen, was Sie sagen.
e Wir können das verstehen.
f Wie sollen wir das wissen?
g Dürfen wir die Tür öffnen?
h Sollen wir die Tür öffnen? **i** Soll
ich das wissen? **j** Wir müssen den
Brief heute zu Ende schreiben.

1.3.1

I **a** wohne **b** arbeite **c** brauche
d esse **e** kapiere **f** interessiere
g fahre **h** lerne **i** komme
k spreche

II **a** höre **b** arbeite **c** schreibe
d esse **e** konzentriere **f** füttere
g bleibe **h** lese **i** unterrichte
j blamiere

III **a** spreche **b** esse **c** trage
d arbeite **e** schaue **f** spiele
g gehe **h** höre **i** lebe **j** verstehe

IV **a** behandele **b** wandele
c sammele **d** gammele **e** tue
f wandere **g** ändere **h** kümmere
i bewundere **j** füttere

V **a** habe **b** habe **c** bin **d** bin
e bin **f** habe **g** bin **h** bin **i** bin
j habe

VI **a** kann **b** kann **c** will
d darf **e** darf **f** darf **g** soll
h will **i** soll **j** will

VII **a** freue mich **b** fürchte mich
c interessiere mich **d** beeile mich
e entschuldige mich
f verabschiede mich **g** erkälte
mich **h** erhole mich **i** lege mich
j entschließe mich

VIII **a** gefalle mir **b** schade mir
c bilde mir **d** vertraue mir
e wasche mir **f** kämme mir
g putze mir **h** putze mir **i** helfe
mir **j** bin mir, sicher

1.3.2

IX **a** sagst **b** trinkst **c** lebst
d schwimmst **e** fragst **f** hörst
g singst **h** spielst **i** studierst
j weinst

X **a** kaufst **b** liebst **c** gehst
d hasst **e** schaust **f** lebst **g** lernst
h stellst **i** machst **j** spielst

XI **a** schreibst **b** wohnst
c spielst **d** machst **e** trinkst
f rauchst **g** sprichst **h** hörst
i arbeitest **j** kochst

XII **a** hältst **b** hältst **c** hältst
d schläfst **e** verschläfst **f** schläfst
g fängst **h** fängst **i** empfängst
j trägst **k** verträgst **l** trägst

XIII **a** gibst **b** trittst **c** trittst
d wirfst **e** wirfst **f** sprichst
g versprichst **h** liest **i** liest **j** liest
k hilfst **l** hilfst

XIV **a** hast **b** hast **c** bist **d** bist
e hast **f** hast **g** bist **h** bist
i hast **j** bist

XV **a** 8 **b** 6 **c** 2 **d** 7 **e** 5 **f** 9
g 10 **h** 1 **i** 4 **j** 3

XVI **a** 5 **b** 8 **c** 10 **d** 9 **e** 1
f 2 **g** 7 **h** 4 **i** 3 **j** 6

XVII   a dir   b dir   c dich   d dir
e dir   f dir   g dir   h dich   i dich
j dich

XVIII   a 4   b 8   c 6   d 7   e 2
f 9   g 10   h 3   i 5   j 1

XIX   a schreibst   b wohnst
c spielst   d fährst   e trinkst
f rauchst   g sprichst   h isst
i machst   j reitest

XX   a sprichst   b spielst
c studierst   d hörst   e fährst
f liest   g spielt   h manipulierst
i singst   j kochst

XXI   a 8   b 10   c 3   d 7   e 9
f 4   g 2   h 6   i 5   j 1

1.3.3

XXII   a lebt   b klettert   c kocht
d probiert   e versteht   f lernt
g bleibt   h taut   i kommt   j bringt

XXIII   a bäckt   b schläft   c gräbt
d wäscht   e trägt   f säuft   g hält
h fängt   i empfängt   j fährt

XXIV   a gibt   b nimmt   c misst
d stiehlt   e stirbt   f tritt   g wirft
h spricht   i liest   j hilft

XXV   a hat   b ist   c ist   d hat
e ist   f ist   g hat   h ist   i ist   j hat

XXVI   a kann   b muss   c darf
d will   e muss   f darf   g soll
h darf   i kann   j soll

XXVII   a duscht sich   b wäscht
sich   c putzt sich   d rasiert sich
e zieht sich   f kämmt sich   g setzt
sich   h beeilt sich   i setzt sich
j trifft sich

1.3.4

XXVIII   a arbeiten   b spielen
c studieren   d essen
e kommunizieren   f tanzen
g leben/wohnen   h kochen
i sprechen   j lesen

XXIX   a haben   b sind   c haben
d sind   e sind   f sind   g sind
h haben   i haben   j sind

XXX   a 3   b 4   c 5   d 6   e 1
f 2   g 9   h 8   i 7   j 10

XXXI   a ziehen uns um   b duschen
uns   c ruhen uns   d beeilen uns
e freuen uns   f verlaufen uns
g filmen uns   h irren uns
i verspäten uns   j verirren uns

XXXII   a müssen   b haben
c schicken   d rufen   e machen
f besuchen   g unterbrechen
h ändern   i sind   j buchstabieren

1.3.5

XXXIV   a Kommen Sie aus
Deutschland?   b Rauchen Sie
Zigaretten?   c Verstehen Sie mich?
d Kommen Sie mit?   e Heissen Sie
Frau Schmidt?   f Trinken Sie
Kaffee?   g Fahren Sie mit dem Bus?
h Fliegen Sie mit dem Flugzeug?
i Fliegen Sie nach Deutschland?
j Haben Sie Humor?

XXXV   a sind   b haben   c haben
d sind   e sind   f haben   g sind
h sind   i sind   j haben

XXXVI   a 10   b 6   c 8   d 7   e 9
f 1   g 2   h 3   i 4   j 5

XXXVII   a Wollen Sie ein
Einzelzimmer?   b Können Sie mir
helfen?   c Wollen Sie die Sauna
benutzen?   d Können Sie mir den
Schlüssel geben?   e Wollen Sie
Frühstück auf dem Zimmer?
f Wollen Sie einen Balkon haben?
g Wollen Sie Ihr Auto auf dem
Parkplatz parken?   h Wollen Sie
eine deutsche Zeitung lesen?
i Wollen Sie um 7 Uhr
frühstücken?   j Müssen Sie jetzt
abreisen?

1.3.6

XXXIX **a** 10 **b** 5 **c** 3 **d** 6 **e** 9
f 2 **g** 1 **h** 4 **i** 7 **j** 8

XL **a** überquert **b** wartet **c** geht
d nehmt **e** passt **f** folgt **g** geht
h schaut **i** fragt **j** seht

XLI **a** seid **b** habt **c** habt
d seid **e** habt **f** seid **g** habt
h seid **i** seid **j** seid

XLII **a** wollt **b** müsst **c** wollt
d könnt **e** müsst **f** sollt **g** dürft
h könnt **i** wollt **j** mögt

XLIII **a** 8 **b** 7 **c** 6 **d** 2 **e** 9
f 10 **g** 5 **h** 3 **i** 4 **j** 1

1.3.8

XLIV **a** 4 **b** 9 **c** 10 **d** 2 **e** 3
f 1 **g** 5 **h** 6 **i** 7 **j** 8

XLV **a** sind **b** sehen **c** scheinen
d tragen **e** kommen **f** sprechen
g trinken **h** essen **i** haben
j gehen

XLVI **a** waschen **b** putzen
c kämmen **d** ruhen **e** legen
f freuen **g** ärgern **h** streiten
i verstecken **j** helfen

1.4.4

I **a** Ich habe **b** du hast **c** wir
haben **d** sie haben **e** er hat **f** Sie
haben **g** sie hat **h** Maria hat **i**
die Kinder haben **j** mein Mann hat

II **a** habe **b** hast **c** haben
d hat **e** haben **f** hat **g** haben
h hast **i** haben **j** habe

III **a** bin **b** ist **c** sind **d** ist
e ist **f** sind **g** bin **h** bist **i** seid
j sind

IV **a** bin **b** sind **c** ist **d** bin
e sind **f** bin **g** ist **h** sind **i** ist
j seid

1.4.5

V **a** bin, habe **b** bin, habe
c haben, sind **d** haben, sind
e hat, ist **f** bin, habe **g** hat, ist
h ist, hat **i** bin, habe **j** bist, bist

1.4.6

VI **a** gesagt **b** geübt **c** gefragt
d gelacht **e** geglaubt **f** gesucht
g gekauft **h** gebaut **i** gebraucht
j gewohnt

VII **a** geraucht **b** gebaut
c gehört **d** gekocht **e** geputzt
f geweint **g** gehasst **h** gemeldet
i geöffnet **j** geteilt

VIII **a** gespielt **b** getanzt
c gesucht **d** gefragt **e** gezahlt
f gewohnt **g** gelebt **h** gemacht
i geschimpft **j** geholt

IX **a** gespielt **b** gekocht
c gehört **d** getanzt **e** geöffnet
f geschickt **g** gelacht **h** geguckt
i gehabt **j** gemacht

X **a** haben, *to have* **b** schauen, *to
look at/watch* **c** reisen, *to travel*
d rauchen, *to smoke* **e** saugen, *to
suck* **f** machen, *to make/do*
g hoffen, *to hope* **h** kochen, *to
cook* **i** planen, *to plan* **j** lieben, *to
love*

XI **a** spielen, *to play* **b** tanzen, *to
dance* **c** suchen, *to search for*
d fragen, *to ask* **e** zahlen, *to pay*
f wohnen, *to live* **g** leben, *to live*
h putzen, *to clean* **i** schimpfen, *to
scold* **j** holen, *to get/collect*

XII **a** besucht **b** betreut
c behauptet **d** bezahlt
e bekommt **f** verhört **g** verkauft
h entleert **i** entkommt
j entlüftet

XIII **a** akzeptiert **b** repariert
c kommuniziert **d** experimentiert

e radiert   f toleriert   g basiert
h attackiert   i poliert
j hereinspaziert

1.4.7

XIV   a geschlafen   b geblasen
c gegraben   d gehalten   e gehauen
f gekommen   g geraten   h gerufen
i gesehen   j getragen

XV   a geschwiegen   b geschrien
c gewiesen   d geschrieben
e geblieben   f gediehen
g getrieben   h gestiegen
i geschieden   j gerieben

XVI   a gerungen   b geklungen
c gebunden   d geschwungen
e gesungen   f gesunken
g gesprungen   h gestunken
i getrunken   j gezwungen

XVII   a hereingekommen
b herausgekommen
c ausgekommen   d weggekommen
e zurückgekommen

XVIII   a weggegangen
b ausgegangen   c heraufgegangen
d hineingegangen   e hingegangen

XIX   a hingefahren
b herausgefahren   c hereingefahren
d abgefahren   e zurückgefahren
f weggefahren

XX   a ausgefallen   b hereingefallen
c aufgefallen   d heruntergefallen
e hineingefallen

XXI   a Wir sind spät
angekommen.   b Wir sind gut
ausgekommen.   c Wir sind schnell
weggekommen.   d Wir sind
heruntergekommen.   e Wir sind
ausgegangen.   f Wir sind
abgefahren.   g Wir sind
weggefahren.   h Wir sind darauf
hereingefallen.   i Wir sind

aufgefallen.   j Wir sind gut
miteinander ausgekommen.

XXII   a aufholen   b aufsuchen
c ansagen   d aufsagen   e ausleben
f zumachen   g ausschimpfen
h abbauen   i anbauen   j weggeben

XXIII   a anhören   b zuhören
c weghören   d anmachen
e aufmachen   f kaputtmachen
g einkaufen   h herausholen
i aufhören   j hinfallen

XXIV   a Wir sind am Freitag
angekommen.   b Ich habe mein
Essen gekocht.   c Ich bin
einkaufen gegangen.   d Ich habe
gefrühstückt.   e Ich habe Tee
getrunken.   f Ich habe
ferngesehen.   g Wir haben uns
einen schönen Abend gemacht.
h Ich habe zu viel gearbeitet.   i Ich
bin früh schlafen gegangen.   j Wir
haben lange geschlafen.

1.4.8

XXV   a Hast du schöne Ferien
gehabt?   b Hast du Tennis gespielt?
c Hast du Pizza gegessen?   d Hast
du Limonade getrunken?   e Hast
du getanzt?   f Bist du oft
schwimmen gegangen?   g Hast du
dich gesonnt?   h Hast du neue
Freunde getroffen?   i Hast du viele
Postkarten geschickt?   j Bist du
segeln gegangen?

XXVI   a Habe ich das gesagt?
b Haben Sie das verstanden?
c Haben wir mehr Kunden
bekommen?   d Haben Sie die
Zeitung gelesen?   e Haben Sie
meinen Kollegen getroffen?
f Haben Sie die E-Mail
rausgeschickt?   g Haben Sie den
Brief geschrieben?   h Haben Sie
ihn angerufen?   i Haben Sie meine
Nachricht bekommen?

1.4.10

XXVII **a** fragte **b** fragtest
c fragten **d** fragte **e** fragten
f fragtet **g** fragten **h** fragten
i fragte **j** fragten

XXVIII **a** atmete **b** atmetest
c atmeten **d** atmete **e** atmete
f atmete **g** atmeten **h** atmetet
i atmeten **j** atmeten

XXIX **a** wartete **b** wohnte
c lebten **d** arbeitete **e** hustete
f spieltest **g** teilten **h** eröffneten
i dauerte **j** badeten

XXX **a** warf, geworfen **b** trank,
getrunken **c** traf, getroffen
d starb, gestorben **e** kannte,
gekannt **f** mochte, gemocht
g sah, gesehen **h** rief, gerufen
i saß, gesessen **j** fror, gefroren

XXXI **a** waren in Berlin **b** war sehr
gut **c** hatten einen Unfall **d** hatten
Glück **e** hatte Kopfschmerzen
f war nur kurz im Krankenhaus
g war fantastisch **h** waren sehr
sauber und schön **i** war nicht
schlecht **j** waren interessant

1.4.11

XXXII **a** wollte **b** wollten
c wollte **d** konntest **e** konnte
f konnten **g** musste **h** musste
i mussten **j** sollte

1.5.1

I **a** Ich fahre nicht. **b** Er fährt
nicht schnell. **c** Ich schmolle
nicht. **d** Er schmollt nicht oft.
e Das Baby weint nicht. **f** Susi
weint nicht im Bett. **g** Ich
verschlafe nicht. **h** Er verschläft
nicht oft. **i** Ich friere nicht. **j** Sie
friert nicht in der Sonne.

II **a** Wir sind nicht bei der Arbeit.
b Er ist nicht in einem
Krankenhaus. **c** Ich bin nicht zu
Besuch hier. **d** Du bist nicht in
einer politischen Partei. **e** Sie
sind nicht auf einer Fähre.
f Ihr seid nicht sehr enttäuscht.
g Ich bin nicht sehr glücklich.
h Anne ist nicht in Berlin.
i Die Musik ist nicht sehr gut.
j Meine Arbeit ist nicht sehr
interessant.

III **a** Wir sind nicht nervös. **b** Ich
bin nicht unhöflich. **c** Ihr seid
nicht verrückt. **d** Sie ist nicht
aufrichtig. **e** Er ist nicht stur.
f Das Lied macht mich nicht
fröhlich. **g** Diese Kinder sind nicht
sehr höflich. **h** Das Wetter macht
mich nicht deprimiert. **i** Geld
macht mich nicht glücklich.
j Wolfgang fühlt sich nicht gut.

IV **a** Ich kann nicht essen **b** Das
Baby will nicht essen. **c** Meine
Tochter darf nicht fernsehen.
d Ich soll die Kinder nicht abholen.
e Er möchte nicht gehen. **f** Wir
dürfen hier nicht parken. **g** Frau
Schmidt kann nicht fahren. **h** Der
Zug kann nicht abfahren. **i** Ich
kann nicht lachen. **j** Sie dürfen
nicht lachen.

1.5.2

V **a** keine **b** kein **c** keine
d kein **e** keine **f** keine **g** keine
h kein **i** keine

VI **a** kein **b** keine **c** keinen
d keine **e** keine **f** keine
g keinen **h** keinen **i** keinen
j keine

1.5.3

VII **a** Wohnt sie in Aachen?
b Sprechen die Kinder Deutsch?
c Telefoniert sie gerne? **d** Fahren
Tobias und Jackie in Urlaub? **e** Ist

ihr Mann sehr müde? **f** Glauben Sie an Gott? **g** Schicken wir eine E-Mail an ihn? **h** Raucht er nicht? **i** Isst du kein Fleisch? **j** Ist sie Buddhistin?

VIII **a** Treibt sie viel Sport? **b** Geht sie regelmäßig schwimmen? **c** Spielt er gerne Golf? **d** Gucken Peter und Gabi gerne Fußball? **e** Gehst du gerne ins Kino? **f** Hört er gerne Musik? **g** Fährt sie gerne Skateboard? **h** Spielt er gerne Gitarre? **i** Ist er DJ? **j** Fahren die Kinder gerne Rad?

IX **a** Kauft ihr gerne ein? **b** Sehen Günther und Anne gerne fern? **c** Fahren sie heute weg? **d** Kommen wir morgen wieder? **e** Packt sie den Koffer aus? **f** Wacht er um 5 Uhr auf? **g** Laden wir Freunde ein? **h** Rufen wir meine Tante an? **i** Fliegt das Flugzeug ab? **j** Kommt der Zug an?

X **a** Können Sie mir helfen? **b** Kann ich etwas für Sie tun? **c** Kann ich die Hose anprobieren? **d** Kann ich Ihnen helfen? **e** Wollen Sie noch etwas anderes? **f** Wollen Sie eine Tasse Kaffee? **g** Können wir bitte bestellen? **h** Wollen Sie eine Vorspeise? **i** Wollen Sie eine Nachspeise? **j** Dürfen wir hier rauchen?

XI **a** haben **b** sind **c** sind **d** haben **e** ist **f** hat **g** sind **h** haben **i** haben **j** haben

XII **a** Where do you live? **b** What is your name? **c** Where do you work? **d** When does the postman come? **e** Why are you laughing? **f** Where are you driving to? **g** Why is the dog barking? **h** What are you doing? **i** Who is Mrs Meier? **j** Why are the children laughing?

XIII **a** wie **b** wie viel **c** wo **d** warum **e** wie lange **f** woher **g** wen **h** wohin **i** wer **j** warum

XIV **a** wie **b** wann **c** wie **d** woher **e** was **f** wer **g** wie viele **h** wer **i** wie viele **j** wie

XV **a** 7 **b** 6 **c** 10 **d** 9 **e** 4 **f** 8 **g** 1 **h** 3 **i** 5 **j** 2

1.5.4

XVI **a** go **b** run **c** cross the road **d** turn right **e** listen **f** come **g** pay attention **h** have a look **i** stop **j** try!

XVII **a** sich **b** iss **c** trink **d** geh **e** schliess **f** öffne **g** zeig **h** sprich **i** komm **j** hilf

XVIII **a** Freu dich! **b** Ärgere dich nicht! **c** Beeil dich! **d** Beeil dich nicht! **e** Erkälte dich nicht! **f** Setzt dich! **g** Wasch dich! **h** Entschuldige dich! **i** Zieh dich an! **j** Trau dich!

XIX **a** 5 **b** 10 **c** 9 **d** 1 **e** 8 **f** 7 **g** 6 **h** 2 **i** 4 **j** 3

XX **a** Amüsieren Sie sich! **b** Erinnern Sie sich! **c** Stellen Sie sich vor! **d** Unterhalten Sie sich! **e** Entschuldigen Sie sich! **f** Freuen Sie sich! **g** Ärgern Sie sich nicht! **h** Beeilen Sie sich nicht! **i** Erkälten Sie sich nicht! **j** Ziehen Sie sich an!

XXI **a** 9 **b** 10 **c** 8 **d** 7 **e** 3 **f** 5 **g** 2 **h** 4 **i** 6 **j** 1

1.6

1.6.1

I **a** werde **b** werden **c** wird **d** werden **e** wirst **f** werden **g** werde **h** wird **i** wird **j** werden

II **a** wirst **b** wirst **c** wirst
d werden **e** werden **f** werden
g wird **h** wird **i** wird

1.6.2

III **a** fliegen **b** besuche
c bleiben **d** fahre **e** mache
f besuchen **g** gehen **h** trifft
i segeln **j** haben

IV **a** 5 **b** 8 **c** 10 **d** 1 **e** 7 **f** 9
g 3 **h** 4 **i** 2 **j** 6

V **a** Wir kommen am Montag um
11 Uhr in Berlin an. **b** Wir
nehmen die U-Bahn. **c** Wir fahren
zum Hotel. **d** Wir packen unsere
Kleidung aus. **e** Danach gehen wir
zum Brandenburger Tor. **f** Wir
machen eine Stadtrundfahrt.
g Wir machen eine
deutschsprachige Stadtrundfahrt.
h Am Abend gehen wir zum
Kurfürstendamm. **i** Danach gehen
wir ins Theater. **j** Dann gehen wir
in einen Club tanzen.

1.6.4

VI **a** in die Stadt gehen **b** im
Garten arbeiten **c** Tennis spielen
d ins Kino gehen **e** eine
Schwarzwälderkirschtorte backen
f meine Freunde treffen **g** einen
Käsekuchen kaufen und ihn essen.
h tanzen gehen **i** meine Freunde
anrufen **j** einkaufen gehen

VII **a** würde, kaufen **b** würden,
machen **c** würdest, aufgeben
d würde, gehen. **e** würden,
verschwenden. **f** würde, legen
g würdet, kaufen **h** würden, fahren
i würde, arbeiten **j** würden,
investieren

1.6.5

VIII **a** hätten **b** hättest **c** hätte
d hätte **e** hätten **f** hättest

g hätten **h** hätten **i** hätte
j hätten

IX **a** könnte **b** könnten
c könnte **d** könnte **e** könntest
f könnte **g** könnten **h** könnten
i könnten **j** könnten

X **a** Ich könnte das tun. **b** Wir
könnten uns treffen. **c** Man
könnte das einfacher machen.
d Wir könnten aufhören zu streiten.
e Mein Mann könnte mir helfen.
f Du könntest mir helfen. **g** Wir
könnten um 6 Uhr da sein. **h** Ich
könnte mit dem Fahrrad fahren.
i Es könnte sein. **j** Er könnte
kommen, wenn er Zeit hätte.

1.7

1.7.1

I **a** Wir haben Recht. **b** Sie
haben Unrecht. **c** Sie hat Angst
vor Hunden. **d** Er hat Durst.
e Sie haben Hunger. **f** Haben Sie
Sorgen? **g** Ich habe Durst. **h** Ich
habe Recht. **i** Sie haben Unrecht.
j Ich habe Angst vor Ratten.

1.7.2

II **a** gibt keine, es gibt **b** gibt
viele, gibt, genug, gab, keine
c gab, gibt es

1.7.3

III **a** weiß **b** weiß **c** kenne
d wissen **e** kenne **f** weiß **g** weiß
h kenne **i** kenne **j** weiß

IV **a** kenne **b** kennt **c** kennt
d kennen **e** kennt **f** kennen
g wissen **h** wissen **i** weiß **j** wissen

1.7.4

V **a** magst **b** mag **c** gerne
d gerne **e** mögt **f** mögen **g** mag
h gerne **i** mögen **j** gerne

1.7.5

VI **a** uns **b** dich **c** sich **d** sich
e mich **f** sich **g** euch **h** sich
i dich **j** euch

VII **a** Ich erinnere mich an
Johann. **b** Er erinnert sich an
mich. **c** Ich erinnere mich an
Alles. **d** Ich erinnere mich an
seine Frau. **e** Ich erinnere mich an
ihr Lächeln. **f** Meine Kinder
erinnern sich an sie. **g** Wir
erinnern uns an den Sonntag im
Schwarzwald. **h** Ich erinnere mich
an unsere Bootsfahrt. **i** Ich
erinnere mich an das wunderbare
Mittagessen. **j** Ich erinnere mich
an den romantischen Abend.

1.7.6

VIII **a** bringe **b** nehme
c bringe **d** bringen **e** nehme
f bringe **g** nehmen **h** bringe
i bringen **j** nehmen

1.7.7

IX **a** noch nie **b** niemand
c noch nie **d** nicht mehr
e nichts. **f** nicht länger **g** noch
nie **h** nur **i** nur **j** nicht mehr

1.7.8

X **a** wohne, seit **b** spreche, seit
c kenne, seit **d** habe, seit **e** bin,
seit **f** wartet, seit **g** wohnt, seit
h bin, seit **i** rauche, seit

1.8

1.8.1

I **a** Wir lernen Grammatik.
b Wolfgang malt ein Bild. **c** Barbara
schreibt E-Mails. **d** Er macht sein
Haus sauber. **e** Ernie wäscht sein
Auto. **f** Jackie fährt mit dem Bus
zur Arbeit. **g** Ich schreibe einen
Brief auf meinem Computer. **h** Wir
mähen das Gras in unserem Garten.
i Wir besuchen unsere Kinder. **j** Sie
hört Musik.

1.8.2

II **a** Ich bleibe am Wochenende
lange in meinem Bett. **b** Ich
verbringe das Wochenende alleine
in meinem Haus. **c** Angelika fährt
dieses Jahr mit der Fähre nach
Deutschland. **d** Wir studieren
montags intensiv im
Deutschunterricht. **e** Klaus und
Gabi fahren am Montag schnell in
die Stadt. **f** Meine Freundin fährt
nächste Woche mit ihrem Freund
nach Hamburg. **g** Ich esse
sonntags gerne im Restaurant.
h Ich gehe morgens nicht so gerne
im Regen durch den Park. **i** Mein
Hund liebt es morgens im Regen im
Park. **j** Mein Auto muss am
Mittwoch leider in die Werkstatt.

1.8.3

III **a** Glücklicherweise habe ich
nächste Woche frei. **b** Am Sonntag
fahre ich nach London. **c** Nächstes
Jahr kommt meine Freundin nach
Schottland. **d** Heute Abend treffen
wir unsere Freunde. **e** Morgen
arbeite ich den ganzen Tag. **f** Zum
Glück haben wir noch Zeit.
g Leider gibt es Krieg in der Welt.
h Dummerweise kommt der Bus
nicht. **i** Komischerweise ist meine
Chefin heute freundlich. **j** Endlich
bist du da.

1.8.4

IV **a** oder **b** denn **c** oder
d und **e** oder **f** entweder, oder
g oder **h** sondern **i** oder **j** denn

V **a** und **b** und **c** und **d** denn
e aber **f** und **g** sondern
h entweder, oder **i** aber **j** denn

VI **a** und ich habe gearbeitet.
b denn die Heizung ist kaputt.
c aber die Kinder mussten nichts
bezahlen. **d** aber es ist immer
noch kalt. **e** und wir treffen uns
um 7 Uhr. **f** sondern wir gehen in
ein Restaurant. **g** denn er war
sehr lustig. **h** denn es war glatt auf
der Straße. **i** aber sie stimmt oft
nicht. **j** sondern er will in die USA
ziehen.

1.8.5

VII **a** 6 **b** 4 **c** 10 **d** 8 **e** 9 **f** 7
g 3 **h** 1 **i** 2 **j** 12 **k** 5 **l** 11

VIII **a** es regnet **b** ich es mag
c ich den Film sehen will **d** er sehr
alt ist **e** ich keine Lust habe **f** ich
einen Urlaub brauche **g** der Krieg
noch nicht zu Ende ist **h** du mit
deiner Freundin telefonierst **i** sie
weg sind **j** wir friedlich und ruhig
sind

IX **a** weil **b** denn **c** weil
d denn **e** weil **f** weil **g** denn
h denn **i** denn **j** weil

X **a** aber **b** damit **c** aber
d aber **e** damit **f** aber **g** damit
h aber **i** damit **j** aber

XI **a** obwohl das organische Essen
teurer ist. **b** weil es verboten ist.
c seit sie in der Grundschule sind.
d weil die Ampel kaputt ist.
e während der Film läuft. **f** wenn
sie nicht rauchen. **g** obwohl es
nicht gesund ist. **h** damit wir
genug Benzin für die Reise haben.
i obwohl sie nicht immer wahr
werden. **j** bevor wir in Urlaub
fahren.

1.8.6

XII **a** weil ich Skifahren lernen
wollte. **b** weil ich noch nie Ski
gefahren bin. **c** weil die Leute sehr
lustig gewesen sind. **d** weil ich
beim Skifahren hingefallen bin.
e als ich mir das Bein gebrochen
habe. **f** dass ich nicht mehr Ski
fahren konnte. **g** während ich in
der Sonne gelegen habe.
h obwohl mein Bein wehgetan hat.
i obwohl es sehr kalt gewesen ist.
j obwohl ich nicht mehr Ski fahren
konnte.

XIII **a** habe ich dieses
Wochenende viel Zeit gehabt.
b bin ich nicht in Urlaub gefahren.
c bin ich schwimmen gegangen.
d haben wir unsere Verwandten
besucht. **e** haben wir viel draußen
gemacht. **f** habe ich viel Deutsch
gelernt. **g** sind wir nach Belgien
gefahren. **h** spreche ich besser
Deutsch. **i** habe ich gestern
Fernsehen geguckt. **j** bin ich nicht
nach New York geflogen.

1.8.7

XIV **a** meiner Professorin meine
Arbeit **b** dem Fremden das kleine
Hotel **c** der kranken Frau Blumen
d den Kindern Geld **e** der Frau
einen Golfschläger **f** dem Fremden
den Weg **g** dem Jungen die Lüge
h der Tochter die Verspätung
i meinem Enkelkind eine Geschichte
j dem Kind das Buch

2

I sister restaurant market morning
vegetables soup lunch dishes night
fridge

II **a** a **b** my **c** his **d** their
e any **f** her **g** his **h** this **i** a
j your

2.1.1

I **a** das **b** der **c** die **d** der
e das **f** das **g** die **h** die **i** die
j der

II **a** die **b** das **c** die **d** das
e die **f** das **g** das **h** das **i** die
j die

III **a** die **b** der **c** das **d** der
e der **f** die **g** der **h** der **i** die
j das

2.1.2

IV **a** der **b** die **c** der **d** der
e der **f** der **g** die **h** der **i** das
j das

V **a** die **b** das **c** die **d** der
e die **f** das **g** die **h** der **i** der
j die

2.1.3

VI **a** Mutter **b** Schwester
c Tante **d** Stiefmutter **e** Nichte
f Frau **g** Oma **h** Cousine
i Stiefschwester **j** Tochter

VII **a** die Frau **b** die Putzfrau
c die Krankenschwester **d** das
Mädchen **e** die Zicke **f** die Kuh
g das Reh **h** die Truthenne **i** das
Huhn

VIII **a** Sozialarbeiterin
b Verkäuferin **c** Ärztin **d** Bäuerin
e Lehrerin **f** Lastwagenfahrerin
g Rechtsanwältin **h** Tierärztin
i Ingenieurin **j** Sekretärin

2.2.1

I **a** Parks **b** Radios **c** Kameras
d Fotos **e** Omas **f** Opas **g** Taxis
h Hotels **i** E-Mails **j** Restaurants

2.2.2

II **a** Abende **b** Schuhe **c** Hunde
d Scheine **f** Filme **g** Briefe
h Ringe **I** Berge **j** Bildschirme

III **a** Beträge **b** Umschläge
c Züge **d** Golfplätze **e** Rucksäcke
f Kämme **g** Pässe **h** Stürme
i Ärzte **j** Köpfe

2.2.3

IV **a** Telefone **b** Feuerzeuge
c Segelboote **d** Geschäfte
e Fahrzeuge **f** Tore
g Tennisnetze **h** Segelschiffe
i Haare **j** Pfunde

V **a** Gläser **b** Gehälter **c** Lämmer
d Clubhäuser **e** Schwimmbäder
f Krankenhäuser **g** Fahrräder
h Dörfer **i** Ämter **j** Wörter

2.2.4

VI **a** Bürokratien **b** Steuern
c Straßen **d** Stufen **e** Strafen
f Schulen **g** Klasssen **h** Feiern
i Inschriften **j** Industrien

VII **a** Versicherungen
b Genehmigungen **c** Feuerwehren
d Verhandlungen **e** Verfassungen
f Rezeptionen **g** Dummheiten
h Frechheiten **i** Informationen
Straftaten

2.2.5

VIII **a** Wagen **b** Zimmer
c Kissen **d** Sessel **e** Fenster
f Teller **g** Theater

IX **a** Bücher **b** Zimmer **c** Rosen
d Kirschen **e** Regale **f** Kinos
g Architektinnen **h** Töchter
i Hotels **j** Dörfer

2.3

I **a** der Laptop **b** die Studentin
c das Fahrrad **d** der Junge **e** die
Frau **f** das Auto **g** das Mädchen
h das Konzert **i** die Schuhe **j** der
Schrank

II **a** *the newspaper* – die Zeitung
b *a gin and tonic* – einen Gin Tonic
c *a new dress* – ein neues Kleid
d *dinner* – Abendessen **e** *pasta* –
Nudeln **f** *a bolognaise sauce* – eine
Bolognaise Soße **g** *the plate* – den
Teller **h** *her new dress* – ihr neues
Kleid **i** *the pasta* – die Nudeln
j *takeaways* – Essen zum Mitnehmen

III **a** *the children* – den Kindern
b *him* – ihm **c** *his wife* – seiner
Frau **d** *her* – ihr **e** *his boss* –
seinem Boss **f** *the baby sitter* – dem
Babysitter **g** *Johnny* – Johnny
h *the children* – den Kindern **i** *his
boss* – seinem Boss **j** *the babysitter* –
dem Babysitter

2.3.1

IV **a** der **b** die **c** die **d** dem
e dem **f** der **g** das **h** den **i** das
j den **k** die **l** die

V **a** masculine nominative,
feminine dative **b** feminine
nominative, feminine accusative,
plural nominative, plural accusative
c neuter nominative, neuter
accusative **d** masculine dative,
neuter dative **e** masculine
accusative, plural dative

2.3.2

VI **a** einen Bruder **b** eine
amerikanische Freundin **c** einen
alten Freund **d** ein altes Auto
e einen alten Hund **f** eine eigene
Persönlichkeit **g** ein kleines Kind
h einen neuen Zahn **i** ein großes
Loch

VII **a** einen **b** eine **c** eine
d einen **e** ein **f** einen **g** einen
h eine **i** ein **j** eine

VIII **a** einen **b** ein **c** ein
d eine **e** eine **f** einen **g** ein
h eine **i** ein

2.3.3

IX **a** kein **b** kein **c** keine
d kein **e** keine **f** kein **g** keine

X **a** keine **b** keine **c** keinen
d kein **e** keine **f** keine **g** keine
h keinen **i** keine **j** kein

XI **a** keinen **b** keinem **c** keinen
d keinem **e** keinem

2.4.1

I **a** meine **b** mein **c** meine
d mein **e** meine **f** meine
g meine **h** meine **i** mein **j** mein
k meine

II **a** meinen **b** meine **c** meinen
d meine **e** meine **f** meine
g meine **h** meinen **i** meine
j meinen

III **a** meiner **b** meiner
c meinem **d** meinen **e** meinem
f meiner **g** meiner **h** meinem
i meinem **j** meiner

2.4.2

IV **a** dein **b** dein **c** deine
d deine **e** dein **f** deine **g** deine
h dein **i** dein **j** deine

V **a** deine **b** deine **c** dein
d dein **e** deine **f** deine **g** dein
h deine **i** deine **j** dein

VI **a** deinen **b** deine **c** deinen
d deine **e** deinen **f** deine **g** dein
h deinen **i** deinen **j** deine

VII **a** deinem **b** deiner
c deinen **d** deinen **e** deinem
f deiner **g** deinen **h** deiner
i deinen **j** deinen

2.4.3

VIII **a** seine **b** seine **c** sein
d seine **e** sein **f** seine **g** sein
h seine **i** seine **h** sein

IX **a** ihren **b** seinen **c** ihre
d seine **e** ihren **f** seinen
g ihren **h** seinen **i** ihr

X **a** ihrer **b** seinem **c** ihrer
d seinem **e** ihrer **f** seiner
g ihren **h** seinem **i** ihrem
j seiner

2.4.4

XI **a** unser **b** unsere **c** unser
d unser **e** unser **f** unsere
g unser **h** unser **i** unser
j unsere

XII **a** unseren **b** unsere **c** unser
d unseren **e** unseren **f** unser
g unsere **h** unsere **i** unseren
j unsere

XIII **a** unserem **b** unserer
c unserer **d** unserem **e** unserem
f unserem **g** unserem **h** unserer
i unserem **j** unserem

2.4.5

XIV **a** Ihr **b** Ihre **c** Ihr **d** Ihr
e Ihr **f** Ihr **g** Ihr **h** Ihre **i** Ihre
j Ihr

XV **a** Ihre **b** Ihre **c** Ihr **d** Ihre
e Ihr **f** Ihr **g** Ihr **h** Ihr **i** Ihr
j Ihr

XVI **a** Ihren **b** Ihre **c** Ihre
d Ihren **e** Ihren **f** Ihre **g** Ihre
h Ihre **i** Ihre **j** Ihren

XLVII **a** Ihrem **b** Ihrem
c Ihrem **d** Ihrer **e** Ihren **f** Ihrer
g Ihrer **h** Ihrer **i** Ihrem

2.4.6

XVIII **a** euer **b** euer **c** euer
d euer **e** eure **f** eure **g** euer **h**
euer **i** euer **j** euer

XIX **a** euer **b** eure **c** euren
d euren **e** euer **f** eure **g** eure
h euer **i** eure **j** euer

2.4.7

XX **a** ihre **b** ihr **c** ihre **d** ihre
e ihr **f** ihr **g** ihr **h** ihre **i** ihr
j ihr

2.5.1

I **a** welche **b** welcher **c** welche
d welcher **e** welcher

II **a** welches **b** welches
c welchen **d** welche **e** welchen

III **a** welcher **b** welcher
c welchem **d** welchem **e** welchem

2.5.2

IV **a** jeden **b** jede **c** jedes
d jeden **e** jedes **f** jeden **g** jeden
h jede

3.1

I **a** er **b** sie **c** ich **d** du **e** ihr
f Sie **g** wir **h** sie

3.1.3

II **a** er **b** sie **c** es **d** er **e** es
f er **g** es **h** er **i** sie **j** sie

III **a** er **b** er **c** es **d** sie **e** es
f sie **g** er **h** sie **i** er **j** sie

IV **a** sie **b** er **c** er **d** es **e** es
f er **g** sie **h** er **i** sie **j** er

3.1.7

V **a** ich **b** wir **c** sie **d** sie **e** er
f sie **g** ihr **h** du **i** Sie **j** Sie

VI **a** Er **b** Sie **c** Ich **d** Sie, ich
e Wir **f** Er **g** Sie **h** Sie **i** Sie
j ihr

VII **a** -e **b** -st **c** -t **d** -t **e** -t
f -en **g** -t **h** -en **i** -en

3.2

I **a** new car **b** it **c** a cat
d a tree **e** the wing mirror
f a bunch of flowers **g** the car

3.2.1

II **a** ihn **b** dich **c** sie **d** sie
e euch **f** mich **g** ihn **h** ihn **i** Sie **j** ihn

III **a** ihn **b** sie **c** sie **d** sie **e** sie **f** ihn **g** sie **h** sie **i** sie **j** sie

3.3

I **a** me **b** her **c** me **d** him **e** me **f** her **g** me **h** him **i** her **j** him **k** her **l** me **m** me

3.3.1

II **a** ihnen **b** ihnen **c** ihm **d** ihr **e** ihnen **f** ihr **g** ihm **h** uns **j** ihnen

III **a** mir **b** sie, ihr **c** ihm **d** ihm **e** ihr **f** mir **g** ihm, ihr **h** ihr **i** ihm **j** ihr **k** mir **l** mir

3.3.2

IV **a** dir **b** ihnen **c** ihm **d** ihm **e** ihnen **f** dir **g** ihm **h** mir **i** ihr **j** ihm

3.3.3

V **a** Er hat sie mir gegeben. **b** Ich habe sie ihr gegeben. **c** Sie hat sie ihnen gegeben. **d** Sie haben sie Ihnen gegeben. **e** Du hast sie uns gegeben. **f** Sie hat es ihm gekauft. **g** Er hat es ihnen vorgelesen. **h** Er hat es uns gegeben. **i** Wir haben es ihr gegeben. **j** Sie haben es ihm vorgelesen. **k** Sie hat es mir geliehen. **l** Wir haben es ihr gegeben.

3.4

I **a** mich **b** dich **c** sich **d** sich **e** sich **f** uns **g** sich **h** mich **i** euch **j** mich

II **a** mir **b** uns **c** dir **d** sich **e** sich **f** sich **g** euch **h** sich **i** uns **j** mir

3.5

I **a** Hören Sie auf ihn! **b** Hören Sie auf sie! **c** Hören Sie auf sie! **d** Hören Sie auf uns! **e** Hören Sie auf sich! **f** Hör auf ihn! **g** Hör auf sie! **h** Hör auf sie! **i** Hör auf uns! **j** Hör auf dich!

II **a** Küssen Sie mich! **b** Tanzen Sie mit mir! **c** Kaufen Sie es mir! **d** Geben Sie es mir! **e** Holen Sie es ihr! **f** Geben Sie es ihm! **g** Bestellen Sie es sich! **h** Bestellen wir es uns! **i** Kaufen sie es sich! **j** Geben Sie es mir!

3.6.1

I **a** die **b** der **c** die **d** das **e** der **f** das **g** die **h** die

3.6.2

II **a** den **b** das **c** die **d** die **e** die **f** den **g** das **h** die **i** die **j** den

3.6.3

III **a** der **b** der **c** dem **d** dem **e** dem **f** denen **g** der **h** dem **i** dem

3.6.4

IV **a** dessen **b** deren **c** dessen **d** deren **e** dessen **f** deren **g** deren **h** dessen **i** dessen **j** deren

3.7

I **a** was **b** wer **c** wem **d** wessen **e** wem **f** wer **g** wen **h** wessen **i** wen **j** wer

3.8

I **a** meins **b** meins **c** meine
d meiner **e** meiner **f** meine
g meins **h** meins **i** meiner
j meine

4.1

I **a** tall, good-looking **b** short,
dark, blue-grey **c** new **d** smart,
casual **e** modern, big **f** small,
bubbly **g** large **h** older, younger
i favourite **j** hot, black

4.1.1

II **a** attraktive, junge, klug
b groß, schlank **c** blonde
d intelligent, gute, viel **e** viele,
interessante **f** kleinen, ruhigen
g billig, schön **h** deutschen
i anstrengend, interessant **j** langen

4.1.2

III **a** schwach **b** alt **c** freundlich
d selbstbewusst **e** unehrlich **f**
laut **g** schmutzig **h** schüchtern
i höflich **j** wunderbar

IV **a** voll **b** klein **c** traurig
d dünn **e** arm **f** kalt **g** faul
h billig **i** neu **j** schnell

4.1.4

V **a** kleine **b** große
c schreienden **d** fröhlichen
e alte **f** schwarze **g** große
h langen **i** wunderschöne **j** kalte

VI **a** kleinen **b** junge
c schreiende **d** fröhlichen **e** alte
f schwarze **g** großen **h** lange
i wunderschönen **j** kalten

VII **a** kleinen **b** netten **c** alten
d freundlichen **e** hungernden
f geizigen **g** großzügigen
h armen **i** verwirrten **j** kranken

4.1.5

VIII **a** kleines **b** neues
c grünen **d** moderne **e** kaputter
f altes **g** hässlicher **h** schlechte
i gute **j** neues

IX **a** neue **b** neuen **c** kleines
d kleinen **e** interessante
f interessanten **g** großen
h spannendes **g** neuen **h** neue

X **a** großen **b** lieben **c** ersten
d netten **e** hilfsbereiten **f** siebten
g großen **h** alten **i** scharfen
j arroganten

4.1.6

XI **a** schönes **b** starker **c** kleine
d alte **e** freundliche **f** ehrliche
g junge **h** agressive **i** sinnlose

XII **a** warme **b** dichten **c** heiße
d lautes **e** entspannende
f spannende **g** neue
h schreckliche **i** positive **j** nette

XIII **a** schlechtem **b** starkem
c großer **d** starker **e** kaltem
f starkem **g** tiefem **h** klassischer
i lauter

4.2.1

I **a** laut, lauter **b** gestresst,
gestresster **c** rostig, rostiger
d schmutzig, schmutziger
e sauber, sauberer **f** cool, cooler
g fröhlich, fröhlicher **h** bequem,
bequemer **i** schnell, schneller
j hilfsbereit, hilfsbereiter

II **a** kürzer **b** älter **c** ärmer
d wärmer **e** grüner **f** klüger
g länger **h** später **i** schärfer

4.2.2

III **a** größten **b** teuersten
c billigsten **d** schnellsten
e bequemsten **f** vollsten

g gefährlichsten   **h** interessantesten
i ältesten   **j** längsten

IV   **a** kleinste   **b** größte
c lauteste   **d** kältesten   **e** stärkste
f kürzesten   **g** schnellste
h langsamsten   **i** herrlichste
j längsten

V   **a** interessantestes
b langweiligster   **c** größter
d schlechtestes   **e** schönster
f schrecklichstes
g schmackhaftestes   **h** fantastischstes
i lustigster   **j** langweiligster

VI   **a** neu(e)sten   **b** ältestes
c neu(e)ste   **d** schönsten
e hässlichsten   **f** bestes   **g** besten
h besten   **i** beste

VII   **a** -en   **b** -en   **c** -en   **d** -en
e -en   **f** -en   **g** -en   **h** -en   **i** -en
j -en

VIII   **a** -er   **b** -es   **c** -en   **d** -e
e -er   **f** -es   **g** -er   **h** -en   **i** -en
j -es

4.2.3

IX   **a–j** so ___ wie

5.1

I   **a** schnell   **b** langsam
c deutlich   **d** richtig   **e** schnell
f langsam   **g** gut   **h** genau
i komisch   **j** ständig

II   **a** hoffentlich   **b** regelmäßig
c links   **d** oft   **e** glücklicherweise
f leider   **g** wirklich   **h** morgens
i selten   **j** nie

III   **a** 3   **b** 10   **c** 8   **d** 7   **e** 4   **f** 9
g 2   **h** 1   **i** 5   **j** 6

IV   **a** Es regnet regelmäßig.   **b** Er
spricht laut.   **c** Die Frau spricht
schnell.   **d** Sie sprechen schnell.
e Sie spricht langsam.   **f** Sie
sprechen deutlich.   **g** Sie sprechen

sehr gut.   **h** Sie macht das gut.
i Er tanzt schlecht.   **j** Sie trinkt
schnell.

5.1.1

V   **a** komischerweise
b interessanterweise
c möglicherweise
d erstaunlicherweise
e normalerweise
f natürlicherweise
g vernünftigerweise
h notwendigerweise
i komplizierterweise
j unglücklicherweise

5.1.2

VI   **a** Gestern bin ich mit dem Zug
nach Dumfries gefahren.
b Allerdings hatte der Zug viel
Verspätung.   **c** Unglücklicherweise
musste ich eine halbe Stunde
warten.   **d** Glücklicherweise konnte
ich in dem Warteraum warten.
e Neulich ist er eine Stunde zu spät
gekommen.   **f** Glücklicherweise
musste ich nicht umsteigen.   **g** Am
Wochenende fahre ich sehr gerne
mit dem Zug.   **h** Gelegentlich
nehme ich auch das Auto.
i Hoffentlich fahren die Züge bald
wieder pünktlich.   **j** Normalerweise
fahre ich genau so lange mit dem
Auto.

6.2.1

I   **a** 3   **b** 7   **c** 4   **d** 1   **e** 2   **f** 6
g 5

II   **a** durch   **b** um   **c** bis   **d** für
e bis   **f** durch   **g** bis   **h** für
i entlang   **j** für

III   **a** Ich bin gegen den Krieg.
I am against the war.   **b** Du kannst
das ohne mich machen. *You can do
that without me.*   **c** Wir kommen so

um 5 Uhr an. *We are going to arrive around 5 o'clock.* **d** Sie wohnt um die Ecke. *She lives around the corner.* **e** Es geht um deinen Unfall. *It is about your accident.* **f** Fahren Sie die Straße entlang. *Drive along the street.* **g** Sie fuhr gegen eine Mauer. *She drove against/into a wall.* **h** Ich komme so gegen 5 Uhr nach Hause. *I am coming home around 5 o'clock.* **i** Paul kommt ohne seine Freundin. *Paul is coming without his girlfriend.*

IV **a** gegen **b** um **c** entlang **d** um/gegen **e** ohne **f** ohne **g** um **h** entlang **i** um **j** ohne

V **a** gegen **b** um **c** ohne **d** durch **e** gegen **f** gegen **g** um **h** entlang **i** für **j** um

6.2.2

VI **a** aus **b** aus **c** bei **d** außer **e** außer **f** aus **g** gegenüber **h** bei **i** bei **j** gegenüber

VII **a** mit **b** seit **c** nach **d** von **e** von **f** von **g** nach **h** mit **i** von **j** seit

VIII **a** von **b** von **c** zu **d** zu **e** von **f** von **g** von **h** von **i** von **j** zu

IX **a** zum **b** zum **c** zur **d** zur **e** zum **f** zum **g** zum **h** zur **i** zum **j** zum

X **a** zum **b** zum **c** zur **d** zum **e** zur **f** zur **g** zur **h** zum **i** zur **j** zum

XI **a** zum **b** zum **c** zum **d** zum **e** zum **f** zur **g** zum **h** zur **i** zum **j** zur

6.2.3

XII **a** dative **b** accusative **c** dative **d** dative **e** dative **f** accusative **g** accusative **h** accusative **i** accusative **j** dative

XIII **a** dative **b** dative **c** accusative **d** accusative **e** dative **f** dative **g** dative **h** dative **i** dative **j** accusative

XIV **a** den **b** dem **c** dem **d** das **e** das **f** dem **g** dem **h** das **i** die **j** der

XV **a** 3 **b** 6 **c** 1 **d** 2 **e** 4 **f** 5

XVI **a** auf **b** auf **c** unter **d** in **e** hinter

6.3.3

I **a** 3 **b** 6 **c** 9 **d** 10 **e** 1 **f** 8 **g** 4 **h** 5 **i** 7 **j** 2